Sergei

Sergei Kourdakov

SERGEI

OLIPHANTS
London

OLIPHANTS
116 BAKER STREET
LONDON W1M 2BB

© Underground Evangelism 1973

First published 1973

ISBN 0 551 00427 4

Printed in Great Britain by
Butler and Tanner Ltd, Frome and London

Contents

List of Illustrations

between pages 84 and 85

I Storm in the Pacific

For several days and nights our ship had been fighting its way through a violently convulsed Pacific Ocean. The storm had started abruptly when a freezing gale out of the north had collided with a cyclone-bearing blast of warm air flowing from Japan. The air masses had exploded in a fury of wind and wave, with us caught in the centre, off the Canadian coast. Though our ship, the Russian trawler *Elagin*, was large and built to ride out the wildest storm, it had, for some sixty hours, bobbed about as if it were no more than a fisherman's skiff on that angry sea.

Many of the most seasoned sailors aboard were sick, because of the unusual circular motion of the storm that kept battering the mountains of British Columbia, then bouncing back to sea in an unbroken circle. After days of such punishment, the trawler, like its crew, was tired. It creaked and groaned, struggled, strained and pulled wearily. Even in the radio room, specially built with noise-killing insulation, I could feel the vessel's great mechanical pulse, as every part of the machine seemed to fight the storm's violence.

I had slept very little during the previous few days. My job as radio operator was to transmit data back to our naval base in the Soviet Union, and the storm had kept me almost constantly on duty. The tempest outside, though, contributed far less to my discomfort than did the emotional storm within me. After months of cautious planning and preparation, I was at last nearing the time for my escape to freedom. Inside Canada's coastal waters, which we had asked permission to enter to ride out the storm, I was fearfully close to my goal. I anxiously awaited my opportunity to flee.

The prow of the ship dipped beneath the mountainous waves, then rose again, and again. The whole ship shuddered from the waves' impact. The night, normally inky dark, was even blacker under the heavy storm clouds. Seafaring men spoke of such a night with fear. This was the night of 3 September 1971. Ten of the Soviet vessels, as well as my ship, had received permission to ride out the storm inside Tasu sound, on Queen Charlotte Island.

Just before 8.30 that evening, the time I was to report for duty in the radio room, I stepped out of my quarters and was almost doubled over by the force of the storm. It took all my strength to inch my way along the slippery deck. Finally I reached the bridge, flung open the door and burst in.

"How far are we from shore?" I asked my friend Boris, on duty at the helm.

He checked his chart. "About half a mile," he replied.

"How far to that village?" I asked, pointing out lights barely visible through the driving rain and wind.

"About three and a half miles," he replied.

"Thanks," I muttered, moving on to my post in the radio room just behind the bridge. Now that we were inside Canada's waters, we were not to transmit; so all I had to do was check on any of our other ships in distress. It would be a short turn of duty tonight, and I was very glad.

A glance at my watch showed me it was 8.30 p.m. I said to myself, "Sergei, in a few hours you might be free or you might be drowned. Or you could be worse than drowned—picked out of the water and taken back to a Siberian labour camp as a naval deserter, then eventually shot." It was a time when anyone in my spot would have second thoughts.

Here I was, Sergei Kourdakov, a second lieutenant cadet officer in the Russian Navy, a decorated Communist youth leader, chosen the head of every Communist youth organization in every school I had been in since I was eight years old, chosen the Communist youth leader in charge of teaching Communism to 1,200 Soviet naval cadets. In five days I was scheduled to head back to the naval base where I would be admitted to full membership in the Communist Party and had a very good job with the Russian police waiting for me. To be completely practical, I had everything in the world to go back to Russia for. But it was not enough. Whatever it was that I needed, I knew I could not have it in the Communist system I had seen so much of.

Three and a half miles, I mused, making some quick mental calculations. I would only be safe in the village itself. That had to be my goal. If I merely reached shore half a mile away, a search party could come and get me. Only the village and people would be safe. That meant it would take about an hour at most to reach the village. I had already checked the water temperature. It was about 40 degrees Fahrenheit. This far north,

2

time in the water would be a matter of life and death. I estimated that I could survive four hours at most in the cold seas. I was in excellent physical condition, due to regular exercises and workouts with weights. "It's now or never," I told myself. I knew in my heart it would have to be now.

The radio shack was between the steering house, at the most forward part of the bridge, and the map room where the captain was on duty. Because of our nearness to shore, he was keeping close watch on our position to make sure we didn't get so far in toward shore that we could be caught on the jagged rocks that shielded the coastline.

I turned three of the radar units on, one for military and two for navigational purposes, and waited for them to warm up. I was hoping there would be no interruptions, nothing out of the ordinary.

But just at that moment, the captain stuck his head out of the map room and shouted to me, "Hey, Kourdakov, how about a game of chess?"

We had played often while at sea. I didn't want to arouse his suspicions now by refusing his invitation, but I couldn't afford to lose the time. The complete darkness was safety and I must make it to shore before the skies brightened. Besides, I was afraid my resolve would disappear if I hesitated too long.

"Comrade captain," I said, "I'm very tired from the long hours I put in these last few days. I think I'd rather rest. I'm just too tired."

The captain made a big joke of it and said, "Listen to the young sea dog!" He laughed. "Three days' storm and he's too tired!"

Inwardly, I sighed with relief. Then I began the final preparations I had gone over so often in my head. First I closed down the radio station, leaving the receiver on emergency frequency, in case other ships might try to reach us. I switched on the remote speaker to the bridge, so that incoming messages from other ships of our fleet could be heard by Boris up forward.

I looked around the radio room to make certain everything was in order, then quickly slipped out, locked the door behind me and started back to my quarters, passing again through the steering room of the bridge, now dark except for the glow of red, yellow and blue lights on the instrument console. The rain was crashing against the window of the bridge, making it impossible to see out. Boris was standing in the dim glow of the instrument lights, anxiously scanning them carefully for any sign of trouble from our overworked machinery. The two of us had passed many lonely hours of duty together these past few weeks. I paused for a few moments of idle talk with him, trying to seem as natural as possible, then excused myself as being dog-tired, and started off to my quarters.

"Boris," I said on leaving, "if anyone calls, don't interrupt me for a couple of hours—not unless it's a great emergency. All right?"

"Right, Sergei," he said and laughed. "Think of me up here, while you're tucked comfortably away in your nice, warm bed."

"Oh sure," I promised and left the bridge, stepping out on to the deck and into the storm. I grasped the rail with all my strength and moved cautiously toward my quarters. The driving wind and rain, again and again, almost sent me sprawling across the heaving walkway. Pushing hard against the wind and wild spray, I reached my quarters. I opened the door, stepped inside and locked it behind me. A surprise intrusion now could be fatal, ending any possibility for escape. Uneasily, I glanced at my watch again. It was 9.45. I had less than fifteen minutes left for final preparation. The casual talk on the bridge had used up precious seconds. Now I had to move fast to make my moves during the few remaining minutes, while the deck was still deserted. The minute the storm let up, men would be all over the ship, checking for damage.

Because of our northerly location I was wearing my heavy-weight uniform—my big military boots; a lighter-weight sweater and over it a heavy, turtle-neck sweater. The weight and bulk of these clothes would create serious problems once I was in the water, trying to swim. But I wanted to walk into that village fully clothed, and with my boots on. There was little time to think about even such important matters. There were others, more important, now.

I reached under my bunk and pulled out something I had been working on for some time—a large, waterproof bag-like belt. I had made it out of heavy rubber for the outside and waterproof plastic for the inside. Reaching into my cabinet drawer, I took out the things I treasured most and planned to take with me: photos of friends, comrades and familiar places back in Russia, none of which I would ever see again.

4

These few cherished items would be all I carried with me out of the old life into the new, except scars—physical and emotional—and lots of memories.

This is all I have to show for my life, I thought, looking at the little pile of papers. *No mother or father. This little pile is my life.* Many of the things would become meaningless—my Komsomol membership card, my naval papers. Others, like my birth certificate, I must keep always. If I survived this night, I would need these documents to prove who I was. If I didn't, at least when my body was found, there would be a name to go on the gravestone.

Quickly then, after stuffing my papers and photos into the rubber belt, I sewed it tightly closed, so the water couldn't get in. I fastened it securely around my waist, then reached into my drawer and pulled out something else that would be very important to me in the hours ahead: the skin-diver's knife which I had smuggled aboard and kept hidden. Strapping the knife tightly to my wrist, I pulled my sweater arm down over it to hide it. I needed to avoid all possible questions, should I be spotted on deck. The knife would be hard to explain, but it would be desperately important to me later on.

Well, I thought, *at last I'm ready. Knife in place, belt securely fastened.* My watch now read 9.55, time to go. The storm had increased in intensity, which would protect me from being seen. Opening my cabin door, I stepped out on to the walkway and was stopped short by a burst of freezing spray. Even here, partly sheltered in the sound, the storm was fierce.

I bent into the wind and clambered down the ladder, holding desperately to the railing to keep from falling. Now down on the main deck, I looked around to see if I had been spotted. I saw no one. So far so good. I felt reasonably sure that everyone was below deck, staying out of the weather.

Slowly I fought my way midship to the spot I had picked a few days before as the best jumping-off place. It was a small area just below the ship's huge funnel, the only spot I could find that was hidden from most other parts of the ship. I struggled toward the chosen spot and after several minutes reached it. A close look at the wild, turbulent waves sent shivers down my spine. I had better quit looking, I thought, or I might give up before I even got into the water.

Then suddenly, directly facing me, a door opened and the light shone out and hit me. I ducked quickly and froze. Whoever had opened it stood in the doorway for an instant, took one fast look outside, then drew back in. Had I been seen? The door closed. Whatever had been in the seaman's mind, the storm had changed it.

But now I had to act fast. The ship rose on the crest of a large wave and I stood about the height of a two-storey building above the water. I planned to wait until the ship was down in a trough, then dive into the water. I waited until the last breaker had hit the ship. Then I climbed over the railing. Balancing myself momentarily, I made ready to dive headlong, straight down into the furious black sea.

2   Battle for survival

I took a deep breath, dived and cut the water perfectly, plunging deep. Then trouble began. Overpowering sensations of shocking cold struck me. The water, when I had tested it earlier, was as cold as any sea I had ever felt. And now that I was immersed in it, my body was shocked by its frigidness.

Driving my numbed arms and legs, I began swimming under water as fast as I could. I had to go as far from the ship as possible before surfacing to avoid being spotted by someone on board who might open a porthole to get some air and see me. Finally, my lungs bursting for air, I desperately clawed my way to the surface and gasped for breath. I looked back. I was still much too close to the ship! I took another huge lungful of air, dived again and swam submerged as far as I could.

Not until my lungs once more screamed for air did I surface. That was better, but I was still too close. Again I went under and swam until, gasping for breath, I had to surface. That was much better.

Only one thing filled my mind—get away from the ship. If I were spotted, lights aboard the ship would be flashed on, illuminating the dark waters, and I would be a sitting duck, even in these tossing seas. I knew the ship carried a high-powered rifle equipped with telescopic sights, and hitting me would be as easy as shooting a fish in a bowl. If I claimed I had fallen overboard, the documents around my waist would give me away.

Again and again I filled my lungs, dived beneath the tossing waves and swam on. Soon I had swum far enough away from the ship to surface, stop and take stock of my situation. Now the numbing cold really hit me. My boots and heavy clothing had become waterlogged and added enormous weight. The boots especially were like a sack of bricks tied to each foot, dragging me down. I had to fight just to stay on the surface. A heavy wave smashed down on me, plunged me under, and I thought I wasn't going to make it. Somehow I reached the surface, coughing and spluttering and gasping for breath. Those boots! What a mistake! I should have taken them off! That little

7

mistake was going to cost me my life, I felt. "Sergei," I said, "you're a dead man!"

I had to get those boots off—fast—or the next wave might smash me under for the final time. Quickly I loosed the knife strapped to my arm, then cut the legs off my trousers. Next I ripped off my big outer sweater. Then I took a deep breath, ducked my head under water and began to cut and hack away at the left boot. Oddly enough, at that desperate moment, I remembered an old saying which I had repeated often: "I want to die with my boots on." But I had never thought of the boots killing me! I hacked and slashed, but the water-soaked leather wouldn't give. Once more I filled my lungs with air and I ducked under the water, slashing desperately. I knew that if I didn't succeed soon, I never would. I put my knife in the top of my water-soaked left boot and began to rip with all my might. The leather was giving! I felt exhilaration as the knife cut through. I surfaced once more for another breath of air, then went down to finish the job. After the third dive, the left boot was off.

But the right boot wouldn't give! I slashed wildly at it, gashing my ankle instead. Finally I managed to get the edge of the knife in just right and pulled—and I could feel the leather tearing. At last I was free of those concrete weights. But I was too drained of energy to feel very good about it. I had been in the water almost an hour.

No sooner had I rid myself of the boots than I became aware of a new problem: fog! Heavy, dense, blinding patches of fog were fast blanketing me and the ship. Soon the driving rain and waves closed off my view of the *Elagin*'s lights, off in the distance, which I was using to get my directions to shore. In the swirling fog and blinding rain I could no longer keep my bearings. In which direction was the land? Which way should I swim? I became confused—and lost! Heavy, pelting rain beat down on my face and head, stinging me. Everything was going wrong!

Without compass, or visibility, I had little hope of finding my way to shore and safety. I was unable to see more than three feet in front of me. By now I had been in the water two long, exhausting hours. That battle with the boots had cost me much precious energy. I had swallowed an enormous amount of water. The cold was now getting to me, too. I could feel the deadening numbness beginning. I gave myself just two more hours. If I didn't make shore by then, it was unlikely that I ever would.

I chose what I thought was the direction of land and headed for it with all my might. I learned the movement of the huge waves and how to use them; when to top the crest of the next one, when to relax and gain strength for another hard push. The cold was bitterly numbing. Next to the fog, it was my worst enemy, consuming my energy and causing me to shiver violently as I swam. But I was making progress. Up one wave, down the other side of it, then up and over another.

On and on I swam until by the luminous dial of my waterproof watch I could see it had been nearly three hours since I had plunged into the water. I had to be close to land now! My heart leaped a bit at the thought.

A violent burst of wind scattered the fog momentarily. Eagerly I strained to see any sign of the shore. Then suddenly there it was, scarcely visible through the fog—a great black object, standing high above the heaving waters. Land! A rock! I had made it! My heart beat faster with excitement. I had done it. *Beautiful!* I thought. *Just beautiful!* No sight in all my life had been so welcome as that mountainous hunk of rock. "You've made it, Sergei! You've made it!" I congratulated myself. I swam on toward the rock, recklessly using up my remaining energy, which I wouldn't need now. Then the fog parted for a few seconds. I stared in utter disbelief.

"Oh no!" I cried in dismay. "It can't be!" But it was. The "rock" was the *Elagin!* Three hours of excruciating cold, most of my energy spent, and here I was, back where I had started!

And now I faced a predicament for which I had made no plans! What should I do? The bright lights shining through the portholes looked so inviting and warm. Perhaps I should cut my rubber belt off and say I fell overboard. With the ship pitching as furiously as it was, maybe my story would be convincing enough. They would pull me in, give me hot food and warm blankets, and my bitter nightmare would be over.

But would it? The unbearable circumstances I was running away from would be back to torment me for the rest of my life.

What then? Strike out for shore again? It seemed so impossible now. I was physically exhausted, psychologically drained. How much longer could I survive in those frigid temperatures? I had estimated my endurance at four hours at the most. And already I had been in the water three hours.

Numb with cold, I sized up the situation as best as my tortured mind would allow. I decided I would rather die trying to

9

find real life than continue to live as I had been living. I would not—could not—return to the life I had known. Even if I drowned I must not go back.

With little hope left, I nevertheless started swimming slowly away from the *Elagin*. I thought of the documents around my waist. Would someone find them? Would anyone know who I was? Would anyone ever learn the story behind the body they found? My mind became dizzy as thoughts drifted in and out. All my life, from six years of age, I had been alone—no mother or father. It seemed cruel that I would die still alone, lost in a watery grave.

I tried to get my bearings. Which way was shore? This way? That way? How could I possibly tell, when I could see only a couple of feet around me? I stopped all forward movement. I was turning in circles, trying frantically to decide which way to go. I realized I was lost, utterly lost.

"Sergei," I said, "you're finished. You're going to die. No one knows. No one cares. No one."

I had been raised on Marx, Engels and Lenin. They were my gods. Three times I had bowed before the lifeless body of Lenin in Moscow and fervently prayed to him. He was my god and teacher. But now in my last moments, my mind turned to the God whom I did not know. Almost instinctively I prayed, "God, I have never been happy on this earth. Now that I'm dying, please take my soul to Paradise. Maybe you can find me a little bit of happiness there, God. I don't ask you to save my body. But as it now goes to the bottom, take my soul with you to Heaven, please God!" I closed my eyes, fully believing this was the end. "Now I'm ready," I said to myself. "Now I can sleep." I relaxed and stopped struggling. My battle was over.

Slowly, ever so gradually, I could sense something strange happening. Though I had been drained of every ounce of energy, I sensed a new strength flowing into my tired arms. I felt the strong and loving arms of the living God in the water like a heavenly buoy! I wasn't a believer. I had never prayed to God before. But in that moment, I became aware of new reserves of power, pouring into my worn, water-soaked body. I could swim again! My arms, which were as heavy as logs only minutes ago, now felt strong enough to get me to the shore! I had now been in the water almost four and a half hours.

And strangest of all, I could sense what general direction to take! I could sense where the shore lay. Even when the tossing waves spun me about, I could come right back to the path I somehow knew would lead to shore.

I didn't understand what was happening to me. All I knew was that my life was going to be spared. For two more hours I swam steadily forward. Then out of the wild seas, I could hear a great crashing noise in front of me. A great wave of doubt flooded my head; I wondered, was it the ship again? Or one of the other ships? Had I swum in a circle again?

I swam strongly toward the sound. As the fog and driving rain cleared for a moment, I peered through; there it was—a huge, tall *rock* rising out of the water! A *real* rock! The noise I had heard was the roar of the breakers crashing against it. It was rock—good, solid rock! I had reached land! "I've made it! I've made it!" My heart leaped for joy.

Then just as quickly my enthusiasm died. I suddenly realized how violent the storm-driven breakers were. Any one of them could pick me up, hurl me against that rock and crush every bone in my body. "You're not out of it yet," I told myself. Then I called out to God once more—and again I felt I *knew* He was with me.

It was amazing! Even after five hours in the water, I was still mentally alert. I watched carefully as a huge wave crashed against the rock. Then I began swimming furiously to slip in between the huge breakers at just the right moment. I made it! Suddenly I was able to grasp the rock. For the first time in five hours, I had something solid to hold on to.

Quickly I mounted the rock and climbed higher and higher to avoid the next breaker which could easily knock me loose and wash me back out to sea. I climbed still higher. Then the next breaker hit—just below me. I clung to the jagged edges of the rocks. After each breaker crashed, I climbed even higher, until at last I found myself looking down at the surging water far below.

But as I relaxed a little, I was suddenly overcome by total exhaustion. I sat for a long time, freezing, shivering, my teeth chattering, unable to control the violent shaking of my body. I had swallowed enormous amounts of salt water. I was so thirsty, so cold! But I knew I couldn't stay here. It was now about five o'clock. I had gone into the water at ten o'clock the night before and knew that my absence from the *Elagin* had long ago been discovered, and I was still on the seaward side of the rock. If the storm eased, I could easily be spotted—through binoculars

—as day dawned. I felt that any minute a boat would come cutting through the fog with an armed search party, and I would be doomed. With orders to bring me back dead or alive, they would capture me, or would shoot me with the telescopic rifle. I couldn't stay on that side of the rock. I had to get to the safety of that village—and people. I began climbing again. It was such a tall cliff, rising over 200 feet above the water. But somehow I managed to get to the top, and I thought at last I was safe.

But no! My heart sank. It seemed I was not on shore at all. The village was across a bay of water—about two miles away. I would have to swim more! By now, I was becoming delirious. I couldn't take stock of my situation. My only thought was a blind, compelling drive to get to the village quickly, before they came for me. But it all seemed impossible. My energy was gone. I was frozen and shaking violently. I moved toward the edge of the high rock, then began climbing down to the water line. Suddenly I slipped and fell ten feet down the sloping edge of the rock. I fell and hit again, and again, and again. I felt like a ball, bounding into the air, hitting the rock, bouncing again, tearing my flesh on the rocks. I felt the searing hot cuts and the blood pouring over my skin as I fell. I hit a jagged rock on my side and felt blood gushing from my hands. Spun backward by the force of the fall, I hit another rock and felt a sharp pain in my back. I landed at the bottom of a ravine. I lay there, bleeding, in pitch darkness. For a second time I felt I wouldn't make out. In darkness and in driving rain, I desperately climbed back out of the ravine. If it had not been for my mountain-climbing experience, I would not have made it.

Back at the top of the cliff I could see the lights of the village about two miles across the bay, so inviting, but so far. Dawn was coming fast. I had lost track of time. I had to get there. I plunged into the water a second time. I screamed in pain as an excruciating, red hot fire engulfed my body. Dimly, through the intense pain, I thought, *God, you are giving me a little of the pain I gave your children.* Blood was coming from my legs and feet. Then suddenly I saw—or thought I saw—something that made me shudder with fear: a small boat, coming my way. They had discovered me missing and had sent a boat out looking for me, I thought.

To this day I do not know whether it was a real boat, or an hallucination from my fevered mind. All I thought of was to swim, to get away. When I tried to swim, the pain increased. Yet despite the agony, I swam on. Soon, however, I began to feel faint. I had lost too much blood and began to lose consciousness. *No! Not here*, I thought. *Not when I'm so close to freedom!* Through the dawning light of the new day, I could see a little fishing village in the distance. Only a few hundred yards to go! *God, after all I've gone through, don't let me die so close to freedom. Please don't.*

Then everything went black. The last sight I remember was of that little village fading from my closing eyes. The last conscious thought I remember was, *I must keep swimming! I must keep swimming!* Then total darkness. I remember nothing else.

What was I doing there, on that cold morning of 4 September 1971, so near death and so far from home? What had caused me to forsake the life of a naval officer and Communist youth leader in Russia and brought me here, at the point of death, to the alien, rocky Canadian shore?

That story really began long ago in Russia with my grandfather and grandmother.

3   The missing family

I never saw my grandfather, Ivan Kourdakov. But I felt as though I had, because of what I learned about him from an old woman who knew him well. What she told me about him left me with the impression of a man I should very much like to to have known.

He was a Russian of Russians—tall, broad-shouldered, a huge man of the soil. Born near the village of Povolgiye on the Volga River, he grew to be self-reliant and independent, building his own farm into a prosperous, thriving enterprise.

During the Czarist times, he had served as a captain in the Cossack army, putting down revolts and uprisings in the southern region of Russia. Later he served with the White Guards as a Cossack captain, joining in attempts to smash the new Communist revolution. It was around that time that his first wife passed away. Then, during the war against the Communists, he met a beautiful "princess" of the Ossetia tribe of people in the lower Caucasus, who later became my grandmother. I was told that she was actually a princess, because her father owned land and sheep, and also because of her beauty. Her hair was black and plaited and reached down to her ankles.

In 1921 my grandfather returned from the wars to his farm village, there to start life all over again with his new young bride. According to the reports I heard, she became the envy of everybody in town because of her upbringing, charm and grace. My grandfather, too, was greatly envied because of the princess he was said to have captured as part of the spoils of war. He kidnapped her, all right, but only in the sense that he stole her heart, for I was told she was very happy with him. Together they worked hard and rebuilt his farm. By 1928 he was firmly re-established in life, owning several horses, a plough and a mowing machine. By no means could he be considered rich, but certainly he was well off, because of his own enterprise and hard work. Here, where he had been born, he and my grandmother were exceedingly happy. But tragedy was not long in coming.

In 1928 Stalin launched his collectivization programme and

all-out war against the farmers and *kulaks*, the landowners. It was a reign of terror, the most fearful to that point in the twentieth century. Representatives of the military simply came on to the farms, brandished a pistol in the face of each owner and confiscated all his food and crops, leaving him and his family behind to starve. It was the first deliberately planned, man-made famine in the world, and millions died of starvation because they resisted giving up their farms and their way of life. At the same time, Stalin increased exports, selling milk, grain and cheese abroad. While this went on, more than a million Russian children died of starvation.

It was in 1928 that the Communists struck out at my grandfather. A local Communist official came to his farm one day, stuck a pistol in my grandfather's face and demanded, "Give me all the goods and crops you have." The man was a drunk and good-for-nothing who had never worked. He ordered his men to begin searching, even digging up the ground, for hidden grain.

But my grandfather was not one to give in easily to anyone. When the intruder turned around, my grandfather grabbed him in a Russian bear hug and, giant man that he was, squeezed until all the man's ribs and backbone were broken, then dropped him in a lifeless heap on the ground. Immediately grandfather was arrested and sent off to a special hard labour camp in Siberia, there to spend nine bitter years, from 1928 to 1937. He never saw my grandmother again, for she was sent to a women's prison camp where she died. At the labour camp my grandfather was given extremely hard work, but though not young he was still physically very powerful and could take the strenuous tasks assigned him.

In October 1937, he was transferred to a lumber camp on the Chulym River in Siberia, and given the job of transporting logs from the river to a narrow-gauge railway. Once when the machinery broke down, my grandfather picked up a heavy log, put it on his shoulder and carried it to the railway car. In doing so, he strained his back and abdomen severely. He died shortly after that.

My recollections of my mother and father are parts of my own hazy memory and a lot of patchwork information from a former friend of my father. I was only four years old when my father was killed. My mother died shortly afterwards.

It was in Povolgiye, on my grandfather's farm, that my father was born. In 1928, when grandfather was exiled to Siberia, father was sent along with him. At that time he was put into a school close by and raised in a state children's home. Soon afterwards, while still quite young, he became an ardent Communist. Because his father was a prisoner in a labour camp, one of the first things he had to do was to "cleanse his record and purge himself of all poisonous family relationships". He renounced my grandfather.

For the short time I knew my father, I remember how I loved him and how, when I was a child of three or four years, he would come into my room to say good night. Even now I can see his piercing black eyes and almost feel his long, curly moustache tickling my face, as he leaned over to kiss me. I remember also that he liked to drink and usually when he came home, he immediately sat down at the table with a bottle in front of him. Being in the military, he was often gone for long periods. But when he was home, we had great fun together.

I recall how he made me dance the *chechotka*, the famous high-kicking Russian dance. When I did well, he gave me a little glass of vodka, and I would drink it and dance some more. But soon he would become dead drunk and plop down on the bed. Often while he lay there, I would go to the closet, take out his uniform and put on his coat, then I would parade up and down in it, bedecked with gleaming medals that tinkled as I walked. Beyond that, I remember little about life with my father.

Because I was closer to my mother, I remember her much better. Her name was Anisia. She was from a very poor home but one in which there were believers in God. She looked after me very well. But most of our early years together have been long lost from memory.

One of my two brothers, however, I remember quite well. He was quite a few years older than I and was my hero. Because we lived on the military base at Novosibirsk (which means New Siberia), Vladimir was sent to the city to go to school. Whenever he had a holiday, he would come out from the city to our house on the military base and then we had great fun. I remember how big and tall he was and how much I admired him.

Once when I was four years old, he came home on a visit. The first thing he said to me was, "Come on, Sergei, let's go for a ride!" Then, putting a pillow over the bicycle handlebars, he perched me on top of it and off we went, racing down the road on the military base and turning off on to a narrow trail through the woods. Up and down the hills we rode, having such wonderful fun and laughing together. I remember coming to a stable, getting off the bicycle and being lifted on to a horse. Vladimir jumped on behind, and we took off at a full gallop, with me clinging for dear life to big brother Vladimir, and he hanging on just as tightly. It was such great sport! But what we didn't know, at the time, was that mother had seen us racing off on the horse and had come running after us, shouting all the way, "Vladimir, Vladimir, bring that child back!"

Mama was so far behind, she never could have caught up to us enough to make herself heard, except for what happened next. Just at the wrong time, as our horse dashed under a tree, Vladimir turned to look at something behind us and we were both knocked off to the ground in a hard fall. Besides everything else, Vladimir landed on my foot, and I began yelling and crying my eyes out. I remember mother finally catching up with us, shouting, "Vladimir, you big oaf! Are you crazy, riding like the wind? And, as if that isn't enough, you get Sergei on a horse and don't have sense enough to know how to keep him on!" I'll never forget mama's lecture and I'm sure Vladimir never did either. He listened respectfully, then reached down when it was over and carried me back to the house. I cried all the way, more scared than hurt.

The last time I saw my brother Vladimir, he came into the room where I was lying on the bed and told me he was sorry for what happened. He told me I'd be a big tough guy some day and that a little accident never really hurt anyone. Then he hugged me and said goodbye and walked out of the room, and out of my life. I have never seen him since, and lost all track of him.

When I was seventeen years of age I was visiting Novosibirsk from my studies at the Leningrad Naval Academy. I was asked by an older friend, "Sergei, do you want to find out more about your mother, father and brother?"

"Yes, of course," I replied.

"Well, then," my friend said, "go to the military base outside the city of Novosibirsk and ask for Lieutenant-Colonel Dobrinsky. He knew your father and can give you some of the information you've been searching for."

17

I had already been told that my father had been shot and my mother had died a few months later. But I had never learned the details surrounding their deaths. Now, at seventeen, I was keen to find out all I could about them. Earlier, when I was thirteen, I had heard that my brother Vladimir might be working in a prison camp in Kazakhstan. I wrote to the Supreme Soviet of Kazakhs Republic asking for their help in locating him. The reply I received later said that he was not found on the records of the population of that republic, nor did anybody know about him.

Afterwards, through a high-ranking Communist official, I sent a request to the Supreme Soviet of the U.S.S.R. in Moscow, asking their help in finding Vladimir. But they could not locate him either. He has so completely disappeared that it is possible he suffered my father's fate in execution or is in exile somewhere in a prison camp. But I have never given up hope that I might some day find him alive.

From the time I was four years of age, I lived in other people's homes, but at six went to live in children's homes operated by the state. After my very early years I never knew the caresses and kisses of a mother and father. I had no one to come to me and say in the morning, "Now eat your breakfast and study well in school." You can imagine, I'm sure, what these simple words mean to a child and the life-long void that not having them left in my heart.

Perhaps this was the greatest void that I, as a seventeen-year-old youth in the Naval Academy in Leningrad, had experienced. Therefore, when I learned that there was a Lieutenant-Colonel Dobrinsky who could tell me about my mother and father, I wasted no time in going out to his military base. I knocked on the door of his quarters and I said, when he opened it for me, "I'm the son of Nikolai Ivanovitch Kourdakov."

At first he looked at me blankly. Then suddenly his face lit up with a smile. "Oh yes, I know you. I remember your father very well. Come in, come in!" He introduced me to his wife, who later prepared a big dinner for me, and we all sat around talking. There was plenty of vodka. The colonel offered me some and I drank a little, but he drank excessively. Soon he was quite relaxed and unable to control his tongue. His words flowed freely, and I began to learn details of my father's life, things that had been hidden from me all these years.

"Certainly, Sergei, I remember him," the colonel said. "Your father was a most interesting and capable man. He felt he had to wash away the sins of your grandfather and so he became a real soldier in the Communist army. Though he had only finished the fourth grade in school, he was such a fine soldier and political activist that he went very high up. He fought in many battles, risking his life for the Communist Party again and again, especially in Turkestan, where he headed the brigade that crushed a number of revolts. Then when the Finnish war broke out, the first thing he did was volunteer for duty on the Finnish front. He led a brigade there and served heroically." I listened enthralled, as the details of my father's life were unfolded.

The colonel's wife busied herself with the entertaining, faithfully pouring the vodka as the colonel demanded more and drank more. I sipped on mine and continued to listen. "When the Second World War broke out, your father took part in that also, commanding a tank unit under General Rokossovsky. He served with great honour and distinction and earned many medals. After the war, your father and I were close comrades and were sent to this very military base where we are now. However, when we came here, there was nothing. We were under orders to establish and build a tank-artillery training base. I was under your father by one rank and was his assistant. He worked very hard and industriously to organize this whole base, as you see it now. You see all this sprawling base? This is your father's handiwork. And though I was able to assist him, it was largely the result of his efforts. So your father was not only a very good soldier but a loyal political activist, as well. He supported Stalin one hundred per cent."

"But what happened when Khrushchev came to power?" I asked.

"Well, *then* things began to get difficult. I remember one night when I was the officer in charge here. A car pulled up and some people came in and asked for your father. I told them, 'He's not here. He's at home.' In the morning your father was due to come to relieve me. But at eight o'clock, when he was due, he hadn't shown up. I sent for him at home to find out what was wrong. But he wasn't there. They had taken him away during the night.

"You ask why they took him away? I can see the question on your face. Well, Sergei, you must understand that Khrushchev was taking power from Stalin and there was a great fight in the higher levels of the party. They cannot change things quickly, but slowly, degree by degree. To consolidate his own power, Khrushchev was ordering the elimination of those high-ranking officers who were known to support Stalin. It had to be done quietly and a little bit at a time so as not to arouse suspicion. That's why your father was taken in the middle of the night. He served Communism as few other men I have known. But like so many others I knew, he just disappeared. The second day after they took him, another man came to our headquarters, here at the base, and announced that he was now the new base chief. He said, 'Kourdakov was a very bad man and is under investigation.' That's the last I heard of your father. He simply disappeared from sight, never to be heard of again. Do you understand, Sergei?"

I understood. Or did I? The lieutenant-colonel told me that my father would certainly have been a general by now if he had survived. He was simply too powerful a figure for Khrushchev to allow to live. So, in consolidating his own power, Khrushchev eliminated my father who had served Communism for almost all his life.

The colonel went on. "Of course, your mother didn't last long after your father disappeared. She died about four months later, I think. Sergei, it was really because of a broken heart from the pain she suffered. She just lost the will to live. I remember when she died and that's when we lost track of you. I don't remember what happened to you after that. If I could have found you, a son of an old comrade and friend, I would have helped you all I could.

"By the way, Sergei," he asked, "what *did* happen to you after your mother and father died?"

4   A street orphan

What happened to me after my father's disappearance and my mother's death, a few months later, is painful to tell. It is a bit unclear to me even now. I was only four years old when I noticed that my father didn't come home any more. "Mother," I would ask, "where is father? Why doesn't he come in to kiss me good night any more?"

Whenever I asked mother this, she would burst into tears or else turn away, bury her head in her hands and say nothing. Even as a four-year-old, I could understand there was something badly wrong that was causing mother to become so upset. Mother's health began to break, gradually getting worse and worse, until finally all she could do was lie in bed all the time, unable to take care of herself or me. The last time I saw my mother, she was very ill; and then the next thing I knew, a friend of the family was saying to me, "Sergei, you don't have a mother any more. She's dead. Come to our house and stay."

At first I couldn't comprehend what that meant. I fully expected to see mother again, if I only waited long enough. I was certain she wouldn't just go away and leave me and never come back. In my little child's heart, I knew that, any time, I might see her at home again and everything would be all right. Though so much about that time of my life is obscured in my memory, I remember that the woman who told me that mother was dead and who asked me to come and live in her home was Mrs. Kolmakov. She was the wife of Professor Kolmakov, a scientist and teacher who has since gone very high in Russia. They were nice people and I liked them a great deal. But I wanted so to stay in my own home and wait for mother. I wanted to be there the minute she got back. Mrs. Kolmakov was very kind and understanding and finally persuaded me that it was best that they should take care of me.

As far as I can recall, I was a little past four when Mrs. Kolmakov and the professor took me into their home and made me a member of their family, which consisted of two sons, one of whom was named Andrei. Though I was very young, I remember how good they were to me and how much Mrs. Kolmakov wanted me to get a good start in life. Being the wife of a scientist, and an intellectual in her own right, she encouraged me to study, right from the time I first came into their home. She herself taught me to read and to count.

The professor was a warm-hearted man and truly brilliant. Later he was to work in Akademgorodok, a city in Siberia given over completely to science. I heard later a report that he became a member of the prestigious Soviet Academy of Sciences. Though always very busy, and having two boys of his own, he still had time to be a kind and loving father to me, and I quickly came to love him.

Mrs. Kolmakov was a small, short woman, very motherly and full of love and concern for her good friend's little child. I could tell she was determined to be as good a mother to me as possible. Even though Mrs. Kolmakov did her best, I was so lonesome for my own mother. But I was glad for the Kolmakovs' care of me and I hoped that, if I couldn't have my own parents, I would never have to leave my adopted ones. And for two years, until I was six years old, we lived comfortably together, except for one thing—Andrei, their son.

Even as young as I was, I knew there was something strangely wrong with Andrei. I later knew that he was mentally unbalanced. He was older than I and big for his age and he kept doing things and acting toward me in ways that frightened me. One day, when I was taking a bath, Andrei came into the bathroom. "Get out," I said. "You don't belong here. You can have it when I've finished."

But Andrei only looked at me and smiled in a strange way. I instinctively knew something was wrong and was terribly frightened. Then suddenly he grabbed me by the shoulders and began pushing me down in the bath tub until my head was completely submerged. I struggled to get free and gasp for breath, knowing now that Andrei was trying to kill me. I tried to shout for help and got a big mouthful of water. I fought furiously, but Andrei was strong. Then in sheerest desperation, I pushed and struggled and splashed until I managed to free myself and scrambled out of the tub. I fled from the bathroom, screaming hysterically, looking everywhere for Mrs. Kolmakov or the professor. Neither one was at home. Frightened by my screams and afraid of what his parents might do, Andrei ran out of the house into the back yard.

Even at the age of six, I knew that with Andrei in the house my life would always be in danger, there in my foster home. So I made a big decision. Hurrying to my room, I gathered up some of my clothes, those I could carry easily, stuffed them into a paper bag and left the Kolmakov house for ever. I was so afraid of Andrei I knew I would never come back, no matter how desperately I might wish I could.

Soon I found myself alone on the streets, an orphan, without home or food. The only clothes I had were the ones I was wearing and a few more in my improvised bag-suitcase. There I stood, in the streets of Novosibirsk, lonely, hungry and frightened, wondering what to do next. I must find food and a place to sleep. I must learn how to survive, alone, on the streets of this huge Siberian city. I was soon to discover it was no easy assignment, especially for a child of six.

When I left the Kolmakov home, it was August and warm, so I didn't have to worry about heavy clothing. But even so, my situation was desperate. And in my own childish way, I knew that it was.

What can I do? I thought. *Where can I go?* And while I tried to plan my next move, I wandered the streets aimlessly. Everything and everybody looked so strange and big. Novosibirsk is a huge and sprawling city in central Siberia, with a population of nearly two million. It is called the crossroads of Siberia.

Before long, I found myself in the heart of the city, near the Novosibirsk Central Railway Station. Milling, pushing throngs of people were moving in and out of the huge, cavernous station. If Novosibirsk was really the crossroads of Siberia, this station was the reason why. Trains departed hourly for such distant points as Vladivostok, in the Pacific Far East; Tashkent, down south in Central Asia near Afghanistan; and west to European Russia. It was a real, teeming, chaotic "crossroads" where one would see many different nationalities, hear strange dialects, as great crowds came and went.

For a six-year-old, away from home for the first time, it was an eye-popping experience. I wandered wide-eyed, taking it all in, bewildered and a little frightened, but most of all curious. "This is it," I said to myself, and began looking around to get the layout of the massive building. In the waiting-room I saw rows of benches and I knew certainly that in these buildings, rooms and track areas, I would have no trouble finding a dark corner where I could bed down at night and sleep unnoticed. With trains coming and going from distant points at all hours, no one would ever pay any attention to a little six-year-old boy asleep under a bench. I would be safe here. No one would find me and send me back to the Kolmakovs.

Now that the problem of my new "home" was settled, I began to think about something to eat. This problem was harder to solve. I had run away with only a few coins in my pocket and already I was getting hungry. The ice-cream stand next to the news stand was so inviting I couldn't resist it.

The ice-cream was so good, and the bar I bought so small that I gobbled it down in a few moments. I started to walk away, but I was still hungry. Looking back at the stand, I dug out the rest of the coins from my pocket, just enough for one more ice-cream bar. Something told me I should save it for later in the day when I would really be hungry. But a boy of six doesn't plan ahead too well. So I went back and said, "Give me another ice-cream bar, please." The woman attendant in her white smock handed it to me, and it, too, was quickly gone.

For some time I wandered contentedly, fascinated by the sights and sounds around me, especially the different languages and colourful dress of the people from down south in Asia. I didn't have a care in the world at that moment. But after wandering for a couple of hours, I was hungry again. My pockets were empty, except for one little coin which wouldn't buy anything. I looked at all the cake, pie and candy stands, full of good things to eat. Oh, how I wanted something from every stand! But all I could do was stare at them, think of my empty stomach and wish.

One stand, loaded with delicious-looking wheat cakes, caught my eye. I sauntered over toward it, then stopped abruptly in front of it. There, guarding over it with a watchful eye and two hundred threatening pounds, was a huge, mean-looking woman attendant. To me she looked like a fire-breathing giant! *She's nobody to fool with,* I thought. *I'd better get out of here.*

A colourful fruit stand a few yards down the track caught my eye. But the attendant at the fruit stand, I quickly realized, would hardly win a prize for friendliness either. He didn't speak; he growled. "What do you want, boy? You ready to buy, hey? No? All right, all right, move on." Slowly I backed away, still keeping my eye on those great big red apples and big yellow pears.

When I had started out to look at the stands, I had in mind begging the owners for a little bit of food—maybe some from several of the stands. But after meeting those attendants, I knew it wouldn't be easy. Besides, I had never begged before, nor told a sad story, and I knew I wouldn't be very good at it. But I couldn't give up. I was hungry.

I'm going to try, I said to myself, then looked up and down the rows of stands. At one, I spotted a little old lady who sold sandwiches. She looked kind. Walking over to her, I mustered all the courage I could and got ready to give my heart-breaking plea. I rehearsed it carefully and had it all organized. It was to go like this: "Please, ma'am, I'm just a little boy, separated from my parents, with no money. And I'm awfully hungry." All of that was very true and should have been easy for me to say. But when I started to say it, everything went wrong. I stammered and repeated myself. The woman eyed me, suspiciously at first, then threateningly. The longer I talked, the more she saw through me. Just then a man came up and ordered a sandwich, and she got busy with him, forgetting I was there.

I ran away, deciding I'd never get any food that way and that I'd better give up begging. But what should I do? If I didn't get some food, I'd starve right there. And I thought, self-pityingly, that would serve them right, all of them, for just standing there and letting me shrivel up and die right in front of their eyes.

Then I remembered the small coin in my pocket and I had an idea. I wandered over to the wheat cake stand once more and had a look around. There at the back on the floor, I noticed a square sheet of metal on which the attendant stood. I walked over to the metal sheet, looking as innocent as I knew how, then, fishing around in my pocket and pulling out my last little coin, I tossed it on to the metal. It landed with a loud noise and began to roll.

The clattering sound on the metal caught the woman's attention and, thinking it was her own money falling on the plate, she swung around and looked down. Quickly I dashed over, grabbed a handful of wheat cakes and ran away as fast as I could. Behind me I could hear her excited shouts: "Stop that little boy! He's a thief! Stop him, stop him!" But I was too far away and quickly disappeared in the crowd. I found a quiet corner, far from the food stands, and sat down to eat. Hungrily I gulped down all but two of the cakes. Those two I decided to save for later. I was learning fast! Then I searched and found a dark corner at the far edge of the station, where I huddled up for a good night's sleep. I had survived my first day in the big world.

For ten days in August 1957, I lived by my wits, getting up early each morning to go out and search for my breakfast. On the tenth day I went "shopping" for food, going first to a fruit stand and trying to trick the woman attendant into looking behind her. But just as I opened my mouth to speak, she began to shout, "It's you again! Now you're going to get it, you little scoundrel!" Of all the stands I could have picked, I had chosen one I had stolen from just three days earlier. The attendant recognized me immediately. I took off, running as fast as I could, with the woman at my heels, shouting all the way. I ran and ran, looking back to make sure she wasn't gaining on me.

And then I ran into a solid object—one that talked and grabbed me in a vice-like grip. "Hey!" it said. "Where do you think you're going in such a hurry?" I didn't dare to look up, afraid I had run smack into a policeman. I had!

My days of living at the Novosibirsk Central Railway Station were over. But my time hadn't been wasted. I had learned a lot about survival that would come in handy later.

The policeman took me to the nearby police station where he asked, "Little boy, where are you from? What's your name?"

I wasn't going to tell. They would have sent me back to Mrs. Kolmakov's house, I knew, and I was sure Andrei would try to kill me again. So I said nothing.

"Where are your parents?" the officer asked.

"They're dead," I said.

"What's your name?" I wouldn't answer. Then the officer shouted at me, and I got scared and said, "Sergei."

"What's your family name?" he demanded.

I replied, "My name is Sergei, and I have no mother or father. They are both dead." And I made up my mind I wasn't going to tell him anything more.

Finally the officer became exasperated and called in another officer and said to him, "What are we going to do with this little boy? He won't tell us anything except his first name and that he's an orphan."

"Well then," the police officer said, "send him to one of the children's homes."

A few hours later someone came in a car and took me to

Children's Home Number One. As I entered the home's front door, a heavy-set woman stood at the entrance waiting for me. Without ceremony, she got right to the point and asked brusquely, "What's your name?"

"Sergei."

She didn't press me further, but just looked over the papers sent from the police station and said, "Well, Sergei, I see you don't talk very much. But we'll take care of that."

Not with my help, I thought. *Nobody's going to send me back to the Kolmakovs to be killed by Andrei*. I was sure that it would do no good to tell her about my fears. I knew no one would believe me. To them, I would be just another little kid, making up stories.

"At least you can tell me how old you are, Sergei," she said.

I guessed there would be no harm in that, so I said, "Eight." Of course I was lying. I was tall and big for my age, and I think she believed me. I thought it might throw them off the track and keep them from finding out who I was.

"Where did you go to school then?" she asked, and I thought, *Oh, oh. Trapped by my own lie.*

Still determined not to give them any more information than I had to, I said, "I can't tell you."

"All right," she replied, "we'll give you a test to find out how much you know."

My tests showed that I was not quite good enough for second grade, but almost too good for first grade. So I was told, "You must go through first grade again."

Again, I thought. I had never been to school at all, since school starts for children in Russia at seven, and I was only six. Whatever score I made in the school test was all because of Mrs. Kolmakov, who had taught me reading, writing and arithmetic. Apparently she had taught me well, because the tests showed I was ahead of my grade. I was put in the first grade to go through it "again".

The school I was sent to was near Children's Home Number One, and I did very well, to my surprise. I was the head of my class, and my studies seemed very easy. Life was looking up, I thought.

But very quickly my hopes were shattered. Professor and Mrs. Kolmakov had been trying to find me and had gone to the police for help. They had finally traced me to the children's home. One day the director of the home called me out of class. "Now, Mr. Smart Kid," she said, "we know who you are."

My heart sank and I pleaded with her. "Don't send me back. Please don't send me back."

"Well, we'll see," she said. "I'll have to talk to the others, but I think you can stay here. But you're not eight; you're six. So you can't go to school yet."

"But I'm doing very well," I protested.

"That's not the point. The rules say you can't, and you can't."

But they did allow me to stay at the home. I really wished I could go back to the Kolmakovs but my fear of Andrei kept me from it.

While the other kids went to school, I spent the afternoons at the home. I'll never forget how lonely I was, sitting in my room, looking out the window. I had plenty of time to think now that I had a roof over my head. And I thought mostly of my father and mother and felt the deep loneliness so keenly. When I thought of my brother Vladimir, I began to grow bitter. Why didn't he come for me? Why did he just go off and leave me all alone? Didn't he care what happened to me?

On 1 March 1958, I celebrated my seventh birthday. It was a big day. Now I could go to school next term! When I was enrolled, the teacher told us, "All children in grades one to three must join the Octobrianiks."

I had never heard the word before. But the teacher explained that it was the Communist organization for children in the first three grades. "You don't belong to your parents any longer; now you belong to the Communist state." Since I didn't have any parents, it didn't matter whom I belonged to. The teacher said that to be Octobrianiks meant we were now "grandsons of Lenin".

Lenin? Who is he? I had heard the name and read it on posters at the railway station, but knew very little about him.

"Lenin is the greatest man who ever lived. He not only lived but he lives now and will always live," she said. "Who wants to be grandchildren of Lenin and go on outings and activities?" the teacher continued. And I, along with the others, joined up eagerly. Me, a grandson of Lenin! That's great, I thought.

From age six to nine, I lived in Children's Home Number One in Novosibirsk and went from grade one to three in primary school. I made friends with the other children at the home, and I also made some discoveries. I had thought this was an orphanage for homeless children who, like me, had no parents. I soon learned differently. One day I talked to a boy who was sobbing and asking, "Why do I have to be here? I have a mother and father. Why can't I be home with them?" That was the first I knew that not everyone in the home was an orphan. Only later did I realize that these homes were primarily for children taken from their parents—mothers and fathers who were declared "unfit" by the state because of their religion or political beliefs or for some other reason.

I tried to comfort this little boy, but I couldn't explain to him why he had to be away from his parents when they were close by. I couldn't understand it myself. He had parents. Why couldn't he be home with them? Whenever I missed my own mother's caresses and father's bushy kisses, I thought about that little boy and wondered why he didn't go home to be with his parents. If I had parents, I'd run away to them. Why didn't he?

But more and more, I came to accept things as they were. After all, a nine-year-old boy has friends and games and other things to think about.

5 Adventures and Terror at Verkh-Irmen

One day in 1960, when I was nine years old, the director of Number One came to me and said, "Kourdakov, get your things packed, you're going to a new children's home."

"Where is it?" I asked.

"Not far away. In Verkh-Irmen." I didn't know Verkh-Irmen from Moscow, and was a little afraid. "It's only forty miles up the river from here," she said. The name Verkh-Irmen literally means "up the river Irmen", the name of the small river it was located near.

When the day of my departure came, my few belongings were packed and ready. It was hard to say goodbye to my friends at Number One, but I had no choice. I got into the truck and it started off. A couple of hours later, we reached Verkh-Irmen, a small community too big for a village, not big enough to be a town.

The Verkh-Irmen Children's Home—or "V-I" as we called it—was located on the outskirts of town. It consisted of four buildings—two dormitories, an administration building and cooking and laundry areas. Close by was the school which served the children from the children's home as well as the children from the village. I was really nervous about my new home. However, the children welcomed me warmly, and I soon began making new friends.

Shortly after I arrived, I joined the Young Pioneers, the Communist youth organization for children aged nine to fifteen, one step higher than Octobrianiks. When I was an Octobrianik, I was a grandson of Lenin. Now that I was a Young Pioneer, I didn't know what I was, except that we were each given a bright red kerchief to wear around our necks. When I looked at myself in the mirror I thought I looked quite dashing with it on.

I quickly sensed that, compared to Number One, this children's home was different. First, there were more children here, around 120. Second, the director and instructors, whom we called "aunts" and "uncles", were much tougher. They were hard and utterly indifferent to our needs and wishes. I had tasted a little of this at Number One, but here I learned that a real hatred existed between the aunts and uncles on one side, and the children on the other. Neither group tried to hide their true feelings.

None of the aunts and uncles became such by choice or because they loved to work with children. The party gave them their appointments to raise "little Communists". These jobs were considered by the aunts and uncles to be the worst Communist Party assignments which party members could get. It was considered dead-end work, jobs for those who had no future, whose careers were at an end. Those unfortunate enough to get them were very unhappy and often would take their feelings out on the children. Here at V-I, and later at other children's homes, they sometimes gave the most harsh and brutal beatings for the most minor rule-breaking. At other times they totally ignored us when we really needed straightening out. Though I didn't understand it, I soon began to sense the tension between the children—especially the older ones—and the aunts and uncles.

Things weren't all bad, however. One of the bright spots of my stay there was the friendships I made. One boy I met, about three years older than I, was Ivan Chernega. Ivan was about average height, with sandy, bushy hair and a friendly, smiling face which looked pleasant even when he was angry. He and I hit it off in a warm friendship at the start, in spite of our age difference, because I was big for my age and a little "experienced" by this time. It pleased me a great deal that Ivan took a liking to me, and we were close friends for a long time to come.

Another good friend was Pavel, about ten years old, who had been at V-I for three years. Though small for his age, he made up for his size with cunning and cleverness. I soon learned that to get anywhere in life, you had to be resourceful, and Pavel surely had his share of that quality.

Late one night we were lying in our bunks talking when we were supposed to be sleeping. Pavel was in the bunk next to mine and said, "Say, Sergei, how are you set for money? Need any?"

I thought, that's a stupid question. Who doesn't need money? "Of course, I need money," I told him, "what do you think?"

Pavel then turned over as if to go to sleep, and said, "Well, any time you really need money, Sergei, just let me know."

He went off to sleep, as I lay there wondering what he meant. All the boys knew Pavel was resourceful. But what did he have—a printing press to print his own money? Some kids had joked about Pavel's "money machine", but never did learn where his money came from. He would just disappear when he needed some, then come back with a fresh supply a while later.

The next day I asked him at lunch time, "Pavel, what did you mean last night when you said if I needed money just to let you know? You sound like you print it yourself."

"It's almost that easy," he said, smiling.

"I don't believe you," I snapped. "It's not that easy for anybody, not even you!"

"I can prove it to you. Come with me tomorrow."

The next day Pavel and I met outside the grounds of the children's home. He was carrying a brown paper bag, stuffed with something. "Come on, Sergei," he said, "we're going in to Novosibirsk."

"Novosibirsk!" I exclaimed. "That's forty miles away. What will the uncles say when they find us missing?"

"Oh, they never pay much attention, if we don't cause them trouble. We leave them alone and they leave us alone. Quit worrying and let's go. We'll be back by midnight." So we boarded a bus and got to the big city at about 6 p.m.

"It's about time," Pavel said mysteriously.

I wondered, *What's he planning to do? Rob a bank?*

"Wait right here, Sergei," he ordered and strode around the corner, carrying that ever-present bundle of his. I found a park bench nearby to sit on and settled down to wait for him. While I waited my attention was attracted to a ragged, dirty, hungry-looking boy walking down the street toward me. Instinctively I felt sorry for him—then suddenly realized there was something familiar about him. I looked more closely.

"Pavel, it's you!" I exclaimed. At last I knew what he carried in that brown paper bag—his ragged beggar clothes! He winked.

"Can you guess my secret, Sergei? No printing press. Just these." He pointed to the smelly, dirty, torn clothes he was wearing and handed me some like them. "Hurry up, Sergei. Put these on. The best time for begging is about dinner-time."

This was all pretty unexpected, but I did what he said. I

went to a public lavatory, took off my regular clothes, stuffed them into a bag and put on the tattered, dirty clothes. Then I walked back to Pavel. By that time, he had smeared dirt on his face and really looked pathetic. Before I knew it, he had rubbed his hands in the dirt and started to smear my face, too. I drew back.

"Now look, Sergei," he told me, "you've got to do this right. Stand still till I get you fixed up." And he proceeded to smear my face. Then he stepped back to look at his handiwork, and said, "Not bad if I do say so myself."

"Where now?" I asked.

"Follow me."

I followed him through the streets until we came to one of the best restaurants in Novosibirsk. It was nothing special to look at from outside but had good food. Pavel paced off a few feet down the sidewalk in front of us. There we sat, like two starving ragamuffins. "Now, here's the way you've got to look," he said, as he put on a very sad face. I tried to mimic him.

"No, that's not it! This way!" And he showed me once again how to look sad. Finally, after several attempts, I got it figured out, and Pavel said, "Not bad, not bad. Keep it that way."

"I'll go first," he said, "and show you how it's done. Now here, play something sad on this." He thrust an old harmonica into my hands from the bottom of his bag. Putting it to my mouth, I tried to find out where the "sad" notes were. I fumbled around at the lower end of the harmonica, thinking I might find them there. Apparently that wasn't where they were because Pavel wasn't at all pleased and gave me an angry look. I tried harder and soon figured how to get sad music, while Pavel put on his saddest face and called out to the people coming out of the restaurant.

"Please, I am an orphan. I have no money. I am hungry. Please help a starving orphan. I have no mother and no father. Please?" he pleaded sadly, while I played away with the saddest sounds I could find on the harmonica. Our performance had gone on for several minutes, with no response. *It's not going to work*, I concluded. But just then a man stopped, looked at us compassionately and dropped twenty-five kopeks into Pavel's filthy hat.

It works! I thought. *This is great!*

Another man, with his wife, dropped in fifty kopeks. By that time I had become greatly inspired and my music became sadder and sadder. Pavel, with his sorrowful face, poured out a story of hunger that moved even me.

More and more pedestrians stopped and dropped money into our hats. Finally, during a lull, I said to Pavel, "This is great, but why here?"

"Don't you know anything by now, Sergei? Look at them coming. Do they look very hungry? No, of course not. They're full. They've just eaten a good big meal. Now, how do you suppose they feel when they see poor starving orphans right outside the restaurant? Don't you think their consciences hurt them? This is my best spot!"

"Your *best* spot? Do you have others?"

"Sure," he said, "at least four others. All right now, Sergei, it's your turn."

"Oh no," I protested, "you're doing too well. You keep right on."

"No," he said, "you've got to learn some time."

He took the harmonica from me and began playing the most doleful sounds I have ever heard. He was really good! I put on my longest, saddest face, and before I knew it, I was saying, "My mother is sick; my father is dead. My brothers and sisters are at home starving. Please give me money for my sick mother. Please give me money for my little brothers and sisters. We are hungry." To my astonishment, it worked! Kopeks came dropping into the hat as the people stopped and opened their wallets.

But then, disaster!

Coming out of the restaurant and heading right toward us was the director of the children's home at V-I. He knew us both well, for we had been called to his office many times, and we were sure he would recognize us, despite our disguises. I thought we were done for! My heart was pounding, and the closer he came, the faster it beat. I figured the best thing we could do was to get out of there as fast as we could, so I said, "Let's go, Pavel, he's sure to recognize us!"

"No," said Pavel, "it's too late!"

The director came over to us and asked, "Little boys, where are your parents?" I had such a lump of fear in my throat I couldn't talk.

Pavel saved us by saying, "Our parents are dead, sir." Even when we spoke, the director showed no sign of recognition. Then

I remembered the dirt and grime Pavel had smeared on our faces. Our disguise was working!

"That's unfortunate," he said, without emotion. He walked a few steps, then hesitated, turned and came back. Looking straight at me, he asked, "Haven't I seen you somewhere before?"

I gulped, hung my head to avoid his gaze and timidly said, "No, sir, I don't think so." And to myself I said, "If I get out of this without being caught, Pavel can have it! I'll survive some other way!"

The director must have had a rare moment of sympathy that day, because he did something quite out of character for him. With a shrug, he patted me on the head and handed me some money. "Here," he said, "go and buy yourselves something to eat."

As he walked off, Pavel and I looked at each other—and without a word, as soon as he was around the corner, we jumped up, grabbed the hat full of money and started running. We ran and ran until we almost fell over from exhaustion.

"Boy! That was close!" Pavel said, as he started counting the money and smiling.

"No more, Pavel, no more. This isn't for me. It's too risky," I said.

We boarded a bus back to Verkh-Irmen late that night, with our pockets full of money.

Since little attention was paid to the inmates of V-I by the home's directors, the older boys, thirteen to sixteen years old, began to roam off the grounds into the main part of town. Among them were many of my "heroes", including Ivan Chernega. And when Ivan and his gang invited me, one of the younger kids, to join them, I was overjoyed.

Without proper attention from the children's home officials, the boys became more and more unmanageable, until the packs of marauding children had begun a reign of terror throughout the entire village. No man's property was safe. Every garden was our garden; every yard our yard. We simply walked in wherever we chose and took whatever we wished.

During those times, the director of our home and the aunts and uncles knew what was going on, but they apparently didn't care. Since they were responsible only for what happened on the grounds of the children's home, and nothing was being damaged there, they took the attitude that what we did in town was no concern of theirs. And we were careful to make sure we saved our worst behaviour for the townspeople.

Before long, Verkh-Irmen was completely in our hands. Any of the "wolf pack" victims who dared to protest, suffered swift and certain retaliation. Usually we smashed their windows, tore down their fences or rooted up their vegetable patch.

The threat of breaking windows in winter was especially effective. I remember Ivan Chernega saying, "Smash their windows! Maybe if they freeze a bit, it will freeze their mouths shut and they'll stop telling on us." Sometimes a "wolf pack" would attack the people themselves. A few were seriously hurt.

Soon some of us decided we didn't want to go to school any more and some of the twelve- and thirteen-year-olds broke out the windows of the school. Of course, they took great care not to hit our dormitory windows, or *we'd* be the ones to freeze! All we wanted to do was to get the classrooms so cold it would be impossible to conduct classes in them. But despite precautions, one boy's rock went astray and knocked out one of our dormitory windows. We all nearly froze because of it. We quickly taught him a lesson that considerably improved his aim!

Night after night the "wolf packs" kept the frightened villagers in a state of siege. Finally, in desperation, the villagers wrote secret petitions of appeal to the provincial government reporting the terror prevailing throughout Verkh-Irmen.

In the summer of 1961 the police and provincial authorities ordered the children's home at V-I closed and the children moved elsewhere.

Ivan Chernega came to me and said, "Sergei, have you heard? They're closing the home here."

"No," I replied. "When?"

"Any day, I guess. I hear they're going to split us up and send us to different children's homes."

"What do you think we ought to do, Ivan?"

His answer was prompt and firm. "Well, nobody's going to move me anywhere! I'm going to move myself. Want to come along, Sergei?"

"Yes," I said.

So we made our plans and one morning very early we packed a few things, slipped out of the door and disappeared from V-I for ever. Ivan and I made our way to Novosibirsk. There Ivan asked, "Sergei, where do you want to go next?"

"Well," I said, "I'd like to stay right where we are. I know Novosibirsk and I'd like to spend some time here."

"They'll be hunting for us, you know," Ivan said. "I think we'll have a better chance if we split up."

"You're probably right," I agreed.

"Where will you go, Sergei?"

"I know where I plan to go, Ivan," I said, thinking of my past experience at the railway station. I remembered that I hadn't done so badly there at the age of six. Now that I was three years older, with a lot more experience behind me, I knew I would do really well. And in an emergency, I could fall back on the begging technique Pavel had taught me. Then we said goodbye and parted. Ivan went his way and I went mine—straight to the railway station. I found it just as I remembered it, only more crowded, with bigger throngs of people coming and going.

I was impressed, as I hadn't been at six, with the chaotic scene before me: train announcements, sounds of steam engines, the noise of great crowds. The station afforded a perfect refuge into which I could disappear and hide for long periods without fear of discovery. I was far wiser and more confident now than I had been during my first brief sojourn here. And much more resourceful.

It didn't take me long to find the place where I was going to sleep at night—a dark, secluded area. If I played it clever and didn't do anything to attract attention, there was no reason why I couldn't continue to live this way for months. Knowing how to snatch fruit and cakes would keep me in food.

Whenever I went to the stands to steal food, I always watched for the new attendants to come and go, because I knew it would be fatal for me if I ever went to the same stand twice. One day I went to a fruit stand managed by a new attendant. I had decided I wanted some apples. Walking up to her, I faked a look of alarm, as though I were seeing something very frightening behind her. She whirled around to see what I was staring at. Those few seconds were all I needed. I reached over, while her back was turned, grabbed some apples and took off running at full speed.

I had taken her completely by surprise and left her totally bewildered. A clean getaway, I thought. But I was unaware that a woman had spotted me and watched my routine. She followed me quietly and came over to where I stood eating my apples and said, "Young man, are you really that hungry?"

"How hungry?" I said.

"Hungry enough to do what you just did." I knew then that she had seen me steal the apples. She was about sixty-five years old with a kind face.

She asked me, "Young boy, do you have a place to live and a place to sleep?"

I replied guardedly, "Yes, I have a place to live."

"Where is it?" she asked.

"Well, it's not far away," I replied.

"You know," she said, "I don't think you have any place to sleep. I think you're sleeping here in the station and you're foraging and stealing your food." She paused for a moment, then continued, "Why don't you come home with me? I have a place where you can sleep and I have plenty of food."

Her face was so sweet and kind, that I agreed. She led me to the outskirts of the city to a little wooden shack along a muddy road. Inside, the tiny cabin was clean and tidy.

During a nice warm meal we talked, and after I had told her a nice story, she said she would be glad to have me stay there as long as I wished. She was most helpful and considerate, and I will never forget her kindness. But after a few days, I realized I was a burden on her because she was very poor, and with an extra mouth to feed, she could not manage very long. So one morning I left her a note thanking her and saying goodbye, then slipped away.

I had been away from the V-I children's home about three weeks when I went to the railway station once more to resume my street life. But within three days the police arrested me for stealing things off the tables in the street stands. I felt badly, not so much because I was caught but because I had lost my touch.

A few days after I was arrested, I was sent to the children's home in Barysevo, a place I'll never forget.

6 At war with the uncles and aunts

Barysevo is a small town located about seventeen miles from Novosibirsk, perched on the edge of a cliff carved out by centuries of fierce Siberian winds. The Barysevo children's home sat on the grounds of a former Orthodox church and school long since closed.

The main part of the church itself had become a club for the showing of movies, while the children's home occupied the former church school building. The priest's house had been converted into the laundry where all the children's clothing, bedding and other linen were washed. Two other buildings had been added, until the complex was large enough to accommodate between 100 and 120 children, ranging in age from one to eighteen.

Though I did not realize it when I arrived, the years at Barysevo were to be a turning point in my life. Barysevo was to be my home until I graduated from high school and went into the military, seven years from the day I arrived.

My first experience in my new home was a happy one. The day I arrived and checked in at the boys' dormitory, whom should I see but Ivan Chernega! "Ivan!" I exclaimed. "Where did they catch you? Have you been here long?"

"Sergei!" he shouted, running up to me and clasping my shoulders. "I see you had better luck staying out than I did." And he went on to tell me how he had been picked up in Novosibirsk and brought to Barysevo.

He listened eagerly to my story and then said, "Well, Sergei, I was going to show you how to survive on the outside, but it looks like you showed me instead!"

"Ivan, what's it really like here?" I asked him. "You know what I mean?"

"Well," he said, "it's a lot like V-I. And let me warn you, there are a couple of people here you'd better not cross. One of them is an uncle named Alexander Nichman—Uncle Nichy we call him. The other is the director, Irene Dobrovlanskaya. All

39

the kids call her Big Irene. They're the two bad ones, Sergei. Stay away from them. Otherwise the aunts and uncles here are about the same as those at V-I. You leave them alone and they leave you alone." I nodded in understanding.

There was a big change in Ivan that I noticed right away. I couldn't quite put my finger on it, but just the same, I saw that Ivan was different. When he introduced me to other friends he had made at Barysevo, I began to feel good for the first time.

My introduction to Big Irene came when I was called into her office just after my arrival at the home. Ivan's warnings were fully justified. She was an imposing, huge, fearsome woman. My first look at her told me that she would not accept any foolishness from anybody, ever.

On her white smock she wore the medal of the Order of Lenin. It was a high order in the Soviet Union, given to those Communists who had rendered outstanding service to the Communist Party. Big Irene was never seen without her medal. She apparently wanted everybody to know she was somebody of importance who had made a significant contribution to the party. But that was in the past, and for some unknown reason she had been sent to Barysevo. She was a woman embittered by disappointment at having been assigned to such an obscure post.

Almost as imposing and fearsome a figure was our chief uncle Alexander Nichman. I have never known another man quite as mean-looking and formidable as he. I met him a couple of days after I had met Big Irene. He was very tall, heavily built and exceptionally strong, with a violent temper that could be touched off by the slightest provocation. The vengeance he would take and the injury he would inflict with his powerful strength could be most horrible. Even without Ivan's warning, I knew Uncle Nichy was no one to fool with, so I made up my mind right from the start I would avoid him like the plague.

Like Big Irene, he had seen better days with the Communist Party. At one time he had been a pilot in the Soviet air force, but for some reason that he kept carefully concealed, he had been demoted and discharged from the military. No one could find out more. Rumours were he crashed a plane while drunk. The slightest hint that anyone was trying to probe into his past would set him off in a violent rage.

Uncle Nichy felt it quite a come-down to end his career as prison warden, as he called it, to juvenile delinquents. He was a

most cruel man, without a spark of kindness in him and con-
tinually taking out his frustrations on anyone who ruffled
him.

Most of the aunts and uncles at Barysevo had been there for
twenty to thirty years. During that time, any love or concern
they might once have felt for their young charges had long since
disappeared. The new young workers who came to Barysevo,
however, brought along many ideas for developing good relationships with the children. But within a year or two they had
changed so radically they could hardly be recognized as the same
eager young overseers. So dominated were they by Big Irene and
Uncle Nichy that they, too, gave up and became as apathetic
as the others.

An atmosphere of fear prevailed throughout the home. We
were afraid of the aunts and uncles. They were afraid of Big
Irene and Uncle Nichy, who, in turn, were afraid of the party
leaders. Barysevo became a camp of hate and fear, divided
between the wardens and the children. Sometimes, during my
first months there, I longed to talk about my problems with an
aunt or uncle. I wanted someone to smile and be friendly,
counsel me and show some approval. But I quickly learned that
the rules at Barysevo tolerated no such "weak" behaviour.

Once we smaller kids realized that these were the rules, we fell
into the hateful attitudes of the older children. And yet, it was
in this hostile atmosphere that bonds of friendship, which were
to last for years, were developed. We children, realizing that all
we really had in life was one another, formed a close-knit circle
to stand against the adult world. Within this circle was an inner
circle made up of our own leaders—the toughest, strongest and
cleverest among us.

How I wanted to belong to that inner circle! But since the
other boys were twelve and thirteen years old and I was barely
ten, I felt there was no chance of it. Then one day Nikolai
Povaleyev called to me and said, "Sergei, come over here. We
want you to give us a hand." I went over to where the boys
from the inner circle were standing. One of them was holding
a box of light bulbs. Nikolai said, "You see, Sergei, we've got to
change the light bulbs in some of the buildings here and we need
your help."

"I'll help," I said. I was flattered at the invitation, especially
when it came from someone like Nikolai, so respected and
admired a comrade. "Tell me what you want me to do."

"Come on, follow me, and I'll show you," he told me.

So off we went, me following Nikolai, and the others trailing after us, all heading for the former main church building which was now the movie and recreation centre.

As we entered the door, Nikolai pointed up to the high ceiling and said, "Sergei, you see that light up there?"

"Yes," I replied.

"Well, it's burned out, and we want you to help replace it with this new bulb."

"All right," I said. "Where's the ladder?"

"Well, that's just it; we don't have a ladder."

"How am I going to get up there?"

"We'll improvise and find a way," answered Nikolai. Quickly he and the other fellows rustled about and came back with about five or six chairs which they stacked, one on top of another, until they reached most of the way up to the light fixture.

I was dumbfounded. "Do you want me to climb that?" I exclaimed. I couldn't believe it, but they did. Nikolai turned to the fellows and said, "Hold the chairs as tight as you can and, Sergei, go ahead. Climb up and get that bulb in. It's all right. You can trust us."

There was nothing to do but start climbing. If I didn't, I'd be branded a coward. I'd never really be accepted. With the light bulb tight in hand, I began to climb, finally getting up to the sixth chair. I paused for a moment and looked down worriedly. But when I saw all of the fellows holding on to the chairs for dear life, I decided I was in good hands. Then just as I reached up to screw the bulb in place, I heard Nikolai, my friend, shout, "Now!" And he jerked the bottom chair out. I fell crashing to the floor in a tangled heap of chairs.

For a few seconds I lay there completely stunned. All the fellows stood and laughed at me while I pulled myself out of the pile of smashed chairs. *Some friends!* I thought. They all turned and walked off, leaving me to disentangle myself as best I could. It's a wonder I hadn't broken my neck. As it was, I had badly bruised my hip and had to hobble back to the dorm, like an old man. Somebody called across the yard, "Hey, Sergei, what happened? You look like you got hit by a train!" And everybody laughed. I didn't know it then, but I had been given the "light bulb treatment".

I finally made it back to the dorm. The pain in my battered body was bad enough, but my disappointment in my "friends" was even worse. None of them said a word to me. I couldn't figure out what was going on.

Then on the third day, Boris came to me and said, "Sergei, you made it! You're in!"

"In? What are you talking about?"

"You're in, Sergei. In! Don't you understand?"

"No, I don't understand," I growled. "All I know is that you guys almost got me killed."

"Sergei, you dumbhead, don't you know that was a test? We couldn't admit you to our group until we could find out if you could keep a secret without running to Big Irene or Uncle Nichy and blabbing about every little thing that goes on and getting us all into trouble. We had to find out if you knew how to keep your mouth shut. You passed the test. Come on with me."

So I followed Boris and we went to the club where we found Nikolai, Ivan, Alex and the others. They all welcomed me, and I thought, *I made it! I guess I really am in the group.* Later I learned it was one of many tests every new boy was put through before he could be trusted. We were two factions at war at Barysevo—the children against the aunts and uncles—and we had to determine which side we were going to be on, then stick together no matter how rough things got.

One by one I began to meet the fellows who were going to be the main people in my life for the rest of my stay at Barysevo. Many of them I met through my good friend, Ivan Chernega.

First, there was Boris Lobanov. Though he was about my age, he had been at Barysevo much longer than I and was wiser in the ways of survival in the home. Boris was a Greek-Russian, heavy-set and as tall as I, strong, dark and rather good-looking. He was the kind of friend you could trust with your life, which I found I would have to do on several occasions.

I also met Mikhail Kirilin. An Asiatic type, he appeared outwardly fierce and forbidding. But inside he was warm-hearted, friendly and totally reliable. He could always be counted on in a tough situation. Mikhail was also about my age, but he had been at Barysevo a year longer. I asked him many things about his background, but he told me little. I knew him as a hard worker, energetic and resourceful. I learned, too, that he had many contacts back in the region of Tashkent in Asia. Later we were to develop these contacts in order to use them in our special business.

43

Nikolai Povaleyev was one of the toughest, strongest and most ruthless fellows I have ever met. When you were on the right side of Nick, you were well off. But woe to the person who rubbed him the wrong way. Once you had won his loyalty, however, you found him a true and constant friend. His contacts and amazing resources were always yours to draw upon in a time of need. There was a saying at Barysevo that whoever won Nick for a friend could afford a lot of enemies. His strength, ambition and natural talents had quickly propelled him into positions of leadership in any situation or group. Remarkable person that he was, Nick was bound to go far in whatever job in life he would choose.

Then there was Alexander Popov. Alex had to be one of the most remarkable fellows I would ever run across in any children's home and certainly one of the world's best pickpockets. After a two-minute conversation with you, he could walk away with almost anything you carried or wore, from your wallet to your shoes! He was a fellow of unusually good humour, always even-tempered. At the same time, he was another one it was far better to have on your side than against you.

Alex was always good for a few roubles. Whenever we needed cash, he would go to Novosibirsk, ride the streetcars and come out at the other end with his pockets bulging with wallets and money. He was often the "provider" for our four-man gang, comprised of Nikolai, Ivan, Boris and me. We nicknamed him Light Fingers and called him our treasurer. Whenever we ran low on funds, all we had to do was turn to good old Alex.

There were other young fellows at Barysevo that I came to know and appreciate, among them two brothers, Alexander and Vladimir Lobuznov. They proved themselves good friends but were never allowed into the inner circle because Alexander had a fierce temper he was unable to control. It eventually caused his death. The loss of their parents was, I heard, especially tragic, but I never did learn the full story.

Others came in and out of our group, like Sorokin and Pavel Kiryakov. Though they were liked by our group and proved their loyalty to it, they never quite made it into the inner circle.

One remarkable young fellow, Nikolai Saushkin, was a bit older than the rest of us and always stood off to the side, never really becoming part of us. Because he was nearing eighteen, he was soon to leave Barysevo. However, he left the home under unusual and unexpected circumstances and I was to meet him again.

Homes like the one at Barysevo, wherever they might be, were to serve as factories turning out tomorrow's Communists. Propaganda was everywhere. Huge placards and slogans were painted in yellow letters on flaming red boards reading:

"We will defeat American imperialism!"

"All support to the people of Vietnam!"

"Long live peace, freedom, and solidarity!"

"Proletarians of the world, unite!"

These slogans were in all the children's homes where I ever lived. We could hardly turn around without seeing them. They were in the dormitories and rooms, the dining hall and washrooms, posted on outside walls, hanging on fences and anything else that would support them. Images like, "We will defeat American imperialism!" were burned into my mind, until they became a part of me.

The school and children's home at Barysevo were separate. The school was in the village of Barysevo itself. We kids from the home went to school there along with the children of the village. This was fortunate. It meant that we could develop good relations with our teachers, even though the relationship with the adults of the children's home was one of mutual hatred. School to us was a break from the pressures of life at the home, a welcome opening into a different world.

As a member of the Young Pioneers, I underwent an indoctrination programme much more intense than it had been in the Octobrianiks. Lenin peered at us from every wall. His slogans, sayings and Communist ideology so saturated the classrooms that arithmetic, language and other studies took a back seat. For the Octobrianiks, school indoctrination in Communism is mostly an introduction to "Grandfather Lenin". But as we got into the fourth grade, it became more intensive. But one thing stayed the same: almost every morning, the teacher started the class by saying, "Good morning, children. How are you today? Remember there is no God." I thought, *They must sure be afraid we'll learn about God, whatever God is.*

I had great enthusiasm and eagerness to learn. In the fourth and fifth grades I was such an active Young Pioneer that when I reached sixth grade I was appointed leader for the school.

We were trained to march and to shout slogans, such as, "Long live Communism; long live Lenin". And as we marched up and down the streets of Barysevo we held our heads high and proudly displayed the red kerchiefs around our necks. I think the townspeople got a little tired of all our marching and shouting of slogans of "long live this and long live that". They often slammed their windows closed whenever one of our marching groups passed by. But I didn't mind. I felt I "belonged" for the first time in my life.

The activities of the Young Pioneers were perfectly geared to the interest of our age level. We were given mock machine guns and organized into brigades and battalions to fight make-believe military battles and take towns by storm. We hardly needed to be pushed. We charged across Barysevo, down streets and across lanes in simulated battle. Sometimes it became all too real when we got over-enthusiastic and crashed through fences and across gardens, leaving behind a trail of enraged and shouting villagers. Boris, Nikolai and I thoroughly enjoyed such exercises and jumped into them with both boots.

Meanwhile, life back at the children's home continued.

As time went on, we boys found it harder and harder to understand the cruelty of our leaders at the home. For minor infractions of the rules, we received brutal punishment.

One of the rules of the home was a nap every afternoon for everybody. But I certainly had no intention of obeying a rule like that. I was about twelve years old, big, muscular and full of energy, and I couldn't imagine anything more boring. Reading was one of my favourite pastimes and I did a lot of it, even during the afternoons when I was supposed to be sleeping. I took a flashlight to bed with me and read under the covers. I did it almost every day and nothing ever happened.

Then one day Uncle Nichy was in a foul mood, partly drunk and trying to find someone to take out his hostilities on. It happened to be Sergei Kourdakov he was after. There I was, reading under the covers, not suspecting a thing, when suddenly I felt a heavy fist in my side, knocking me out of bed. Startled and shaken, I looked up. There was Uncle Nichy standing over me, looking ten feet tall, instead of his usual six. He was yelling, "Kourdakov, I caught you this time. You're a worthless, no good boy. I'm going to beat you to within an inch of your life. I'm going to teach you a lesson you're never going to forget!"

I was really scared. I didn't know what to expect. I was big for my twelve years, but I was no match for Uncle Nichy. Next thing I knew, he grabbed me by my pyjama top, dragged me across the room and shouted, "I'm going to give you some Vitamin P, Kourdakov. Vitamin P. You know what that is, Kourdakov?" He laughed drunkenly. I trembled. We all knew what Vitamin P was! The Russian word for belt buckle is *Pryazhka*. When he used it, he called it giving us our "Vitamin P".

I watched him as he took off that big heavy belt with the huge metal buckle. Even a thrashing with the leather part of it would have been terribly painful, but he had to beat us with the buckle, which would leave us really bruised and broken. "All right, Kourdakov," Uncle Nichy said, with hatred in his voice. "Get ready for your Vitamin P! Maybe it'll teach you a lesson." By this time all the startled kids had jumped up from their nap and were looking on, scared and wide-eyed.

The last thing I ever would do was beg for mercy, from anybody. Even though I was about as scared as I had ever been before, I tried to put up a big front. But that only infuriated Uncle Nichy more. And he began to beat me, hitting me with the edge of that heavy belt buckle again and again, not caring where it landed. I jumped about trying to dodge his blows, but he held me in such a grip in his left hand I couldn't shake loose. Everywhere that buckle landed, it felt like it broke a bone. I wondered if he was trying to kill me. I was bleeding from behind my ribs, where the edge of the buckle had cut deeply into my flesh. Finally, when he was so exhausted he could hardly stand, Uncle Nichy pushed me away and shouted, "Now get out of here, you dirty little punk, and don't ever let me catch you reading again."

I stumbled back to my bed and fell across it, hurting everywhere in my body. I was sure I must have broken bones. That beating hurt me more than any I had ever had in my life, but I wasn't going to let Uncle Nichy have the satisfaction of seeing me show any pain. So I covered my head with my blanket and writhed in agony—but I wouldn't cry. That brute of a man would never see me shed a tear for anything he could ever do to me. And neither would anyone else!

From the day of that merciless beating, I could think of hardly anything else but getting even with Uncle Nichy. I hated him more than ever. My chance was soon to come.

Several days after the beating, Nikolai Povaleyev came to me and said, "Sergei, it's time we taught Nichman a lesson."

"What can we do?" I asked.

"Just leave that to me," he said. "I've been around a little longer and I can think of something."

"All right," I said eagerly, "I'll go along with anything. But let's just make sure he gets everything he deserves."

When Povaleyev set his mind to something he wouldn't let up until he got what he wanted. So the next day he came back with Boris and Ivan and a great idea. "Sergei," Povaleyev said, "we've got it all planned, how we're going to take care of Nichy and give him some of his own Vitamin P." We huddled together and he told me what we would do. The idea sounded perfect, and I could hardly wait to get started on it.

Every night, around eleven o'clock, Nichy would come into the dormitory to check on everybody. This night we would have a surprise for him. The room was dark and still, and we listened intently for footsteps, big heavy ones. It was not long till we heard them. Nichy was coming.

The dormitory door opened, and Nichy walked in, not suspecting a thing. Then we went into action! Povaleyev and two others jumped on his back and quickly pulled a cloth sack over his head so he couldn't see who we were and what was going on. Two others had unscrewed the light bulbs so he couldn't turn the lights on. Others jumped on him, hit him with their fists, beating and kicking and pummelling him to the floor. I took special delight in giving him a couple of good hard blows right on the nose. I hoped I had broken it. We swarmed all over him kicking and beating, while he shouted, his yelling stifled by the sack over his head. The kids who were not in on the plan knew what was going on, but they just kept their heads under the covers. They saw nothing and we knew they would say nothing.

Nichy took a good beating that night. Three boys sat on him and held him down while the others dashed to their beds and jumped under the covers. Then they turned loose and jumped into bed too. Nichy, shocked, shaken and bleeding at the nose, jerked the sack off his head and staggered out of the door, cursing. We heard him raging and bawling all the way back to his quarters. Then we all braced for the explosion.

But there was none. Not that night, nor the next day, nor the next week. He just didn't say anything about it, ever. But we knew he was suspicious of who did it and we figured he was waiting for a chance to get back at us. But we had vowed to stick together, no matter what, and if Nichy ever tried to give anybody Vitamin P again, we'd beat him instead. A balance of terror now existed between us and Nichman, and I can tell you, we felt ten feet tall!

In 1963 things began to get extremely bad at Barysevo. Until then, the food at the children's home had been poor but adequate. But now it began to decline in quality and quantity. We found ourselves getting hungrier and hungrier. What we ate at lunch no longer lasted us until dinner time, and when we protested and asked for more, we were simply told there wasn't any. The food crisis became worse not only in the children's home but in the village of Barysevo as well.

Soon we learned that the shortage extended throughout the country, and was worsening rapidly. We were told that Khrushchev had a weakness for corn and thought he could grow it anywhere, even on the moon. In his eagerness to increase the corn crop, he had dug up land normally used for wheat and other foods and substituted corn for them. It was soon learned that corn would not grow there, and a famine spread throughout many parts of Russia.

It was no secret to us where the food supplies were kept at the home, so we planned a raid. But Uncle Nichy and Big Irene were one jump ahead of us. They made sure all food was under lock and key and guarded. And no matter how cleverly we planned, we could find no way to get to it.

For months, all we got to eat for the whole day was one corn flatcake, something like a hard pancake. The flatcakes were hard and dry, but at least they were something to put in our mouths. I broke mine in two every day, eating half in the morning, a quarter in the afternoon and the final quarter at night. With hunger on our minds, all serious study at school stopped and we formed into wolf packs of children desperately foraging for food and fighting over pieces of potato peels or whatever we could get. After months of this meagre diet, I began to get a bad case of scurvy. My teeth came loose and I could feel my strength waning.

But many of the children were in a far worse condition than I. My very good friend Sasha Ognev was small for his age, but always a most pleasant, cheerful person. I could see he was failing more rapidly than the rest of us, though he had been on the same diet. Day by day, Sasha grew thinner and weaker, his skin becoming very white and his face pallid. Soon we found him spending more and more time in bed, too weakened to move about.

After a few weeks, his stomach and his whole body began to swell. I had never had any experience with starvation before and didn't know it when I saw it. Poor Sasha tried to put on a good face and smile, but I could see that he was in a really bad condition. Our inner circle hung around and tried to help him, but there was nothing we could do. The only solution here for Sasha was good food.

One day I heard a noise of several people at the door of the boys' dormitory. As the door opened, there stood Big Irene, as fat as ever. She was a big shot and it was beneath her dignity to come to our dorm. But there she was, for some reason. I don't know where she got *her* food, but it was obvious she hadn't lost a pound. After hesitating at the door a moment, she strode over to Sasha's bed, with a twisted smile on her lips and that medal of the Order of Lenin hanging prominently from her coat.

I was near Sasha's bed when Big Irene reached it, and I watched as she pulled back the covers and looked at Sasha's swollen body, bloated from hunger and malnutrition. Leaning down, she patted him on his thin little face and said, "Oh, I see you've put on some weight, Sasha! You look pretty healthy. I've got a weight problem too, you know." A half-smile came over her face. She paused, took one sweeping glance at the dormitory, then strode away.

I felt an overpowering wave of hatred for Big Irene at that moment. How could she compare her rolls of fat with Sasha's tiny body, swollen by malnutrition and hunger? I could feel the anger rising from every child in the dormitory. The whole room was charged with tension.

Two days later, when I came home from school about four o'clock in the afternoon, I walked into the dormitory and put my things in the chest at the foot of my bed. Then I walked over to see Sasha and ask how he was doing. I whispered to him. "Sasha?"

There was no response. I peeked under the covers. His face was white and frigid, and I knew he was dead. My friend Sasha had died alone and no one had even noticed that the life had gone from his little body.

Sasha's death hit me hard. Of all that took place at Barysevo, it had the greatest impact on me in changing my attitude and outlook on life. From Sasha's death, I realized many things. First of all, that life is the survival of the fittest. It is a jungle. The strong will live. The tough will make it. The weak will lose or die.

I walked from that room fighting back tears and vowing, *If this is how life is, I will be the toughest, the strongest, the smartest.*

Two other children died in that famine in Barysevo. One little girl calmly said goodbye to her friends, walked into a lake and drowned. Another, only eleven, was found hanging from the rafters. It was just too much for them.

7   King of Barysevo

The leaders of the children's home cared nothing for us as individuals. Because they generally hated their jobs, they left us largely to our own devices to govern our own lives. So long as we didn't damage the buildings or completely bring routine activities to a halt, they mostly ignored us.

We were free to organize our own life with a minimum of adult interference, so we created our own little world. It was as structured as any society in the outside world. The inmates were divided into three distinct categories: the slaves, the lieutenants and, on top, the king.

The slaves were the younger children, smaller and weaker than the others. It was their responsibility to carry out the jobs given them by the older children. Assigned to manual labour and menial work, they were forced to serve those above them. Most of the children belonged to that category.

The lieutenants who gave the slaves their assignments and supervised their work were a small, more exclusive group. They exercised control in the day-to-day life in our own society at Barysevo. They were an élite commander corps that delighted in ordering the others about. Above the lieutenants, reigning supreme over all, was the king. He was the unchallenged ruler in the home over all the children there. He was selected on the basis of two tests, one physical and one psychological. Physically, he must be big and strong. He must prove his physical superiority by being able to beat any other boy in the home, who might himself want to be king. Psychologically, he must command the respect as well as the fear of the children. He must be one cunning enough to beat the hated system at the home.

The king's life was relatively easy, mainly because he had his lieutenants below him to carry out his orders and all the slaves in the school to look after him and obey his every command.

I don't remember the boy who was king when I first went to Barysevo. He was much older than I and ready to leave the home when I arrived. Nikolai Povaleyev became his successor, and I was merely a slave.

My first job as a slave at Barysevo was to polish the king's shoes. After they were ready, I had to stand at attention and wait for the king to decide whether they were acceptable. As he examined them carefully and critically, I stood there trembling, hoping I had pleased him. And usually I had, because I was a good shoe-polisher. I was never hit or shouted at for doing a poor job.

Sometimes the king would decide to lie in bed and summon one of his slaves to comb his hair carefully, so it would be in perfect order when he got up. His clothes, also, would have to be carefully arranged, his boots polished and ready to put on. Then his breakfast would be served. Everything had to be done so he could truly live in a manner fit for a king. After the king had arisen and was prepared for the day, he would summon his lieutenants and begin to issue orders and instructions, sending them out to organize the slaves for their day's tasks.

Any dispute among the slaves had to be settled by the king, who would instruct the lieutenants to bring the dissenters to him, so that he could listen to them, sometimes kindly and patiently, sometimes angrily. After hearing all sides of the story and the arguments, he would render his verdict and it would be the final law.

But the king's throne was an uneasy one. Always there was some lieutenant eyeing him carefully, looking for the slightest sign of weakness and hoping that he might overthrow the king and take his place.

When I first became aware of the little society the children had created, I wondered what Uncle Nichy and Big Irene would say when they discovered the king and lieutenants and the whole system. To my surprise one day, I saw Uncle Nichy talking to the king. They were discussing rules Uncle Nichy wanted carried out. Then I understood! This complete system wasn't kept secret from Uncle Nichy and Big Irene at all. They knew all about it and they used it for channelling their wishes to the king and through him they ran the children's home.

I remained a slave for only a short time. When I became a little bigger and a little stronger, I challenged a lieutenant and beat him up and took his place. Before long I was one of the top lieutenants in the home. Most of my friends of the inner circle—Boris, Alex and the others—also became top lieutenants when Nikolai was king, and we were able to do pretty much what we liked.

I was determined to become the strongest boy in the home,

and eventually to become king. That was my goal, and no one, including Nikolai, was going to stop me from reaching it! But because Nikolai was my friend, I only hoped that I wouldn't have to take him on personally.

Then one day in late 1965, when I was fourteen, Nikolai called me and said, "Well, I'm going to be transferred to another children's home, Sergei. You should be king here at Barysevo. You've got what it takes!" I didn't tell him that's what I was planning, but I did say I was sorry to see him leave. "Don't worry, Sergei," he said, "I won't be very far. I'm going to a home near Novosibirsk."

"Great!" I said. "Let's get together there in the city."

"Sure," he said. "I'll introduce you to some of my friends." It was rumoured around Barysevo that Nikolai knew murderers and narcotics pushers by their first names. And to think he would introduce me to them! Criminals, individuals who could beat the system, were greatly admired by the Barysevo boys.

I said goodbye to Nikolai, and he left for the other children's home. As I expected, in a short time he became king there. I was very glad I didn't have to fight him to become king at Barysevo.

But even at that, I knew the throne he was vacating at Barysevo would not be easy to win. There were four other boys who wanted to be king. One by one, I took them on and beat every one of them. Only one gave me a hard time, but I was able to finish him by smashing his face in.

Soon it was very clear who was the new king. We had fought by the rules of our society, and I had won. If at any time some lieutenant thought he could whip me, he had the right to try. But for now I had won, and I was crowned the new king at Barysevo. For a fourteen-year-old, that was not bad.

I appointed my inner circle of friends my top lieutenants. With them, I was able to control and run most of the home. Boris, Mikhail Kirilin, Alex and the others in my group were ready to cater to my every wish. If I needed money, I just told Alexander, our pickpocket "treasurer", I wanted "fifty roubles by sunset". At sunset, sure enough, Alexander would come back from Novosibirsk with the money I had asked for. I'm sure he kept that much, or more, for himself.

The most objectionable part of being king was the fact that I had to deal with Uncle Nichy and Big Irene. I detested them. They could sense this and kept their distance from me. I told

Boris, "I'm going to have as little to do with them as I can. I want you to make contact with them. I hate them!" Boris accepted my order although he didn't want to deal with them any more than I did.

All in all, life at Barysevo went on fairly well for me. I was in the Communist Youth League at school, and king at the children's home. And I felt good about that.

As kids reached the age of sixteen, seventeen or eighteen, they left the home and their places were taken by new children whom we didn't know. We had no idea how reliable they were, or anything about them. So we had to put them quickly to the light bulb test, the same one I had been through years earlier. If a boy told one of the aunts or uncles, he'd never be trusted by us. He was branded a spy. On the other hand, if he kept his mouth shut, he'd be accepted by the other kids as reliable.

Because of the trouble the spies could get us into, we developed special treatment for any we caught informing or spying on us. Once one of the fellows got mad at another and reported him to Uncle Nichy. Uncle Nichy beat the offending boy. The spy was found out. Under the rules of our little world, he had to pay. He had to be taught a lesson.

I sent Boris and Mikhail to get him. They taped his mouth while he was sleeping and, with him kicking wildly, dragged him out. A couple of other boys emptied his locker at the foot of his bed, leaving his toothbrush, clothing and other belongings spread out all over the floor. We carried him and his locker to a ravine in the grounds of the home.

"Open up the locker," I ordered. "Now stick him in." Boris and Mikhail crammed the boy into the locker, closed and locked it, then carried it to the very edge of the ravine. As we lifted it on end, I shouted, "All right. Let it go!" With that, we gave it a big shove, and the locker, with the spy inside, tumbled down the steep hill end over end, bouncing and crashing all the way, until finally it came to rest at the far bottom.

"All right, somebody go down and let him out now," I ordered. "Maybe he's learned his lesson."

That trick shut the mouth of that spy right there. The poor kid could hardly walk for the next two weeks. He had bruises all over him. But it was a lesson he had to learn. In our world of conflict in the children's home at Barysevo, there was no room for spies.

I ran a tight ship. But I wanted all the children to know that if they did right and were fair, they need not worry. I tried to make sure that I never abused my position of power and authority.

As king, I made it my business to learn as much as I could about the children in the home. Almost a third of them had been taken from their parents and sent to Barysevo, and I was curious to find out why. It was a question that had bothered me, off and on, for a long time.

I was amazed at what I learned. Some were there because their mothers were prostitutes or their fathers were drunkards or because their parents were believers in God. Such parents had been declared unfit by the state, had been stripped of their parental rights, and their children sent to Barysevo.

One of those whose parents were Believers was a thirteen-year-old boy. He was always a bit of a mystery, very different from all the others. He was small for his age, bright, intelligent and always studying. He did his duties as a slave without complaining but then kept to himself. Whenever he did talk to other children, he always talked about God. When I heard about him, I was fascinated. Nobody had ever talked about God before around Barysevo. Or anywhere else I had been. Somebody drew a cartoon of the little fellow on a wall and made him look like a priest, with a halo on his head and a greased beard on his face. One of the other kids came along and wrote under the picture in pencil, "The Deacon".

The nickname stuck, and from that time on, it was the only name we ever used for him. "Hey, Deacon," I shouted once when I saw him. "Come here." Well, to be called by the king was something, and he came running. "What's this I hear about you going around talking about God? Is it true?"

"Well, yes . . . yes it is," he stammered.

"Are you a Believer?" I asked. I was really curious. I had never seen a Believer up close before. To me, it was like asking if somebody was from Mars or the moon. I had heard some things about Believers, even rumours that my mother had been one. I put my arm around his shoulder and began to walk and talk with him. I found that the Deacon was a real "missionary". Though grim and gloomy-faced most of the time, when he started talking about God, he promptly came alive. His face would light up and you couldn't turn him off! He'd begin to give the background and the history of God and man and fill his story with examples from the Bible. I was dumbfounded. He was an object of curiosity to me and I took him under my wing and talked with him often.

One day in winter, after a heavy snowfall, we were all very happy because we could ski down the sharp slopes of the ravine. The Deacon was out there watching us, and I called him over and said, "Hey, Deacon, does your God hear our prayers?"

"Yes, He does," he answered. I could see his face begin to beam and I knew he was about to give me another message about God.

"Hold on," I said. "I'm not ready for a sermon now. All I want to know is, does your God answer prayer?"

"Yes, He does."

"Good," I said. "You mean that when I get ready to ski down this slope, if I ask God to help me ski better, He will?"

"Of course," the Deacon said.

"Even over there?" I asked, pointing to the sharpest and most dangerous slope on the ravine, "where no one has ever skied before?"

"Yes, even there. God will hear your prayers, Sergei."

"I'm going to give it a try," I told him.

With everybody watching, I walked down the ravine to a slope which fell off sharply. I stood at the top with my skis on, ready to shove off. But I gulped. It was the steepest slope I had ever dared to try. I was scared.

"Start praying!" I shouted to Deacon, and off I went. Swift as a bullet, I zoomed almost straight down. To my amazement, I stayed on my feet, then came to a neat stop at the bottom of the hill! Looking up, I shouted, "Hey, Deacon, it worked! It worked!" I carried my skis back up the slope, slapped the Deacon on the back, and said, "Boy, that's not bad. You and I have got to stick together, Deacon. You do the praying and I'll be the ski champion."

Once more I went confidently down the side, picked up speed then tumbled and fell flat on my face. From that point down, I skied more on my nose than my feet and came to a crashing stop at the bottom of the ravine. Everybody started laughing, until I looked up, and then they stopped. The Deacon stood there, a little afraid.

"Hey, Deacon," I shouted, "What happened this time? Did God go to sleep?"

I climbed back up the hill, threw my arms up and said,

"Well, I guess even God can't hear all the time, hey, Deacon?"
And he was relieved.

Some of the boys at the home hated the Deacon because he did so well in school and made all the others look bad in class. Fortunately, he was not in my grade, or I might not have liked him either. When some of the boys picked on him and beat him up several times, I heard about it and ordered it to be stopped. But still they teased and tormented him.

One day I asked him, "Deacon, what do you want to be?"

"Well," he said, "all my life I've wanted to go to Bible college and study the Bible more. That's what I'm hoping for, Sergei, and I'm praying that some day God will give me that chance."

He wouldn't talk about his family. One day I overheard one of the other boys asking him, "Deacon, where are your mother and father? Why are you here?" Deacon grew very sad. I don't think I've ever seen sadder eyes in all my life. He had a faraway look and a big lump in his throat. He couldn't talk, just got up and went into the dormitory. I followed him and found him lying on his bunk face down, with his head covered by a pillow, sobbing.

It was later that I learned his mother and father were Believers in God and lived in Ogurtsovo, only seventeen miles away. Because they were Believers and had taught the Deacon about God they had been brought before a judge, declared unfit parents and stripped of their parental rights for life. The little Deacon was pronounced officially without parents and made a legal ward of the state until his adult life. He would never see his mother and father again, even though they were only seventeen miles away. It was a great load for a boy to carry, a tragedy that he will carry with him for the rest of his life.

Just now, however, he had other burdens to bear. Persecuted severely for his faith by the aunts and uncles, he was tormented at every turn. At the slightest provocation, they would shout at him and mistreat him. Uncle Nichy especially hated him. Frequently he would come storming in shouting angrily, "Where is that Deacon? Where is the little devil? I've got some Vitamin P for him." Deacon would slip off his bunk and walk over to Uncle Nichy, who would grab him roughly by the coat and drag him out to where he would give him a brutal dose of Vitamin P.

I never learned what finally happened to the little Deacon, but I knew there was no place in Russia for anybody like that.

Later I discovered that there were hundreds of Barysevo-type children's homes across Russia and hundreds of other Deacons who had been taken from their parents. The little Deacon was my first close contact with anybody who believed in God, and I will never forget him.

8 Training ground for criminals

When I was fifteen, something happened that helped change my life. I began to get special, helpful attention from Comrade Skripko, the Communist director of the school. He was the first man ever to show any interest in me. Through his guidance and teaching of Communism I became more interested in the Communist Youth League group at the school. He began to channel my restless energy into work with the Youth League, and I plunged into it eagerly.

One day the director came to me and said, "Kourdakov, I've been watching you in the Youth League. I think you're good leadership material. How would you like to work really hard next year and see how far you can get? If you really apply yourself, you could go far. You could be leading the Youth League here at school."

Wouldn't that be great! I thought. *Leader of the Communist Youth League!* Why not? I was king of Barysevo and could easily make it, so set out with all my might to study Marxism and Leninism and the goals and aims of Communism.

I can't think of anything that had a greater impact on my life in school than my studies of the principles of Communism, Marxism-Leninism and their objectives: the unity of all peoples and the brotherhood of man. From each according to his ability, to each according to his need. Those truths rang a bell for me. Until I learned them, I had had nothing to believe in, no time to develop any strong commitments or beliefs. Now I had a belief: Communism.

It wasn't the Communism which I saw in Big Irene and Nichman, however. What they had wasn't Communism. Their personal brutality and failures had nothing to do with Communism and its ideals. How could it? Communism taught the brotherhood of man and the equality of all people, yet Nichman and Big Irene created an atmosphere of hate in the children's home, of survival of the fittest, of might makes right—exact opposites of equality for all.

But the hope that I found in Communism was not shared by my friends at Barysevo. The harshness and hatefulness there were working tragic effects on them, one by one. My good friend Alexander Lobuznov and his brother Vladimir ran away to Novosibirsk. Absences from the home of a few days or even a week weren't noticed. Alex and Vladimir hung around the park in the centre of Novosibirsk, sleeping there and living off food they stole. One day they stole several bottles of vodka and soon were drunk. They attacked a young man in the park and beat him fiercely. They didn't intend anything serious, but in their drunken state, Alex put a leather belt around the young man's neck and dragged him about a thousand feet across the park. On the other side of the park, Alex unloosened his belt and shouted at him, "If you know what's good for you, get out of here fast!" But the fellow didn't move. Alarmed, Alex looked down. The man was dead, strangled by the belt. Alex and Vladimir took off, running as fast as they could, but the police finally caught them.

Alex, my good friend, two years older than his brother, was executed by a firing squad. Vladimir went to prison and is still there.

Others in the children's home, when they became fifteen or sixteen, ran away to enter a life of crime, narcotics or prostitution. The criminal underworld was very strong in Novosibirsk and easily accessible.

My inner circle stayed mostly intact until one day when Ivan Chernega disappeared from the home. I didn't think too much about it, because I knew Ivan could take care of himself. I figured he was probably off having a good time in Novosibirsk. What I didn't know was that he had got mixed up with a notorious element of the underworld and was robbing trains— and was very successful at it too, for a while.

One day Boris came running up to me all out of breath. Excitedly, he asked, "Sergei, have you heard about Ivan?"

"No. Why? What's up?"

"They caught him."

"Who caught him?"

"The police. He's been running with a gang of train robbers and they were caught trying to hold up a train."

"Ivan, a train robber! Boris, you're crazy," I said.

"No, Sergei, it's true. He's at the Central Police Station in Novosibirsk. They're going to send him to prison."

"Can we go and see him?"

"It won't do any good, Sergei. They won't let anybody near him."

Poor Ivan, I thought. *My good friend.* We had had many adventures together and shared all kinds of experiences ever since I had first met him, when I was eight years old. He was then a young, wide-eyed happy boy, always with a smile. And he always saw the best in everything. Somehow those years at Barysevo had changed him. He was given a long sentence at hard labour and is still in prison somewhere in Russia.

Meanwhile, I was at the top of my class, not only in Marxism-Leninism but also in physics, mathematics, language, geography and politics. I had developed an excellent facility for language and had studied German and was able to speak it quite well. I suppose that being the favourite of the Communist director of the school was a great help. But only initially. Ever since the tragic death of my gentle friend, Sasha, my driving ambition was to "go ahead". And I put my motto into practice, studying with determination. I scored 100 per cent, or perfect, in most subjects.

The Communist director came to me one day and said, "Kourdakov, I want you to speak to the younger classes on Communism and Marxism-Leninism."

"All right," I said, realizing that was a great honour.

I was allowed to stay out of my own classes and go into the classrooms of the younger children to lecture them. My subjects included imperialists, the war in Vietnam, which was then beginning to be very much in the Communist literature of Russia, and other political themes, as well as Marxist doctrine.

The Communist director of the school was pleased. "Keep this up," he told me, "and you've got a great career ahead of you—and an excellent record to show from school."

His praise meant a lot to me, because not only was he a director of the school but he was an important Communist official in the region, and I knew that to get ahead in Soviet life, you have to have a top reference from the local Communist Party official. Everything seemed to be going my way.

During the school holidays, in the summer of 1966, Boris, Mikhail Kirilin and I spent a lot of time in Novosibirsk. We could come and go at the home as we pleased. One day when I met the two of them in Novosibirsk, they were bubbling with enthusiasm. I wondered, *What are these guys up to now?*

"Sergei," Mikhail said, "back home where I come from in Tashkent, there are a lot of Moslem people."

"I know. You told me about them."

"I've got plenty of friends and family acquaintances, Sergei. You know, they smoke a lot of hashish down there and I think I can use my connections to buy some."

Oh, oh, I thought. *Here it comes.*

"We could bring it up here," Mikhail continued excitedly, "and sell it!"

I thought it over for a minute. Offhand, it didn't seem like a bad idea.

"Why not?" I said. "We could make a lot of money."

"Right, and it wouldn't be difficult."

"But," I asked, "where would we store it?"

"Where else? In the children's home."

"Mikhail, are you crazy?"

"No, I think it's a great idea. Who'd ever think of looking in a children's home for drugs?"

"Hey! That's not bad."

"Sure, and then we can go into Novosibirsk and sell it a little bit at a time. The city's running over with young people who will buy it."

"How would we get started?" I asked.

"Nick—that's my partner—and I have already talked it over. We're going to be leaving for Turkestan by train in three or four days."

We scraped together all the money we could, with our "treasurer's" help, and Mikhail and Nick took off by train for the southern regions of Asiatic Russia to make contact. In about three weeks they were back at Barysevo, grinning from ear to ear. I knew by that they had been successful. We found a place to hide the hashish in the home, which became a perfect front for our new business.

Mikhail started selling it almost as soon as we got it unpacked. Some of his first customers were the older kids at the home who bought it and smoked it secretly. We didn't have to worry much about Uncle Nichy and Big Irene and the other uncles and aunts because by this time, especially during the summer, they just let the home run itself. There was very little surveillance and few controls. Anyway, we kids were pretty resourceful by then and knew how to get around them.

Then we went into Novosibirsk, made some contacts with

young people, and the stuff sold as fast as we could handle it.

One day on one of our business trips through the streets, we ran into Nikolai Povaleyev. We hugged and slapped each other on the back. It was the first time I had seen him since he had been sent away from the Barysevo home to another children's home. He told me about his association with the criminal organization in Novosibirsk, part of a nationwide system. I learned later that each major area in the U.S.S.R. is divided into regions, and each region is assigned to a criminal organization. Povaleyev told me of attending a conference near Moscow where criminal chieftains from across the Soviet Union met secretly for three days to divide up the country. He told me he had become good friends with some of the top criminal leaders.

"I'm not surprised, Nikolai," I told him. "That's you, able to get in anywhere."

"And what have you been up to, Sergei?" he said.

"Mikhail, Boris and I have a little business."

"I heard you were the Communist Youth League leader at Barysevo. Is it true?"

"Yes, it's true," I replied.

"So can't you make up your mind? What are you trying to be—a Communist or businessman?"

I laughed. "Well," I said, "we've all got to eat. Even Communists." I thought of what had happened to Sasha.

"Look, Sergei," he said, "I want to see you in a couple of weeks. I've got something in mind for you. How about meeting me right here at this time—two weeks from today?"

"Right," I promised, and we went our separate ways.

When we met again, Nikolai got right down to business. "Look, Sergei, you're wasting your time on this little stuff. You're working your head off and taking all kinds of risks and where's it getting you?"

I had thought I was doing pretty well. But next to Nikolai's operation, it was not much. Nikolai saw the effect his sales talk was having and he began to put on the pressure. "Sergei," he said, "the people I'm with need guys like you. You're young and fresh in the business. You don't have any police record so far as narcotics is concerned. You're just the kind the police wouldn't suspect."

It all sounded great to me, so I said, "All right, Nikolai, what do you want me to do?"

"Well, we need couriers. All you have to do is pick up merchandise and deliver it where we tell you."

"That sounds easy."

"It *is* easy. That's all you have to do."

We walked on and continued talking, and I said again, "It sounds good. I'll do it."

"Great!" he said and slapped me on the back.

But before I could start with Nikolai, I had to finish with Boris and Mikhail. We still had quite a bit of hashish on hand that we needed to get rid of. We decided to take it to Ulyanovsk, Lenin's birthplace, and sell it all.

It was summer time, and lots of sightseers were coming in to see where Lenin was born. We figured it would be a good place to make some sales. We made the trip by train, and it didn't take us long to sell out our goods at Ulyanovsk. I saw Lenin's birthplace, too, so it was a great experience for me both ways— as a Communist and as a businessman. Before long we were on the train and back in Novosibirsk.

Soon I was in my new courier routine, going into the central market place in Novosibirsk and making contact at a certain stall. There I would be handed a paper bag under the counter and told a street address for me to take it to. I would then carry the bag to the assigned place. The police didn't suspect me; I was just a sixteen-year-old kid.

I was paid well and it was easy work.

I myself never took narcotics or smoked the hashish. I was a physical fitness fanatic and I knew drugs would ruin my body. I disciplined myself, determined to get very strong and stay that way. What I was doing was just a job to help me get money in order to take care of myself in life. Nothing more.

Then something happened that upset my comfortable life. It was a hot day, and I was wearing light summer clothes, carrying hashish in my shirt pocket to give to some of my friends at Barysevo. On the streetcar in Novosibirsk we were jammed in tight, which made everyone even hotter. Somehow in the jostling and pushing, one of the packages split open and the hashish spilt out into my shirt pocket. Hashish has an odour all its own and can be easily detected because of its distinctive smell.

I came to my streetcar stop, got off near a small kiosk selling newspapers and went over to get a newspaper. Then a man, tall and strongly built, came over and said to me, "Come here, boy, I want to ask you something." I began to suspect something was wrong, but I followed him over to a dark alleyway. I wasn't afraid of him. I was strong and was skilled in judo. I could take care of myself with *one man* any time. It didn't worry me that he was bigger and taller than I. So I followed him without fear.

When we reached the alley, he said, "You've got narcotics."

"No, I haven't," I lied.

He grabbed me by the shirt, and I reached up to give him a karate chop and follow that up with a judo throw. But I didn't know what was going on behind me. As I raised my hand to let him have it, I felt a hot pain in my back, as if boiling water had been poured on me. One of his comrades had sneaked up behind me and stabbed me with a knife. My head began to spin. I became faint and dizzy and fell to the ground, unconscious.

The next thing I knew, I was in a hospital, asking the nurse what had happened. "You were found in an alleyway," she said. "You lost a lot of blood. If they hadn't found you when they did, you'd have bled to death. The stab punctured a main artery."

I got word to Boris and Nikolai where I was and they came to see me. During his visit, Nikolai came close and said, "Sergei, give me a description of those guys."

I said, "Well, I only saw one."

"What did he look like?" I remembered him well and was able to give a good description. "Don't worry, Sergei. We'll take care of him."

A few days later, Nikolai came in. He said, "Well, Sergei, we've taken care of your two friends. They won't be causing anybody any trouble any more."

"What happened to them?"

"Well, I put the word out to my friends and they soon found those two guys. I'm not going to tell you what happened to them, but they won't be bothering anybody else any more ever." Knowing Povaleyev, I guessed they were at the bottom of the Ob River.

After about two and a half weeks I was released from the hospital, and Boris and Nikolai took me to the children's home to rest. It had been a narrow escape. The doctors said that if the knife blade had gone in just a little farther to the side, the stab would have been fatal. Or if I hadn't been found when I was, I'd have bled to death.

As I lay in my bunk at the children's home, being waited on

by my lieutenants and slaves, I had lots of time to reflect during my recovery from my stabbing.

I could see that my life was beginning to come to a crossroads. Either I had to follow the course Nikolai Povaleyev was taking and become deeply involved in the underworld, or start seriously developing a career of my own in the Communist organization. I had tasted both, and wasn't certain which would suit me better. There was no moral question involved. After all, just a few yards away, in the tiny cemetery behind the home, lay the body of Sasha, a good person, but not tough enough and hard enough to survive. If I did not take care of myself, I would meet the same fate.

I must admit I was a little confused by it all. There was Big Irene, strutting around with her medal. She had been rewarded by the Communist Party and made sure she took care of herself. But she had less scruples than some of the people I dealt with in the underworld.

But I realized my real interest was in politics and studies. Comrade Skripko, the Communist director at school, said I had a real knack and ability. I had a growing love and enthusiasm for Lenin's teachings and the goals and aims of Communism. I wanted to be in party work or politics.

So, lying there on my bunk, I made my decision. I would pursue a party career with the help of the Communist director of the school. I would talk things over with him as soon as possible and get his advice on how to shape my life and career. I would put aside everything but my work as head of the Youth League and plunge into my studies. The reckless phase of my life was over. Now I needed study and discipline.

9   A military life for me!

More and more I lost contact with Nikolai Povaleyev, Boris and Mikhail Kirilin, who continued their work in drugs and narcotics in the criminal underworld. I saw them occasionally at weekends when I went into Novosibirsk. My life was increasingly taken up with my studies and my duties as the Communist Youth League leader. I pushed our Communist Youth League hard in all its projects and goals. I began to win a reputation for getting things done. I determined that my youth organization was going to be the best in our entire district. This was a tall order because our district took in the city of Novosibirsk and the huge surrounding area. But it was important for my career that my group be the best.

The months passed by rapidly, and I was doing excellently in my studies, and my Communist Youth group was at the top of the entire district. I graduated from school in late June 1967, at the head of the class. Three top students in the school were to be given medals. A girl won the gold medal, and I won one of the silver medals.

Then the big day came. It was time to judge all the Communist Youth League organizations in the District of Novosibirsk. High Communist officials were there, and I was sitting in my group, nervously waiting for the awards to be announced.

"The Number One Communist Youth organization in the District of Novosibirsk is . . ." The announcer paused and I listened breathlessly. " . . . Barysevo!"

I couldn't believe it. I had won! All eyes turned in my direction and people slapped me on the back as I made my way to the podium to receive the award as leader of the Barysevo Communist Youth League. It was a great day for me. There was long and loud applause. Handshakes and congratulations from Communist leaders of our district. And as I received the public award, the Communist officer who gave it to me stated, "This boy will go far."

That was my goal in life—to go far, to go ahead. As I stood there with the applause and congratulations ringing in my ears I knew this was my life. I knew that I understood the rules of the game and the rules of life and that I could play by those rules and win. All the years at Barysevo and V-I and even way back at Number One, the hard knocks I had taken, the hard lessons of self-reliance I had learned, though I resented them then, had toughened and hardened me. These lessons gave me an advantage over those who had lived a soft or sheltered life and who had a mother and father to look after them. In the game of competition, I could go ahead. My life and career lay in front of me, and I knew that I was prepared. I was a creature of the system. I understood it and knew I could go to the top.

Now it was time to decide what career I would choose. First of all, I would have to face military service. Would it be the army or what? I had talked to some fellows who had been in the army and they said, "Sergei, that's the last thing you want to do. Stay away from the army. It's a hard life, and there's no way to get ahead. You come out of the army and you start as a factory worker. What kind of future is that?" I had already observed that the life of the factory working man was not very good. I didn't want that. I wanted something that would help me get ahead.

Then I talked to some friends who had been in the navy. After hearing them tell about their experiences, I decided the navy was for me. But I wanted to be an officer, not just a seaman. I had been a leader in every children's home where I had been except Number One, both in class and in the Communist Youth organizations. Now I wanted to be a leader in the navy.

Comrade Skripko promised to help. "Kourdakov," he said, "I'll write up a very good report and recommendation for you. You take this report and give it to the naval recruiting authorities in Novosibirsk and have them contact me."

So he prepared a record of my work in the Communist youth organizations, from the time when I was an Octobrianik to the present, and gave it to the authorities in Novosibirsk along with his endorsement. He also sent a copy on to Leningrad along with my application for admission to the Naval Academy.

In early August 1967, the word came back to me at Barysevo that I had been accepted for training at the Officers' Naval Academy in Leningrad. That was great news! I had Comrade Skripko to thank for that. It was hard to say goodbye to my close friends—but my mind was fixed on going ahead and not looking back.

When it was time to go to the Novosibirsk railway station to board the train for Leningrad, I looked around at the familiar sights from ten long years ago, when I was there as a street child. Finally I heard the last "all aboard for Moscow". I boarded, and in moments we began chugging out of the station. Suddenly I was struck by the realization of what a big part of my life I was leaving behind. Peering out of the window, I took one parting look at that massive old station.

My mind filled with reflections, I settled down for my long ride to Leningrad. The train chugged out of the station and through the outskirts of the city. As we entered the countryside and picked up speed, the clickety-clack of the wheels began to speak to me. They seemed to be saying, "*Clickety-clack, clickety-clack,* you made it, you made it. *Clickety-clack,* you made it, you made it."

"Yes," I said to myself, "*you* made it, Sergei. But what about all your friends who didn't?" As I reminisced, the faces of those who *didn't* make it flashed before me. There were seven boys who entered Children's Home Number One at about the same time, when I was six. We grew up together. Of those seven, I was the only one who finished high school and had any hopes of making something of life.

As I stared absent-mindedly out the windows at the flat Siberian landscape rushing by, other faces began to appear. There were Ivan Chernega, Alex and Vladimir Lobuznov. There were Nikolai Saushkin, Nikolai Povaleyev, Boris Lobanov, Mikhail Kirilin, Alex Popov, our "treasurer", and all my old friends. Some had turned into thieves, narcotics pushers, even murderers. Nearly everyone had been in serious trouble of some kind. Ivan Chernega, my good friend, was to spend years in prison, and Alexander Lobuznov had been shot by a firing squad. I was shocked to realize how many of the boys and girls in the home at Barysevo turned out to be criminals, gangsters or prostitutes. The weak, like Sasha Ognev, died or committed suicide.

I remembered the Deacon and wondered what would happen to him. Where would he go? Would he ever get to his dreamed-of Bible school? Of course not. Where would life find a place for a kid like him? And my mind raced back to all those other "official orphans" taken from their parents. What would happen to them?

The train sped across the vast flatness toward Moscow and a

new life, and soon the wheels seemed to change their message, saying, "Be strong, be strong." And I realized that above all else I must heed the message of the wheels.

After a long and tiring journey, my train pulled into Kazan Station in Moscow. I got off the train and began a two-day stay there in the capital city of our country.

The first place I went was the tomb of Lenin. There I got in line and stood patiently for several hours, until it was my turn to go in. As an Octobrianik I had been his grandson and as a Communist Youth League leader, his son. One day, as a member of the Communist Party itself, I would be his comrade.

As I entered the quiet sanctuary and approached the mortal remains of Father Lenin, I was overcome with a sense of awe and reverence. I stood close, quietly looking at the body of the man about whom I had studied so much and who was a god to me. He was the founder of my "religion", which had given me something to believe in for the first time in my life. He taught equality, brotherhood and the strong helping the weak. I bowed my head and prayed to him. Yes, it was a prayer. I cannot describe it in any other way. I prayed, "Help me, Father Lenin, in my life. Give me the guidance and direction I need. Help me to have the understanding to follow your teachings. Remove obstacles and danger from my pathway and from life. Heed me and guide me. Help me, Father Lenin." I lifted my head, looked a few minutes more at the remains of Lenin and left. Somehow I felt stronger and more able to face what was ahead of me.

The next day I boarded the train for Leningrad, 400 miles north-west of Moscow, and arrived in a short time to begin another chapter of my life, a career as a future naval officer, studying at the Alexander Popov Naval Academy. Back at Barysevo I had kidded "my" Alex Popov that the academy was named after him.

When first I saw Leningrad, I immediately understood why it was called the queen of Soviet cities and why Voltaire, in the eighteenth century, had said, "The united magnificence of all the cities of Europe could but equal St. Petersburg" (Leningrad's former name). Leningrad contained a rare mixture of Russia's timeless grandeur and its modern culture. It was often spoken of as the capital of the Czars and the cradle of Communism. Founded by Peter the Great, centuries ago, it was named for him. It had received its present name in 1924, in honour of Vladimir Ilyich Lenin, who on an October day in 1917, launched an uprising that transformed Holy Russia into the Union of Soviet Socialist Republics. In founding the first Communist government in history, he set off an ideological explosion that was to change and shake the world. A huge 100-foot billboard picture of him towered above the streets, dominating Leningrad's famed Palace Square. Just as I had read about it and seen it pictured, it was a city of bridges, with nearly 600 of them spanning numerous canals and rivers that intersected the streets.

I remember how low the skyline seemed for a city of four million inhabitants. But I had already read that it was because of a law limiting all buildings except churches—their spires, that is—to a height not to exceed the ninety-two feet of the Czar's winter palace.

As we rode down Nevsky Prospekt, the city's main thoroughfare, I recall the numerous shops, restaurants and cafés that lined the sidewalks for the avenue's entire three-mile length. A description by one of our poets, Alexander Blok, popped into my mind. He called Nevsky Prospekt "the most lyric street in all the world". It was a true description.

Leningrad is also a city of museums, one of the most remarkable of which is the State Hermitage Museum housed in the 1,100-room winter palace that originally belonged to Catherine the Great. Guides there tell visitors that if they were to spend just one minute looking at each object on display, it would take them twelve years to complete the tour. More than three million visitors pass through its doors each year.

The general citizenry of Leningrad more fondly think of it as the hero city, a title well earned by its gallant, unyielding stand against Hitler's three-year siege and slaughter of 200,000 of its soldiers and a million of its citizens. On one of the worst days of the Nazi siege, more than 8,000 Leningraders died in a twenty-four-hour period. While the city itself had recovered remarkably from the devastation, wrought by the unprecedented bombings and shellings, more than a million of its former population remained forever anonymous in huge, mass graves. I had studied all of this in preparation for my coming to Leningrad.

Of course I was looking forward expectantly, not only to being in Leningrad but to my arrival at Alexander Popov Naval Academy. Finally my bus came to it, on the outskirts of

Leningrad in a wooded area quite far from the centre of the city.

On our first day we were called in to muster where all new recruits were being assembled. Because the older cadets were on hand to observe us, all of us new recruits were a bit nervous. But the ice was quickly broken when the older cadets got up and began to shout, "Who's from Moscow?" or, "Who's from Kharkov?" or Donets or Bashkin. Whenever any hands went up, the older cadets and the new ones from the same place would get together. It was the way in which the older cadets, who had come from all over the Soviet Union, could find some new recruit from their old home towns. From that, friendships developed.

Somebody called out, "Who's from Novosibirsk?"

"I am," I shouted excitedly and looked around, soon spotting one of the old-time cadets smiling. We met, shook hands and introduced ourselves. Vasil was his name, and he was two years older than I, a friendly sort of guy. I was glad I met him because he helped me get adjusted to the Naval Academy routine and to avoid a lot of problems. As in most schools, it was customary for the older class to harass the newcomers, as well as befriend them. Vasil and I hit it off well and spent many long hours talking. Soon a strong friendship developed that was to last several years.

In my studies, I was offered two separate kinds of courses I could take, one in mechanics, the other in radio. I wanted to become a radio officer. I had always been good at physics and mathematics and was fascinated by radio and electronic equipment.

Three days after we arrived at the academy and got settled, all the new cadets in the radio section met to elect the leaders of the Communist Youth League organization for their section of the academy. Names were submitted, and somebody said, "I propose Sergei Kourdakov." I was surprised, since I was new there; and I was more than a little flattered when the vote was taken and I was elected their leader.

Later I learned that my record of having the best Communist youth organization in the Novosibirsk District was responsible. Based on that, my name had been proposed by the party chief at the Naval Academy. So my "election" was automatic. In any event, I took charge of the Communist youth organization in the radio section of the Naval Academy for the year I was there.

I organized classes and taught Communist theory and, for my own further learning, attended lectures in geopolitics and current affairs.

The regimen and discipline were tough and hard at the academy, but for me, after my life in the children's homes, the academy was a pushover. While some of the other cadets who had had more sheltered lives couldn't take it and dropped out, I thrived on it and was able to maintain an excellent record, especially with my work in the Communist Youth League.

During those early days, I met Pavel Sigorsky, who became a dear friend of mine. He was a senior naval cadet and had come from that part of Poland which had been taken over by Russia after the war. Being a Polish nationalist, he spoke only Polish in my presence. We laughed about it, and he said, "If you want to speak to me, you'll have to learn Polish." I thought that was a good idea, so I asked him to teach me, and he did. We were soon able to speak to each other entirely in his native tongue.

Often I was assigned to guard duty at the entrance to the Academy. On a Sunday morning I saw some people walking across a nearby field.

"Who are they?" I asked the other fellow on guard with me.

"Believers."

I looked at them. To me they had always been, and still were, an object of great curiosity. "Where are they going?" I asked.

"Oh," he replied, "there's a church there behind those trees and they're going there."

It was true. Here on the far outskirts of Leningrad, there was one church allowed open. All the Believers in the whole city who wanted to worship had to walk out into the countryside to get to the church. I was impressed. I remembered reading in school in our constitution of the Soviet Union, that every citizen had the full right of religious worship and religious freedom. And I thought, *It's true! There is religious freedom in Russia.* Believers were openly going to a church. That proved there was religious freedom.

The months passed quickly through the winter of 1967 and on into the spring of 1968. My work at the Naval Academy in Leningrad became increasingly demanding. I was keenly interested in all my studies and especially enjoyed the lectures on Marxism-Leninism and politics. They attracted me very much and I studied hard.

74

I was very glad when April came, so I could get away for my spring vacation on the trip I had planned back to Novosibirsk and Barysevo. The holiday turned out well. I had a great time with all my old friends. But the experience which impressed me most during the two weeks of my vacation took place on my short bus trip from Novosibirsk to Barysevo, on my way to visit friends at the children's home. As we passed through the suburb of Inskaya, I noticed a bus ahead of us was caught in a traffic jam. Looking out of the window, wondering what it was all about, I saw trucks blocking the road, police cars, two fire wagons and people by the hundreds and hundreds, thronging about.

It was a hopeless tangle. Everyone on our bus knew we'd be delayed for some time, and we kept looking ahead to see what was going on. None of us could figure it out. All we knew was that there was a lot of frantic activity up in front of us. Then some of the people from the milling crowd came back and boarded our bus. We asked them what was happening.

It turned out that they were Believers. I had thought Believers were grandmothers or grandfathers, old and bent over. But these Believers weren't like that at all. They were all ages. Many were as young as I, and they looked and dressed pretty much the same as I did.

We asked them what was going on and they told us that many churches in Novosibirsk had been closed. But just now, after much petitioning, they had succeeded in getting the government to allow one small prayer house to open here in the suburb of Inskaya, on this day. They said the news of its opening had spread among the Believers and though they expected quite a few people to be on hand, they never imagined there would be a crowd like this. The prayer hall held about 150 people standing. But many hundreds of Believers had shown up, jamming the streets and blocking the roads, all trying to get in. And no wonder there were so many! Novosibirsk was a city of one and a half million people and for years it had been without even one Protestant church. So the day this one church was allowed open, everybody came.

It didn't take the police long to get out there and order the Believers out of the area. We asked the Believers on our bus how they ever expected to get in to worship, and they said, "Well, we were going to take turns. The plan was for one group to go in for half an hour, pray and worship, then leave. Then the second group of a hundred and fifty would go in, and so on, until everyone had a chance."

I shook my head in amazement. I was really dumbfounded. First, I had been told there were very few Believers, and here were hundreds upon hundreds of them, spilling out into the streets of this small suburb. Then I had also been told that only the old continued to believe in God, but there were lots of young people in that milling crowd trying to get in to pray.

Finally, after the police drove the Believers off and got the traffic moving again, the bus went on to Barysevo. I was lost in my thought about what I had witnessed. It all made a deep impression on me, and I was to think about it again and again for a long time to come.

The rest of my holiday I spent with friends in Barysevo and Novosibirsk and had some good, happy times. But soon my time was gone and I had to return to Leningrad. Before long, I was back, working harder than ever.

In July 1968, after completing almost a year at the Naval Academy in Leningrad, I was assigned to continue my studies at the Naval Academy at Petropavlovsk in Kamchatka Province. I was *really* pleased. This was a choice assignment. The Petropavlovsk Naval Academy was a large one in the Soviet Far East, on the Pacific coast of Russia, north of Japan. Kamchatka was known as the "eyes of Russia". To be assigned to the Naval Academy there was a big step upward. Most of the Soviet fleet was in that area and I was happy for this good fortune.

I said goodbye to my friends, including my Polish comrade, whom I was not to hear from again for quite some time. My military pass gave me a month and a half holiday before I was to report to the new assignment. I decided to spend my holiday with my friends in Novosibirsk.

My last look at Leningrad brought a lump to my throat. I felt I would never forget those busy, exciting days of training, and of course I would always remember the unsurpassed beauty of that great city.

From the time I left Leningrad until my train neared the suburbs of Moscow, the trip was uneventful. Then things began to happen. In the car ahead of me I heard a big commotion going on and, being curious, I had to find out what it was. So I sauntered through our coach into the next one.

There I saw three big, tough young guys shaking the life out of a small, studious-looking boy with big glasses and pale white skin. "Give us your money," they told him, "or we'll break your arm!" The kid was trembling like a leaf in a windstorm. One big guy stood facing the other passengers to make sure no one interfered while they worked over the boy. I've never liked bullies and what I saw instantly made me mad. I whipped off my military belt and wrapped it around my fist, so that the big, heavy buckle would be like brass knuckles, and moved toward the boy. When the guard made a move to stop me, I rushed him and grabbed him around the neck with a judo hold, then threw him against the wall and smashed him in the face with my improvised brass knuckles. He went out cold.

The two others were pulling the money out of the boy's wallet. "Drop that money," I said, "or you'll get the same treatment!" They saw their comrade sprawled unconscious on the floor. I moved to take them both, and they backed off, saying, "Okay, okay. We're going, we're going." They got off at the next station, taking their friend with them.

The young boy, of course, was completely shaken. I helped him gather up his money, then took him by the arm, comforted him and suggested we sit down. As we talked, I found out his name was Mikhail Koptelov. For a while I hesitated to ask about that name. It was such a remote possibility that he would have any connection with the person I was thinking of. But finally I said, "Are you, by any chance, related to the great writer, Konstantin Koptelov?"

"Oh yes," he replied. "He's my father."

"Your father!" I exclaimed. I was really impressed. Anyone in Russia who loves literature knows the name Konstantin Koptelov. He is one of Russia's greatest and most popular writers and won the Lenin Prize for Literature. His books are famous throughout the whole Soviet Union. From then on, I talked with more interest than ever. Mikhail asked who I was and where I was going, and I told him.

"Look," he said, "while you're here in Moscow, Sergei, why not break your journey and come up to our apartment and meet my parents?"

Great, I thought, *a chance to meet Konstantin Koptelov!* It didn't take me long to decide. "All right," I agreed. "I've got several hours to wait anyway." I found myself very excited over the prospect of meeting one of Russia's famous writers.

When we got off the train, we took a subway to Mikhail's apartment, where he introduced me to his parents and told them what had happened on his way home. His father shook my hand and thanked me for my help, and his mother smiled and was very grateful, too. Then she said, "Sergei, can you take time to have dinner with us? Everything's about ready. We can have a nice visit and you can catch the train to Novosibirsk." I was delighted and accepted the invitation readily.

Before long we were at the table, enjoying a wonderful, home-cooked meal and talking like old friends. Mr. Koptelov began to ask me about my background and what I was doing now and what did I expect to do in the future. So I told him the story of my life in the children's homes. He seemed fascinated. Listening intently, he asked for more and more details about it. When dinner was over, we retired to the living room for more conversation and a few drinks before they were to take me to the station. "Sergei," he said at last, "as I've been listening to you talk, I've been thinking. I'm convinced your story and the story of the children's home at Barysevo would make a fascinating book."

I was taken aback. I had never thought of that. He began to ask more questions and said, "I could write a book about your life at the children's home. It would be like a Russian Tom Sawyer." I was certainly flattered, but I told him I honestly didn't know whether there was a story there or not. Of course, he would know best, because that was his business. I assured him I would be glad to tell him all I knew about it.

"All right, we'll do it," he announced. "I'll be in contact with you soon. We're trying to buy a summer country house near Novosibirsk. It'll be close enough to the children's home to interview you and the other fellows." Then my new friends took me to the station, where we said goodbye and I boarded the train for the rest of the trip to Novosibirsk.

When I arrived at the Novosibirsk railway station, there was Boris Lobanov to meet me. Good old Boris! I set my suitcase down and threw my arms around him, and he hugged me too as we exchanged greetings, both talking at once. Soon we were at his one-room apartment and after I got cleaned up, we went to see some of our other friends. The first we saw was my good friend Nikolai Povaleyev.

"Just look!" he shouted. "Who's that smart looking officer walking with you, Boris? He goes off a wet-behind-the-ears kid and comes back an admiral! Boy! They sure aren't particular who they put a uniform on these days!"

After we all had a good laugh and greeted each other, I got serious and said, "Listen, Nikolai, I've got some great news for you." I proceeded to tell them about how I met Konstantin Koptelov and how he wanted to write a book about the children's home and the people in it, including Nikolai. "I told him the whole story," I said, "and, Nikolai, he wants to tell your story, too. It'll make you famous!"

Nikolai listened with a growing look of horror on his face and exclaimed, "Sergei, how stupid can you be? Of course it will make me famous. But it'll also put a noose around my neck! The last thing I need is to be famous, or written about! Don't you understand," he said, "what that would do to my business? Sergei, how could you do this to me, your good old friend?"

Then it dawned on me. Of course! How stupid could I be? "Look, Nikolai," I said, "I'm sorry. I didn't think about it from that point of view."

"Well, you better begin to think about it," he muttered. "The kind of activities I've been in—well, we just don't talk about them. Boris and I and some of the other guys have a good thing going here, Sergei, and a nosy writer would end it all fast!"

I started to interrupt, but he wouldn't let me. "I know you haven't made much money at the Naval Academy, Sergei. And I've been making pretty good profits lately. Look, I'll give you the money to make up for what you lose on the book, if you'll just call this whole stupid idea off. All right?"

By this time I was getting irritated. "Listen, Nikolai," I almost shouted, "if you'll stop talking for a minute, I'll tell you what I'm trying to tell you! I didn't realize what you've just said. I hadn't thought of it that way. So you can consider the idea dead. You don't have to pay me off. I'm your friend."

Nikolai relaxed. A little smile crossed his lips. "That's the old Sergei I knew. Thanks a lot."

Later Koptelov wrote me at the address I had given him and told me he had bought a summer cottage nearby and was coming out to it soon. When he got there, in a few days, I went over to see him to explain about the book, that I didn't think the idea was too good after all and I'd rather not collaborate on it. He wasn't at all happy that I'd changed my mind, but I told him that was the way it had to be. And we ended it right there.

The twenty days of my holiday before I would have to leave

for Petropavlovsk were filled with fun and excitement and happy reunions with friends. But there were also unexpected incidents. One day Nikolai said, "Sergei, I want you to meet the big man of our organization." I had heard a lot about this underworld figure while I was a courier. I had wanted to meet him, but I was so far down the line in the business that I didn't have a chance. I regarded this invitation as a rare opportunity.

We went right across Novosibirsk to a little, out-of-the-way room in a neighbourhood I'd never been in before. Nikolai walked in, with me at his heels. We stood for a minute, then Nikolai whispered, "Here he comes, Sergei." The door opened.

I was flabbergasted! I couldn't believe my eyes. I looked at Nikolai and said, "*That's* 'Mr. Big'? That's Saushkin!"

"That's right, Sergei. Saushkin. I am the—shall we say—Number One of this business."

So I finally found out what had happened to Saushkin! It all flashed before me, how he had been caught and arrested at Barysevo when he had once tried to kill Big Irene with one of the deadly home-made zip guns we had secretly made at the children's home. Nobody knew where they had taken him. "They took me to a children's prison," Saushkin said, as he started to answer the questions on my face. "That's where I made the contacts that led me into my present—er, profession."

Saushkin's "profession" was drug-pushing. He was the biggest pusher in all of Novosibirsk. Here was one graduate of Barysevo who had really gone far. I stood looking at Saushkin, hardly daring to believe what he and Nikolai were telling me. But when I remembered how tough he was at Barysevo, I knew it was true.

Actually, I didn't think Saushkin remembered me, since I was so much younger than he was when we were at Barysevo. But he did. "Of course, I remember you, Sergei," he said. "How've you been? I see you're in the military now."

"Yes," I said. And we had a good time talking about Barysevo and everything that had happened to us since.

That day was the first I knew that Boris and Nikolai Povaleyev had been working closely with Nikolai Saushkin in the narcotics business in Novosibirsk. After we had talked a while, Saushkin made me a proposition. "Sergei, you're going to be here on holiday for a few days. How about making some money while you're here?"

"I could use it," I answered. "Tell me more." So he did.

"For the time that you're here," he said, "you can work with Boris and me and Povaleyev. Business is very good. We're selling a lot of narcotics and we're getting other merchandise in from Japan and selling it on the black market."

I leaned over to Boris and asked, "What are you selling?"

"Tape recorders, lipsticks, things like that," he said.

"All right," I said, "I'll do it." I was thinking of the lesson I had learned long ago, that in this life you look after yourself.

I worked closely with Boris, Nikolai and Saushkin for a few days. Then disaster struck. Saushkin was arrested and sentenced to eight years at a rugged old prison near Tomsk.

But business had to go on. It couldn't stop because "Mr. Big" was gone. Nikolai Povaleyev figured he was next in line and promptly took over Saushkin's territory. One night he and Boris invited me to go along with them to a special meeting of local underworld chieftains. "Since Saushkin was arrested," Boris explained, "we've been having some trouble with another organization. They've been getting into our territory."

I said to myself, "Well, this ought to be pretty interesting. I think I'll go along." On the way, Boris told me there had been some shootings and somebody had been killed in the fight between the two organizations. That's why they needed this peace conference. They wanted to get things settled so they could get on with their business and not get in each other's way any more. The meeting was to be held in a dilapidated building in an out-of-the-way part of town.

When we arrived, we went up a small stairway and down a long, dark corridor to a dimly lighted room on the third floor, where we found the other gang leader already waiting. I stood off to the side while Nikolai and the other leader began to talk. After they had argued for a while, Nikolai began pounding the table and shouting, "If you don't stay out of our area, we're going to talk to you out of a gun barrel. We've tried to work things out, but you won't listen to plain talk. You've got your area—you stick to it! You got that clear?"

Nikolai got up, then the other leader and his henchmen got up and stormed out. I looked at Nikolai and winked. He was the same tough guy I knew back at Barysevo, the same guy who had "taken care" of the two men who stabbed me in the alley.

I figured the meeting was over and I told Nikolai, "I'm going to go down and get some fresh air. I'll meet you outside." I walked down the corridor, the two flights of stairs and out of the door to the street. The moment I stepped outside, an explosion ripped the air and blew up right in my face. I felt a hot, burning sensation beneath my ribs and a fierce impact that knocked the wind out of me. In a daze I looked down and discovered I was bleeding profusely; my shirt was already covered with blood and my military jacket was starting to get soaked.

All I could think was, *I'm shot! I'm shot!* I dropped to my knees. Then, from behind, I heard footsteps. Someone came racing down the hallway and down the stairs. It was Nikolai and Boris charging out with two guns each, one in each hand, ready to blaze away at my assailants. But they had disappeared. Nikolai and Boris put their guns away, helped me to my feet and half-dragged me inside. The raincoat I was wearing over my jacket had a pocket full of documents—papers, my orders, identification cards, other items.

"You've got to be the luckiest guy around, Sergei," Boris exclaimed while he emptied my raincoat pocket, just over my left breast. The bullet had passed straight through everything, my thick address book, all my identification papers, plus all my clothes—raincoat, jacket, shirt, undershirt—to hit me. It was imbedded in my skin. Even so, my clothes were soaked with blood, and when Boris looked at the wound and then at the hole through the documents, he gave a long, low whistle. "If it hadn't been for that pocketload of stuff taking the impact of that bullet, you'd be dead right now," he told me.

We improvised some bandages from our handkerchiefs and Boris's shirt and stopped the flow of blood. They helped me up and took me to the hospital. It had been a very close brush with death.

After that, I rested for a few days at Boris's place, and drank. I was never a really heavy drinker. I did drink some at Barysevo, along with the other kids, and I drank quite a bit afterwards, too. But I usually stopped short of getting drunk, because I was determined to stay in good physical and mental condition. I knew that too much alcohol could be harmful. Only on the rarest occasion would I really get drunk.

One morning about nine o'clock, after a big party that Boris had thrown for me the night before, I woke up and found everybody else still out cold. Still groggy, I got up to walk outside and clear my head. Just then I found somebody else with the same thought in mind. He was about fifty years old, heavy-set and had a wooden leg. Since we both wanted to brush the cobwebs from our brains, we decided to walk together in the park across the street. After a few minutes we found a bench where we sat down and talked. I told him who I was and where I was going and asked him about himself. To my surprise, I learned he had been a major in the police force in the city of Norilsk. At the mention of that name, my ears perked up. Norilsk is one of the most famous of all cities in Russia. It is a fabled master-piece of far-north technology. Built in the very northern part of the country, it stands as a shining example of Soviet skill in building cities in the frozen north and actually making them habitable.

"That's great!" I exclaimed. "I've read about that fabulous city in my school books. I understand that it's a great techno-logical achievement for the party."

"Technological achievement!" he snorted. "All you kids know is what you read in books. That's the trouble with you! You believe everything they tell you and everything you read."

"Now don't get upset," I replied. "I'm only trying to be friendly and tell you what I read."

"Well, forget what you read! Not a word of it is true. I know. I'm *from* there. I was a major in the police force there."

"But," I protested, "I understand we developed special machines and special technological abilities just so we could handle difficult jobs like these."

"Machines!" he said and laughed. "Do you want to know what machines we developed? The machines were *slaves*. Tens of thousands of them died building that city, and their bones are still there. That's the 'technology' that built Norilsk—the blood and bones of slaves."

I couldn't believe what I was hearing. I'd like to have been able to brush his words away as the confused ramblings of a drunken moron, but how could I? The man was a former police officer and, if he was telling the truth, he had not only lived there but had helped build the city. "I saw them die by the thousands," he continued. "They died from hunger or cold or both."

He went on to tell me how he had given his life to Commun-ism. When the Hungarian Revolution of 1956 broke out, he had been sent to Hungary to help put it down. But there, while fighting as a tank commander in Budapest, he was shot through the leg and had to have it amputated. "After that," he said, "I was considered worthless, of no use. They sent me to Norilsk to ride herd on those poor devils up there. That's all they thought I was good for!"

Such talk was to me sacrilege. This man, a stranger, was attacking the system I believed in and I didn't like what I was hearing. I tried to close my ears to it, but he raved on, and I listened. "Do you know what they gave me, son? Oh, they were good to me, all right. They gave me this wooden leg and a handful of roubles every month, which I can hardly live on, then threw me out! Oh yes"—and it seemed he was saving this for last—"they gave me something else, too. You know what? A handful of medals." He reached into his pocket and dug out a bunch of them. "You see, I served them well in Hungary. And up in Norilsk, too!"

He dangled the medals in my face and continued. "Medals! What can I do with them? Eat them? Pay my rent with them? Look at me, son." He paused, as though I should really study him from head to foot—and I did. I had to agree with what he was saying. He called himself old and worthless and pointed out again that he had one leg and forty-five roubles a month. He wasn't my idea of what a loyal, retired Communist officer should be. The medals, yes. But not the poverty, the bitterness and the hopelessness of it all.

Then he began coughing. The medals fell from his hand into the mud around us. He began coughing up blood. Taking a handkerchief from his pocket, he wiped the blood from his mouth, then fell to his knees in the mud and began scraping around with his fingers, searching for his medals. I got up and left.

Well, I thought, if what the old man was saying was true, it was all in the past anyway. I had *my* future to live for, and I had to look to that. Only fools dwell on the problems of the past, we had been taught. Certainly our party had had difficulties in the past, when our country was new. Our country had been embattled and had suffered greatly in the early days of the new regime. Some slight injustices had to be accepted. In what country aren't there slight injustices?

But all those deaths in order to build a city! Could that be considered a slight injustice? I debated with myself, then decided to dismiss it from my mind. Anyway, I had no real answer to my questions, and life for me had to go on, whether

1 Sergei points out the spot on the Canadian coast where he swam ashore to freedom

2 With friends at the Barysevo Children's Home. In the top picture are (*left*) Mikhail Kirilin and (*right*) Nikolai Povaleyev

3 (a) Pause for rest in a park when on a drug-peddling trip to Ulyan-ovsk, Lenin's birthplace

(b) Back from hospital after treatment for a stab wound suffered while acting as courier for drug-pushers

4 Outside the headquarters building of the local branch of the Communist youth organization

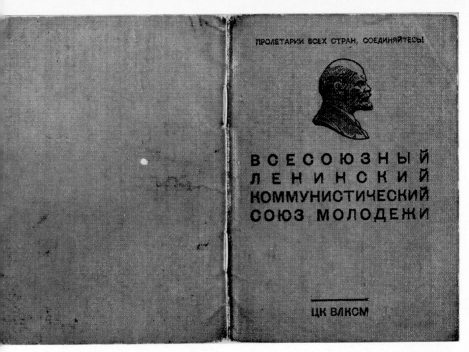

5 ALL-UNION LENINIST AND COMMUNIST YOUTH UNION
Komsomol Membership Certificate

Surname: Kourdakov
Name: Sergei
Patronymic: Nicholaevich
Birthday, year and month: March 1951

Date of entry into VLKSM:
April 1965
Novosibirsk District Committee
Date of issue: February 8, 1967

6 Sergei as "king" of the children's home, with one of his lieutenants. He lost his tooth in the fight which won him the position of king

7 (a) King, with one of the younger slaves, the lowest order in the children's private hierarchy

(b) Barysevo in winter

8 Sergei (second from left on ground) with a group of army officers visiting the children's home. Behind them is the slope down which the boys pushed spies who carried tales to the staff

9 (a) As a student in the Leningrad Naval Academy during his first year of military service

(b) The Commander of the Petropavlovsk Naval Academy (centre), Viktor Yelisayev

10 (a)   CERTIFICATE OF MEMBERSHIP NO. 51
Kourdakov Sergei Nicholaevich is a student of the Petropavlovsk-Kamchatski
Navigation School
Valid: Until December 31, 1969
Extended: Until September 1, 1970
Extended: Until September 1, 1971

(b) Sergei (in sunglasses) with fellow-members of the Petropavlovsk Naval Academy
wrestling team

11 (a) Sergei (in back row) with some of his fellow cadets

(b) With a group of friends, Sergei (without shirt) enjoys cross-country skiing. It was on these outings that they glimpsed concentration camps hidden among the mountains

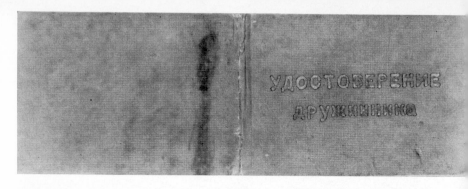

12 Licence to harass

VOLUNTARY PEOPLE'S BRIGADE FOR MAINTENANCE OF CIVIL ORDER

Kourdakov Sergei Nicholaevich is a member

Has a right to demand presentation of papers in situations of public disorder, to make reports on disorders and deliver the involved persons to the brigade headquarters, militia stations or local Council

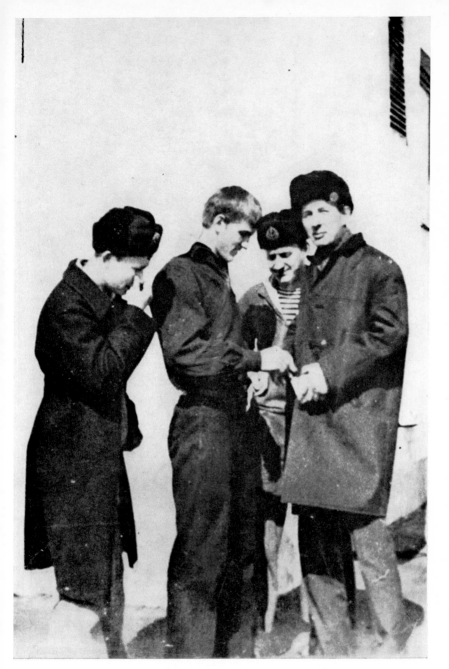

13 With three members of the police operations group which he led against Believers and secret churches. *Left to right:* Sergei Kanonenko, Sergei Kourdakov, Alexander Gulyaev and Yuri Berestennikov

14 (*a*) Three more members of Sergei's anti-Christian attack squad are in this group: *far left*, Vladimir Litovka; *third from left*, V. Shorohov; *far right*, Victor Lazarov

(*b*) On a sea coast outing with friends soon after his graduation from the Naval Academy and shortly before he went to sea for the last time

15 (a) Part of Petropavlovsk from the harbour. In one of these houses Sergei led a raid hunting for Bibles

(b) On board the *Elagin*, off the Canadian coast, Sergei continued to build up his strength for his escape attempt

16 Following his escape and his conversion to Christianity, he was in great demand as a speaker in Canada and the United States

or not it did for that pathetic figure grovelling in the mud for his medals. Trying with great difficulty to erase the whole disturbing incident from my mind, I went off to prepare for my departure. Soon I would be on my way to the Soviet Far East and my new and exciting career in the Soviet navy.

10   Assigned to "The Eyes of Russia"

My first stop after leaving Novosibirsk, travelling across the endless stretches of Siberia, was "the magic seaport"—Vladivostok. I spent two weeks there at the naval base. Then I was moved for a three-week stay at Blagoveschensk, right on the border of China, where there has been a lot of military tension, even actual gunfire, between Russian and Chinese troops on the Amur River.

I was in a military unit of the navy ordered into action against the Chinese and was involved in a machine gun battle with Chinese troops on one occasion. Later I received my orders to report back to Vladivostok, where I boarded a ship for Nakhodka, a major Soviet seaport city, and continued on to my main assignment at the Naval Academy at Petropavlovsk, arriving in late September 1968, to begin two-and-a-half years of study to become a radio officer.

Petropavlovsk is the main city of Kamchatka Province, with a population of 150,000. It is a port, with paved streets and lights in the middle of the city, and dirt streets away from the centre of town. The citizens are from all parts of the Soviet Union. Due to the numerous naval and military bases, Kamchatka has a high percentage of young people. But there are also many retired military personnel who stayed on following their service there.

The Naval Academy at Petropavlosk was headed by Commander Viktor Yelisayev, a young officer who had climbed rapidly to this important post. The base was a great sprawling area with 1,200 young naval cadet officers in constant study, training and preparation. These 1,200 were the "cream of the crop", carefully chosen from all over the Soviet Union, handpicked future officers.

Life at the academy was divided into two basic parts: naval studies and Communist Party activities. The naval studies were divided into several areas: navigation, radio, mechanical and others. We studied intently, concentrating on our chosen area.

Because everything in Russia has its political aspect, the Communist Party reaching into every phase of Soviet life, it was only to be expected that here, where future naval officers were in training, party activities would be intense and strongly emphasized. It was as expected.

One day shortly after my arrival, Commander Yelisayev called me to his office. Several officers were there as well as a man in plain clothes. He was introduced as the Communist Party chief for the city.

"Kourdakov," he said, gesturing with my file in his hand, "we have been examining your records as a party activist as well as the records of the other cadets. We have to pick one of the men to be chief of the Communist Youth League here at the academy. There are twelve hundred men here, and we are all agreed," he said with a sweep of his hand towards the others, "that the job is yours. Your record is perfect. You've been an activist since your first year. Your group won the district award for Novosibirsk and we see your good record at Leningrad. So, it's you, Kourdakov. You're our man."

I was a little stunned. I would be responsible for the Communist education and development of 1,200 future officers! And I was only eighteen years old.

As I walked across the naval base, back to my quarters, I couldn't help saying to myself, "Sergei, this is a once-in-a-lifetime opportunity. You're going to go far."

About three-fifths of our time at the academy was spent in political studies and two-fifths in technical studies. As officers of the Soviet navy we would carry great responsibility with its warships. And because of the military power we would command, we had to be politically stable and utterly trustworthy. This is why so much time and effort were devoted to political development.

We had adult overseers who assisted with day-to-day naval training, but the political responsibility was in our hands. I had six lieutenants who supervised groups of fifty, 100 or 200. We were the top seven leaders. They were my cabinet.

My duty was to lead them in organizing and supervising all political training activities. I received directives from the Communist League headquarters in Moscow, and it was up to me to see that those directives were carried out. I assigned work responsibilities and political studies to the cadet officers through my cabinet.

In general, the purpose of my job was to make sure that each cadet who graduated and assumed high responsibility in the navy was tough, highly disciplined and totally committed to Communism. The Communist Youth League was the party's watchdog over the political beliefs and dedication to Communism of every one of the 1,200 officer cadets. If any cadet had a problem with anyone on his level, or even with the academy Commander, he had the right to come to me with his grievance. Then I was expected to represent him before the Commander and to argue in his favour if I was convinced he was right. Of course, the veteran career officers resented such double authority on the base. They wanted their authority to be supreme and final. But the party gave equal authority to the Communist Youth League. In some cases, the League could even overrule the purely military officers in deciding the merits of a case. Political purity was more important than technical skill.

Whenever a cadet showed signs that he was beginning to waver or err in his Communist commitments or political zeal, I would call him in and give him a hard lecture. Then I would bring him before a general meeting of the Youth League and shame him publicly. By these methods I was to try to shock him into better performance.

One word from the Youth League over my signature could ruin a young officer's career. He could be discharged, reduced to an ordinary seaman or assigned to the army at low rank.

Other punishment was fast and severe, even for the slightest mis-step. Any infraction could bring the offending cadet fifteen days in the brig on bread and water. Other offenders would be assigned twenty-four hours a day on patrol watch. When they fell asleep, they would be arrested. The object was to toughen them to the point where they would obey any order of their superiors without thinking first. Every command had to be executed without consideration or hesitation. We were to become officers and lead others. But before we could lead, we had to learn to follow.

I determined that I would exercise my authority with caution and care, seeking to help the cadets as much as possible. I understood human weakness, and it was my job and personal intention to make sure as many of the officer cadets as possible would come through successfully.

But it wasn't always possible. The pressures were extremely

intense. The constant marching and drilling, the technical naval studies, the studies of Marxism-Leninism, the long, hard hours devoted to the *subbotniks* (volunteer labour brigades) brought incredible pressures to bear on some of the cadets. The first year I was at Petropavlovsk three cadets shot themselves—or hanged themselves in their barracks. The pressures were too much for them.

One boy, I remember, was accused of sleeping on duty, and was ordered to go on watch duty and patrol for another twenty-four hours straight. Of course, he couldn't take it and he disappeared. We immediately assumed he had deserted, but the next day we found his body hanging from the rafters.

One particularly sad case I had to deal with was that of a young fellow officer whom I had tried to help. He finally jumped out of a third-storey window and killed himself. We were ordered to spread the word around that he was drunk and didn't know what he was doing. I knew better. I knew him well and it was plainly suicide. But like the others, I had to obey orders and make it appear that he was drunk when he jumped.

In some cases I used my position as Youth League leader to intervene for cadets even though naval authorities were determined to expel them. I would arrange to meet with the officers to try to persuade them that the cadet in question was salvageable. I would urge them to give the cadet another chance, promising that I would personally see to it that he was more thoroughly indoctrinated with Lenin's teachings and that we would make him into a good Communist officer yet. "Just give me another opportunity to make him right," was my plea.

"All right, Kourdakov," they would often reply. "You have three months to see if you can turn him around and straighten him out." Usually I succeeded.

I reported directly to the local Communist Party Committee in Petropavlovsk. There my duties put me in direct touch with Communist Party leaders in Moscow. From them, I received the directives, training manuals, lessons and copies of lectures I was to give to the cadets. I met many of the top Communist officials of Kamchatka Province and of the city of Petropavlovsk in the local *Gorkom*, the city Communist Party office. The direct link these contacts provided with Moscow gave me an opportunity to see the inner workings of the party.

One pleasant duty I had was to organize recreational and

cultural events for the academy. These came under the heading of "political development". Often we brought in entertainers for the cultural events from Moscow. They were always well received.

The least well received were the lecture meetings. I had to get a good turnout for the bigwig Communist lecturers visiting from Moscow, or else! Many such lecturers came through regularly.

During this time, from September 1968 to May 1969, I was asked by the *Gorkom* to go to some of the local schools and the university and give lectures on Communism and world politics. I lectured on American involvement in Vietnam, the dangers of imperialism, the importance of the military might of the Soviet Union, Leninism, Marxism and other political subjects. I tried to speak forcefully and soon became a popular speaker, with my lectures well attended.

In addition to such activities, I also participated in all sports at the academy: wrestling, judo, karate, long-distance running, track. I was always on the go, with never a moment to relax. It was the busy, active life I enjoyed very much.

One day when I was in the *Gorkom* headquarters in Petropavlovsk, one of the party officials put his arms around my shoulders and said, "Kourdakov, we want to tell you that you're doing a Number One job. We've had less trouble at the Naval Academy here than in any of our military institutions. You've really got things organized. Keep it up, kid!" I beamed all over, really pleased and stammering for words.

Then, as I turned to leave the office, the city party leader walked into the room and said, "Young man, keep it up; you've got a great future! We need men like you. Keep your head on straight and you can go far."

I almost floated back to the base. This was my life. These were my kind of people. The party was my "family". I was now a part of something I could believe in, belong to and give my life for. I understood discipline, authority and hard work, and the party knew how to reward such. It was one of my proudest moments! I felt in perfect harmony with the world.

11 An order from the secret police

One day in early May 1969, I sat working in my office at the Communist Youth League building on the naval base. There was a rap at the door and I called out, "Come in."

The man who entered was a stranger. He was short, powerfully built, combed his thick black hair straight back in a severe manner, and wore civilian clothes. When he spoke, in a rapid-fire staccato, he betrayed a defect in his speech which made him difficult to understand. I had to listen closely to catch what he said. He introduced himself as Ivan Azarov.

I had heard his name before. He was a major in the K.G.B., the secret police, here in Kamchatka. The K.G.B. is the Soviet's élite secret police unit, operating with far greater authority than the uniformed police. When I heard the name, I gulped. What did the K.G.B. want with me?

Azarov pulled some files from his briefcase and, as he placed them on the table between us, I noticed one set of papers with my name on the folder.

"Kourdakov," Azarov said, "I've been studying your record back to the time you were at Children's Home Number One at age six. You've piled up quite a record for a young man."

I shrugged, trying to effect a gesture of modesty.

"You see," he continued, "we've got a very serious problem in our country that we have to deal with in a special way. As you may know, I'm involved in police work." Then he told me about a special police group to be formed to operate as an official secret branch of the police in Petropavlovsk.

"This special action squad will be given assignments and take on very special jobs the regular police can't handle for a number of reasons," he explained. "Similar special operations squads are being set up all over the Soviet Union. We've got orders from the party and Moscow to set one up here." He paused, then continued, "We've been looking for a man to head up our special police group here."

So, I thought, *that's what he's after!* I began thinking up reasons why I couldn't accept the assignment. I already had my hands more than full right now. But Azarov went right on in his rapid-fire way. "I don't know whether you remember it," he said, "but I was in one of your meetings at a school where you spoke." I didn't. "You made quite a rousing speech there, young man, one of the best on Communism that I've ever heard delivered to young people. Those kids were eating right out of your hand." And then he came to the point. "We're looking for leadership like that, Kourdakov. The man we choose must be able to recruit and train his men, organize and direct their activities. I've studied this file closely," he added, tapping it as he spoke. "We think you might be the man to organize and lead our new police operations group."

He could, of course, order me to take the job but I was nevertheless trying to think of a reason to say no. When I started to speak, he began talking again. I could see he wasn't accustomed to interruptions. "And you understand that for this very special work you would be given very special pay, out of a special fund set up for this purpose—twenty-five roubles per operation."

I couldn't believe what I was hearing! Had I misunderstood? After all, he spoke like a machine gun. I couldn't have heard right. "Would you repeat that sentence?" I asked.

He smiled and said, "I know what you're thinking; but you heard me right. This is a special police squad, with its operating expenses paid from special funds set aside by Moscow. You will be given twenty-five roubles per operation."

As a naval cadet I received seven roubles *per month*. And here I would be paid twenty-five roubles per "operation"! Even as a commissioned officer in the navy, following my graduation from the cadet programme, I would earn only seventy roubles per month. In just three "operations" with the police unit, I would earn more than a whole month's navy pay! Azarov saw the gleam in my eyes.

"You agree to accept our offer?" he asked.

"Yes, of course," I said. "But why did you pick me?"

"For three simple reasons. First, you're in military school as an officer cadet, and your time already belongs to the state. You don't have to quit a job. It's a simple thing. I'll make the arrangements with your commanding officer for time off for your police work. Second, I can't forget your talks on Communism and world affairs at the university. You showed the kind of leadership that this job needs. Third, and this is the most important reason, you have the contacts to pick the kind of men we need in the police operations group."

He was certainly right on the last point. As head of the Communist Youth League on the base, I had developed friends among all the party's secretaries under me. They, in turn, knew every naval cadet on the base. All I'd have to say was, "Give me your top three toughest guys," and they would do it. I had the contacts and authority to pick from all the 1,200 officer cadets on the base.

"How many men do you want?" I asked Azarov.

"At least twenty," he replied. "They won't all be needed at one time, nor in all cases, but we want at least twenty to draw from, in case a few can't make it at a particular time." My mind started working on who my twenty men would be.

"Pick your men, Kourdakov, and bring them to me no later than ten days from now. I want to brief all of you and turn you over to the man who'll be directing your operations group on a day-to-day basis."

"All right," I replied. The major stood and went out.

I wasn't born yesterday, I thought. I knew what he had in mind. We would be expected to take on drunks, murderers, wife-beaters, and other law-breakers the regular police couldn't take time to deal with. There were some pretty tough elements around Petropavlovsk, being a seaport. I knew I'd better pick some rugged, tough, fearless guys, strong and skilful enough to break up a gang fight by taking on *both* of the gangs involved.

I was sure I could handle myself. I'd always been strong on physical fitness, had wrestled and recently become judo champion of Kamchatka Province. I had to pick twenty other guys like me. I thought of my athlete friends first. By the time I got to my barracks I had already decided on several. They were men I had met through our Communist Youth League sports programme—champion boxers, judo experts and other good athletes.

My first choice was Victor Matveyev, a very strong man about six feet six inches tall and weighing 230 pounds. Though built like a bear, he was exceptionally fast on his feet. And despite a warm, friendly face, he had a cold heart. He was a close friend of mine and one of my deputies in the Communist Youth League, in charge of 200 cadets in the radio department. He was a top player of our hockey team. The only time we had any problem with each other was when we'd get into physical competition. At first it was just a friendly judo or wrestling match, but sometimes it got beyond friendliness and became a real battle, with both of us losing our tempers.

Inside his own circle of friends, or people he worked with, Victor was congenial enough. But when he got into a fight, he was crazy, completely given over to animal instincts. At those times he could do terrible harm to those he was attacking, as he was later to prove during the police actions.

Victor had a frustrated ambition: to be an air force pilot. He never quite made the grade in the air force and lost two years trying. Though two years older than I, he was one grade lower in rank. This frustration nettled him.

But in judo he achieved one of his goals by becoming champion of all East Russia. After he won his title, I once fought him in a city judo competition and, though he was in a heavier class, I held him to a draw.

My next choice was Anatoly Litovchenko, a playboy in Petropavlovsk, tall, strong and handsome, with an outwardly charming, friendly personality. His long black hair and dark moustache gave him the appearance of a "Latin lover". And his big, dark eyes added to his striking appearance. But though he looked like a ladies' man, no one but his close friends dared to call him that, and even they did so only in fun. Anatoly was a highly skilled, classical boxer, ranking third in all the Republic of Russia. It was generally agreed that he would have been champion, but he suffered a shoulder separation in one of his bouts. Until his injury, he had been popularly known as Kamchatka's hope for the world Olympics. He was in that class.

The next man I picked was Alexander Gulyaev, nervous, tense, with an explosive temper that later cost him his life.

Alex was no athlete, just big, strong and violent. He was impulsive, jumping into things before he thought. He was from my own home city of Novosibirsk and we had become good and fast friends. Probably the most determined of all my men, once Alex set his mind to something, nobody on earth could stop him. He had a round flat face with a nose that was shaped almost exactly like Victor's. In fact, we called Victor and Alex "Brother Nosey".

Vladimir Zelenov was one of the smaller men I chose for our squad, not tall but an extremely skilled boxer and quite strong. He was a happy-go-lucky guy, to whom life was supposed to be all fun and nothing else. He went to the Naval Academy not because he wanted to, but simply to avoid the army. In fact, Zelenov didn't want to be in anything, but he figured the navy was better than most of the other military choices. "All that army marching," he used to say. "Anything's better than that!"

Once in the navy, he did everything possible to get out. Some of the cadets cut their fingers or tendons, or tried to contract tuberculosis or some other dangerous disease to get release. Vladimir never actually tried any of those things, but he often talked about a plan for getting out—breaking a leg, cutting off a finger, faking a heart attack, or whatever else came to his mind. He never went beyond idle boasts, however.

The only activity he took seriously was boxing. He was the middleweight boxing champion of Kamchatka Province.

The tallest member of our attack squad was Yuri Berestennikov. His mother was director of Public School Number Fourteen in Petropavlovsk and had many friends in the Communist Party. Yuri was exceptionally strong and dearly loved to fight, especially on buses. Often he would go for bus rides, not to get anywhere in particular but just to get a good fight going. Our buses were usually crowded, often with military personnel.

Once Yuri was on the bus, he could always count on someone bumping him when the bus started up with a jerk. That gave him an excuse to let go with a good punch at the offender. Sometimes all the younger passengers would take up sides and Yuri would have a pitched battle going. One time he got all the civilians fighting all the uniformed military men in a wild free-for-all. The bus driver looked back at the brawl and drove straight for the police station with his load of fighting passengers.

That was Yuri. He lived for a fight. But still you had to like him. He had had a good education, was smart, very witty and always doing something crazy.

I'm sure he was also the most unmilitary guy ever enrolled at the academy. I think he got in only by the pull of his well-placed parents. In class, when he was called on, he would go to the blackboard to give an answer to the instructor's question. There he would stand at rigid military attention and soberly give the wrong answer. When the instructing officer told him it was not correct, he would drop his head in a show of mock shame and let out a very unmilitary yell, setting the whole class off in a roar of laughter. Once he patted a bald senior officer on the head and said, "Grass doesn't grow on a good roof."

Of course, Yuri got called down often for his undisciplined behaviour, but he didn't care. His fun in life was to get people laughing or fighting together, preferably with him in the middle of it.

Finally his superiors concluded he simply wasn't officer material and, despite his parents' influence, took him out of officers' training, making him just an ordinary seaman. But while he was on my attack squad, he proved to be one of my toughest, most dependable men, fearsome when he got into a fight.

Another key man was Sergei Kanonenko, a Ukrainian, who was one of my assistants in the Youth League. He was tough, reliable, brutally cold, with almost no show of emotion, and very efficient. He was also on our wrestling team, a powerful man, weighing about 210 pounds and standing six feet three inches tall. He loved to use a knife in fights, and I'd have to keep an eye on him to make sure he didn't use it unnecessarily.

There were other friends, like Vladimir Litovka and Victor Lazarov, all strong, powerful athletes and big guys. They and myself would form the nucleus of my police squad. For the rest of the positions, I asked my deputies in the Youth League to give me the names of the strongest, toughest men they had, men skilled in boxing, wrestling or judo. I really don't think a tougher group could ever have been put together in all of Russia. Azarov had asked for the best, and that's what he was going to get.

After making my list, I approached each of the men. Generally there were complaints and excuses. "Sergei," some said, "I'm too busy. I've just got too much going right now." They talked that way until I mentioned the money they were going to get. After that, I didn't need to say a word. They did the talking. "Sergei," they would say, "when do we get started? Let's go!" Those twenty-five roubles for just a few hours' work were a magnet none of us could resist. But Yuri, I think he would have accepted just for the fighting alone!

Soon I had rounded up a group of twenty-one and had assembled them together. I don't think I'd seen a room full of so many big, tough-looking guys in my life. As soon as we got together we all enjoyed a good drink, several in fact. I told them to report the next day to Ivan Azarov at Communist Party headquarters in Petropavlovsk.

The next day we all showed up at Azarov's office. We were all assembled in the room when Azarov entered. He looked at my men and said, "All right, Kourdakov, I see you took me seriously when I told you to choose well." As he checked out the fellows, I could see he was impressed. Azarov was overshadowed in the crowd of tall, heavily muscled young men, but with a great air of authority, he ordered us to sit down, proceeding to explain why he had called for such a group.

"I've asked Kourdakov to bring you here for a special reason. Throughout our country we have problems with enemies of the people. To combat them we're forming special police operations groups to work closely with the police.

"Technically, men, you will work for the police here in Petropavlovsk, but you will be directed behind the scenes by my office at party headquarters here. You will become a special unit, organized by direct orders from Moscow, to deal with special enemies of the state. You will *not* be used for general police work. Any questions?"

There were none, so he continued. "After this briefing, I will have you meet your police commander who will be in day-to-day charge. I will be ultimately responsible and will keep check on your reports. I know most of you are at the Naval Academy with Kourdakov. I'll inform your commanding officers that you're being assigned to special outside police operations work. That way we'll be sure you get the passes needed to leave the military base at any time you're called by police headquarters. There's no question that you are responsible first to the base, where you are cadet officers. But your police duties and responsibilities, as part of the operations group, definitely come next. Any questions?"

Still there were none. "We're going to give you a preliminary group of assignments first, and then I'll be seeing you fellows again shortly for further briefings. Now I want you to meet your police commander, the one who will be giving you your assignments."

A few moments before he said that, a man in plain clothes had walked in and seated himself off to the side. One glance at him said he was military or police and that he was out of place in civilian clothes. His coat, though not designed to be, was buttoned to the top, and he wore it as if he would have felt more comfortable in a strait-jacket. Now Azarov said, "I want you to meet Police Captain Dimitri Nikiforov."

Nikiforov got up and acknowledged Azarov's introduction by awkwardly thanking him and stammering a greeting to us. At first I wasn't much impressed, but I realized that appearances were often deceiving. He was short, stocky, with slightly blond hair and cold, steel-blue eyes. Though not tall, almost everything else about him was big—large, bulbous red nose; bigger-than-average mouth; big bones but no muscle. Puffy, dark semi-circles under his eyes gave him a weary look. I could guess he was no man to fool with, and was certain it would be dangerous to underestimate him in any situation.

Nikiforov had come to Kamchatka Province as a young man in 1947. In 1953 he was promoted to police chief of Petropavlovsk, succeeding a man who had gone on a drunken rampage and from a window in the police station had begun sniping at passers-by with a hunting rifle, killing several before he himself was killed.

I learned that Nikiforov was no big improvement over his trigger-happy predecessor. He, too, had such a craving for action that he often neglected his administrative duties to go on raids. Nikiforov never married but lived with a prostitute in a big, second-floor apartment which, except for absolute necessities—refrigerator, bed, chairs and table—was devoid of furnishings. His whole life belonged to the police and the state. His home meant nothing. We nicknamed him "Iceberg Niki".

He had well-placed contacts in police circles and strong connections with Communist Party leaders in Kamchatka. As I looked him over, I thought I'd surely hate to have him on my track.

His awkward introductory remarks concluded, Nikiforov began speaking slowly, deliberately, giving every word meaning. "You men," he said, "have been picked to be a special operations group attached to police headquarters. As such, you will work directly under my command and follow my orders. I, along with Comrade Azarov, will be responsible for your training and your assignments." He shifted his feet, looking us straight in the face. "We have growing problems in our country with enemies of the state. They operate internally, attempting to undermine the authority of our government. It's our job to find these enemies and root them out.

"At first I am going to give you routine assignments for a short period of time, to let you get your feet wet. After that, Comrade Azarov and I will conduct another group of lectures as part of your training. You will be on call at all times and when you are ordered out, you will report to me at police headquarters as quickly as possible. You will be given some assignments which the police do not have time to take care of, as well as assignments which must not look like official action. That's why you will wear street clothes at all times. To the public, you'll simply be ordinary citizens aroused into taking action against criminal elements. Do you understand?"

We nodded that we did. Then he continued. "Now I want to speak to your leader, alone. You're dismissed—all but you, Kourdakov. Come up here, comrade."

The others filed out. Nikiforov then told me that my responsibilities with the police operations group would begin at once. He ordered me to report to headquarters with my men in three days.

When the three days had passed and we gathered again, Comrade Nikiforov told us we would be on routine assignment for the next several weeks and should report to the police headquarters for three hours each day. Soon we were being sent out to assist the police in routine arrests. It was not unusual for murders to take place two or three times a week. Fights broke out often among drunken sailors, in from the sea. We were sent to break up the fights. We would charge into a bar full of brawling seamen and soon would have the situation in hand.

On one occasion Victor, Vladimir, a few others and I were sent to break up a brawl in a club near the city docks. On such assignments, we used a police truck, with the driver and two passengers in the cab and the other men on benches fitted around the sides of the bed of the truck. Such a truck would hold ten to fifteen men. This particular night we raced to the scene of the brawl and charged in. Nikiforov had said, "Don't worry about who's right and who's wrong. Just get it stopped by whatever means is necessary." For boxers, judo champs and wrestlers, that was like throwing red meat to a dog! Victor promptly floored four guys, knocking them cold, with one blow each. I was in the middle of the brawling crowd when two guys jumped me at the same time. They were both bigger than I, but I got rid of them in a hurry, one with a karate chop across the back of the neck and the other with a judo throw. It was really great sport!

It took us about twenty minutes to get the brawl stopped, and by then the inside of the club looked as if a hurricane had struck. I looked around to see how we had made out. There were Victor and Anatoly and three of our other men standing around and laughing. And Yuri! He was in heaven. He didn't have to start a fight. It was already waiting for him. He was beside himself with joy. It was a big joke to us. Where else could we get a licence to fight as much as we wanted to and be *paid* for it?

Well, the fight was over. Most of the guys who started it were lying around the floor groaning. Drunken seamen weren't much of a match for a trained disciplined group of fighters. We made no arrests. Our job was just to break up the fight. We had done that, so I shouted, "Come on, let's go!" We all piled into the police wagon and took off back to the station, reporting our results to Nikiforov, who commended us.

"Good," he said. "You boys are doing a fine job."

Time went on and we were called out three or four times a week to break up brawls or help police search for someone. Sometimes we'd all go to the station and just sit there and be available for duty, having a drink, smoking and talking. The phone would ring, somebody would report to Nikiforov that a brawl was going on, or a murder was taking place, and Nikiforov would say, "All right, Kourdakov, get moving." We'd tear out of the police station, leap into the truck, driven usually by Victor, and head for the address given us. We raced through the streets with our sirens screaming and red lights flashing, without a care for anybody else.

After every raid, we'd collect our twenty-five roubles each and head for a bar or club where we'd eat, drink, dance with the girls and have a grand time before going back to the base. It was a good deal all around. We could get off the base at any time, something none of the other cadets could do, and we could stay out after our assignments, for a drink and a good time.

The work brought us in contact with the worst kind of people, and we soon developed complete disregard for them as humans. When we got a chance to beat up a killer, why shouldn't we beat him to a pulp? And Nikiforov would laugh and congratulate us on "changing faces". If we didn't beat someone enough, he mocked us as "little softies". We got the message. Pity the next guy we caught!

Then one day Nikiforov phoned me. "Comrade Kourdakov," he said, "I want you to get your men over here tomorrow afternoon at four. Azarov is coming and we both want to have a talk with you."

I notified my men and we assembled at the police station. Azarov spoke first. "Well, I've heard good things about you boys," he said. "I hear you're coming along really well. Now we're going to get down to the real heart of your job, down to the really important work." I wondered what he was talking about. We'd been doing our work for several weeks now. What more was there to do?

He went on, "I wanted you fellows to get some experience in the job before giving you the really important assignments. In the Soviet Union we have many types of criminals. We have anti-state people who are murderers, drunkards and prostitutes. You've been dealing with that kind. But they are really nothing.

"Then there are criminals who are a far greater threat to our country's security and our way of life. They are more dangerous because they work quietly in our midst, undermining the foundations of our system and threatening the existence of our country. The people I'm talking about look innocent on the outside. But don't be deceived. They spread their poisonous beliefs, threatening the life of our society, poisoning our children's minds with false teachings and undermining the doctrines of Leninism and Marxism. These are the *religiozniki*, the religious Believers."

I didn't catch what he said at first. But he repeated it. "It's the *religiozniki*." He wanted to make sure we all got what he was saying.

"These are the Believers," he continued, "who have organized an action programme which threatens the great accomplishments of the Soviet people. They actively aid the enemies of our country. They go hand in hand with the imperialists and attempt to overthrow or set back the achievements of the Communist Party of the Soviet Union." By now he had become greatly impassioned. We could tell how deeply he felt about what he was saying. "They are even more dangerous because they do not appear to be dangerous. Murderers and thieves are direct. These people are deceptive and cunning and clever. Before you know it, they have undermined the things we've worked so hard for, poisoned the people and done their damage.

"Now, that's why you've been selected as a special police operations squad—to be an action group against these enemies. You've been given practical experience; now it's time for your real work. Your unit is one of many that are being established throughout our country. It's time we put a stop to these enemies.

"We must take *direct action*! That's your job. The orders for your operations come directly from the Party Bureau and Comrade Brezhnev. From Moscow your orders come directly to *Gorkom* here, and we pass them along to Comrade Nikiforov, who will be your immediate superior, as before. You're being paid from special funds set aside for the purpose of combating the evil and contaminating influences of religion in Soviet life."

I listened with amazement. Ever since I had seen those Believers, almost 2,000 strong, in Inskaya near Novosibirsk, I had wondered about them. I knew, of course, that there was no God and that religion was the opium of the people. I realized that religion had no place in modern Soviet life. All this I knew well; I had taught it myself many times in the lectures I had given in the schools and universities and in my Youth League meetings. What surprised me was that religion and the Believers were so strong they created a special threat to our country and had to be dealt with so severely. Of course, I thought, they do grow and spread, like a disease that will infect you before you know it. Certainly they must be stopped and uprooted from our society.

"You see over there," Azarov said, pointing to a group of "wanted" posters on the wall. Beside the posters of several murderers was a photo of a man wanted for "action against the people".

"That man," Azarov stated, "poisoned children with the narcotic of religious beliefs. He had secret Bible-teaching sessions. When he's caught, he's going to get seven years."

I was glad for the pay I was already getting, but somehow, dealing with murderers, thieves and other criminals seemed outside my interests as a Communist activist. But now, dealing with the enemies of our party, that would be far different, far more relevant and direct. These were problems I had often discussed in my lectures. Now I could do something about them and get well paid for it. This was great news.

About this time, "Loverboy" Anatoly asked, "Comrade Azarov, you say these people are worse than the murderers we've been dealing with. In what way?"

"Comrade Litovchenko," Azarov said, "murderers kill a few people and are caught. But these Believers kill the soul and the spirit of our Soviet people and spread their poisonous beliefs to many, many thousands. In the past two years in our country, this problem of religious Believers has become a far greater one. Instead of dying out and ceasing their struggles against our state, they have spread their poison throughout our country and managed to beguile and win over many followers. Wherever they can, they poison the minds of our Soviet youth. Finally now, our party has to take action. A special action order to fight the *religiozniki* has come from the top in Moscow. You boys are part of that action programme. All organizations engaged in warfare against religious beliefs have been brought together under the party's central leadership. A co-ordinating body has been set up to direct the battle plans against the Believers and their superstitious beliefs. Our best brains and finest professors are studying this problem theoretically. At the same time, a new body has been established with large computers to keep records of all of the Believers, so that we can identify and keep track of the enemies in our midst. Part of your assignment will be to prepare reports, record names and all details of the Believers among us. These reports will be sent back to Moscow and fed into the computers. That way we'll be able to keep track of these cunning and dangerous foes.

"Another organization and department branch has been established in Moscow to study the teachings of these Believers, so we can better oppose and defeat them. There our finest scholars are studying their literature, including their Bible, in order that they can learn how better to fight their religious beliefs. It's sort of a complete and full-scale Bible college."

When I heard the term "Bible college", my mind immediately flashed to the Deacon back at Barysevo, who wanted to go to Bible college. But I don't think it was the kind Comrade Azarov was describing. I tuned in to Comrade Azarov again. On and on, he went.

Looking about, I saw that the others were as fascinated as I. Never before had we realized the great threat that religious Believers were to our way of life. But now we knew. And we were hearing of a dynamic action programme that was being established in defence of our country. It convinced us of the vitality and vigour of the Communist Party. Behind it all were men who knew what they were doing. Because of them, our Communist Party was on the move. They weren't sitting back, waiting for our enemy to destroy us from within. We were men who admired action and we listened with admiration as we heard of the massive efforts being mounted. And to think that we were part of it! My sense of pride in the Communist Party welled up inside me. *At last we will strike,* I thought. Our enemy had pushed us just too far. We, the Soviet people, would show them. The Communist Party has patience, but when pushed too far, it knows how to act. And here I was, in the mainstream of it all.

Azarov told of another special force whose speciality was to seal our borders and prevent the smuggling of Bibles or literature into our country. I had never heard that anything like that was taking place. Azarov continued, "Men, it's up to you to get all the religious literature you can. We'll examine it and send it to Moscow. They'll study it to find out what country it's from and how it's being smuggled in. When we learn that, then we'll soon put a stop to it.

"Cut off the heads," Azarov said, "and the body will die. Get rid of the leaders, the brains behind the secret organization of Believers. Then their deceived, disillusioned followers will drift back to the right way."

By the time Azarov had finished talking, we saw Believers as evil, plotting, cunning people who gathered secretly in homes to plot the overthrow of our government and poison children. We wanted to get right in, teach them a lesson and finish them off.

Azarov's speech was followed by a number of other almost identical lectures over the next two weeks. We learned the methods and techniques used by the Believers. During one of those lectures, I asked why the term "religious people" or "Christians" wasn't used, instead of "Believers".

Azarov replied, "That's a good question, Kourdakov. Let me answer it. Didn't Comrade Lenin teach us long ago that it's not religion that we have to fear, but beliefs? That's our great enemy. We can crush religion and close the churches. Look about you here in Kamchatka. What do you see? Any churches here? Of course not! We don't allow them. There's not one place of religion in all Kamchatka. The *church* represents no threats.

Religion represents no threat. It's the *Believers* themselves who are the threat."

He paused for a moment, glancing over his audience to see what effect his words were having. Apparently satisfied, he continued, "Comrade Lenin said that we can close the churches and put the leaders in jail, but it's very hard to drive faith and belief from the heart of a man once he is contaminated by them. This, Comrade Kourdakov, is why *belief* is our enemy, *not religion*. This is why we don't call them Christians or church-goers. We call them *Believers*. They believe inside, and to root this belief from their hearts is a very difficult task."

It made a lot of sense to me.

After all, our club building back at Barysevo Children's Home was a closed church building. It's not hard to close churches. I understood it now. Our job was to keep belief from taking root in our people, especially our youth and children.

"Thank you, Comrade Azarov," I said on behalf of my men. "These have been most revealing sessions. We had no idea what problems those innocent-looking people have been causing."

12 The first raid: disaster!

A few days later, while I was busy with my radio engineering studies at the academy, a voice came over the loudspeaker: "Kourdakov, Kourdakov, report at once to the patrol office!" My teacher nodded, and I put down my textbooks and reported as ordered.

The patrol officer in charge said, "Kourdakov, there's a telephone message for you from Captain Nikiforov. You're to report to him at the station tonight at ten o'clock with your men. He said you would understand what it's all about."

"Yes, I do," I said. "Thanks." At ten o'clock that evening, fourteen of us, all I could get at that short notice, met at the police station.

"Send your men into the back room," ordered Nikiforov. "Let them relax a little. It's too early to go yet." So I sent the men into the small lounge at the back of the police station, while I stopped to talk to Nikiforov at his desk.

"Here are your instructions," he said. "We found out about a meeting of Believers that's starting at about eleven o'clock tonight."

"Where is it?" I asked.

On the huge street map on his office wall, he pointed to an area of private houses, in District 75, across the city. Nikiforov continued with his instructions. "There'll be only twelve to fifteen people there. You shouldn't have any trouble."

I asked, "How do you know all this?" The meeting hadn't started yet, so word about it couldn't have come from neighbours reporting suspicious activity.

A sardonic smile came on his face. "Why, a little bird told me, of course, Kourdakov!" he said. "You'd be wise not to ask too much."

I had only tried to be friendly, and had learned how difficult Nikiforov could be. I decided I'd better take it slowly with him. I wanted eventually to get on close terms with him.

Meanwhile, my men were sitting around at the back. "Go ahead, comrades, drink up and relax a little," Nikiforov called out, gesturing to the vodka bottles and glasses on the table. We needed only one invitation. Victor had already started pouring his glass full, and soon everybody was drinking and chatting.

When Nikiforov saw that everybody was loosening up with the vodka he said, "You should start out from here at about eleven o'clock. That'll give those Believers thirty minutes to get their meeting started, and they'll be relaxed, thinking everything's all right. It's the ringleaders, their secret pastors, we want. Here are the names of the two men I want brought in."

"Yes, comrade," I replied. "What about the others?"

"The others? Oh, just rough them up a little. Give them something 'nice' to remember. But don't fail to bring in the leaders," he said firmly, gesturing to the names on the paper as he handed it to me.

"Yes, comrade," I replied again. Then I began wondering why all the instructions. Was this going to be so different from our other raids? When we were sent out to break up a brawl in a bar, "Niki" was straightforward and direct. But I could see that tonight he was nervous and I wondered why.

"Make sure that no one on the street sees you," he went on. "You shouldn't have any trouble; it's eleven o'clock at night. But if there are still people passing by, just wait a minute till they go before you move in."

During one of the briefings which Azarov had given us on the Believers, he had emphasized the need for secrecy. Under no condition was the public to know what was going on. I was curious about that, because when we took on the drunken brawling gangs, we ploughed right in and there was no problem. I asked why, and he replied, "Well, Kourdakov, some people could misunderstand what we're doing and why we have to do it. Some people don't appreciate the danger that these people represent to our society. Also, there are always enemies of our country, agents of imperialism, who would really like to spread the word that we're persecuting Believers. Therefore, it's absolutely vital that you do everything possible to keep out witnesses, especially anyone taking photographs of what's going on. We can't have enemies of our country telling the world that we persecute Believers and don't permit religious freedom, now can we?" he said, and laughed. *That makes sense*, I thought.

I assured Nikiforov we would wait until the street was clear before we moved in. "All right, Kourdakov," he said. "Go back and join your men, and I'll call you when it's time."

Back in the lounge, with my men, I had a couple of drinks. I could see that everybody was feeling the vodka. The tension was gone, and Vladimir was telling a story. Everybody was laughing. Before long Nikiforov came in and said, "All right, Kourdakov, it's eleven o'clock. Time to get going." As we got up from the table, Alex bumped it and knocked over the glasses. He apologized.

Nikiforov gave me last-minute instructions at the door on the way out, saying, "Now, Kourdakov, I want you to make a thorough search for Bibles or literature. These people have some anti-Soviet literature, we know, and we need as much as we can get to send in to *Gorkom* for them to mail to Moscow. So search the place carefully for any literature and bring it in!" I nodded in agreement.

Behind the station, where the police truck was parked, Victor got into the driver's seat, I joined him in the cab, and the others piled into the back. Off we went. There were no sirens this time, no need for them because it was late at night and the traffic was light. Anyway, we didn't want to alert the Believers that we were on our way.

The city has street lighting only in the major centre, which leaves the outlying areas dark. So we had to pick our way in and around the darkened areas in the outskirts, as we tried to locate the house in which the Christian Believers were meeting. Finally we found the street and drove quietly along, looking at the house numbers. We slowly made our way up the muddy, unpaved street.

I was watching to see if I could spot any people outside. The street was deserted. Victor looked through the darkness on the left, and I looked on the right, both of us watching the house numbers. Finally I said, "It's in the next block up ahead, Victor. Stop here."

He pulled over, cut the engine and we got out. I told the fellows in the back to be very quiet. We didn't want to make any noise and have a lot of peering eyes looking out of windows or curiosity seekers coming out on the street to find out what was going on.

I got out and they followed me as we walked toward the house. It was a few houses to the left, a cabin made of wooden logs with a wooden roof. It stood behind a little picket fence and was like thousands of other houses in Petropavlovsk. The curtains were drawn, but a dim light shone through.

Now what to do? Suddenly I began to feel a little embarrassed. This was far different from breaking up a fight in a bar. There we just took off running and plunged into the wild free-for-all with fists flying, feet kicking, swinging punches until we'd cleared the floor of brawlers.

But here, instead of fighting and screaming and cursing, a few people were simply holding a meeting. We could faintly hear them singing inside. We looked at one another. What do we do next? Well, it was up to me to get things started, so I walked up to the door and tapped on it. Then I tapped a little louder.

We stood awkwardly waiting for the door to open. This was utterly ridiculous, and we knew it. What a sight it was! Fourteen tall, strapping men, standing in line on the narrow pathway leading to the front door of a little house on a deserted street at night, with one of the men up front politely knocking on it!

Soon I heard footsteps from inside. The door opened, and a man of medium height stood there and asked politely, "Yes, what can I do for you?" He sized us up, looking around my shoulders at all the other men behind me and understood what it was. His face became downcast, but he kept his dignity and said, "Come in."

As we entered, I looked around. It was a one-room house, poorly furnished with a cooking area at the back. Twelve or thirteen people were sitting on the edge of the bed and chairs that were pulled up together. They were softly singing a Russian hymn and continued singing—though with nervous glances—even as we spoke.

The man who opened the door talked in a soft whisper. "Are you from the police?" He knew, of course, that we were.

I replied, automatically picking up his whispering tone of voice, "Yes, we are." And I thought, *This is stupid! We were sent to break up the Believers' service, and here I am, conducting a conversation in whispered tones so I won't disturb the meeting!*

By now they understood that their meeting was over. But, amazingly, they continued singing. We kept on talking and soon their hymn came to a close. Then they all turned and looked at us. The little house was now packed with the Believers and my men.

Defensively, feeling more than a little embarrassed, I began to assert my authority. "What are you doing here?" I demanded.

The leader of the group said, "We're worshipping God."

"But there is no God," I said.

"Well, we believe there is, and all that we're doing is worshipping our God," replied the man who I guessed was the secret pastor.

"You can't!" I said firmly.

"Why not?"

"Because it's against the law. And we've been sent with orders that say it must be stopped."

Then he said, still politely, "But we're not breaking the law. Comrade Lenin himself said that citizens of our country have the right and freedom to worship God."

I was really at a loss what to say. Seeing the advantage he had gained over me, he began to press his point. "Comrade Lenin said that every citizen of our country has the full right to exercise his belief in religious worship, or not to believe as he chooses."

"Is that really so?" I asked.

"Of course it's so. If you want, I can show you where Lenin said that."

I was getting nowhere. I was confused and bewildered; my men behind me were embarrassed, and I could see we were losing this argument. Then the Believer began to quote the Soviet constitution, pointing out that a certain section states that every citizen has the right to fulfil his religious beliefs. "All we're doing, comrade," he said, "is using the rights which the founder of our country and our Soviet constitution provides. Are we harming anybody? Look around. We believe in God and are worshipping Him. That's all. It's our right, and we're harming no one. What have we done wrong?"

I was trapped because I knew the constitution does say that, and I remembered that Lenin did say something about religious freedom somewhere. I also recalled how, back in Leningrad, I had seen Believers going to church, and how I had thought then that our country does give religious freedom.

I protested, "But you're violating the laws of our country. Don't you understand?"

"Please explain to me how," the leader asked.

"Well, I only know that you're violating the laws of our country, and I'm sorry but I have the names of two people who must come with us."

The Believers looked at one another and realized that somebody had to go with us. The man I had been speaking with was one whose name I had. As the two men put on their coats to be taken to the police station, the confusing contradictions went through my mind. At last our two prisoners were ready. They quietly shook the hands of their fellows, said something about "pray for us", then came out of the door. As we left, I could hear the remaining Believers begin to pray.

Back in the police truck and bouncing down the darkened streets of Petropavlovsk, on our way back to the police head-quarters, I was really confused. I would rather break up bar-room brawls and fight twenty knife-wielding men than go through this kind of experience again! I didn't like it at all.

We parked the truck behind the police station and got out. Niki was waiting at the door, a big smile on his face. The smile quickly disappeared as we walked in. He took one look at us and at the two men we had arrested and became furious. He turned to one of his lieutenants and shouted, "Get these prisoners out of here and lock them up!" Immediately the two were shoved into a cell. Then Nikiforov turned to us. We were a sheepish-looking bunch. Fourteen grown men coming back from a raid, with nothing to show for it but two small, middle-aged men who had put up no fight at all when we arrested them.

It hadn't taken Nikiforov long to size up the situation. "Well, my children," he said sarcastically, "it looks like you have been on a nice little picnic." Then he abruptly dropped the sarcasm and roared, "Where do you babies think you have been anyway?" He proceeded to give us a tongue-lashing none of us would soon forget, raving angrily as he paced the floor.

"But, Comrade Nikiforov," I protested, "these people didn't fight back. This wasn't like the other police actions we were on. They're a different kind of people. We have to use different techniques sometimes!"

"Different techniques!" he shouted. "Different people! I'll tell you about these 'different people'! These are cunning, deceptive enemies of the state! You go out to bring them in and protect our state, and they almost convert you!" He went on to tell us how evil and treacherous they were. The very fact that we thought them harmless, he said, and had arguments for their rights, was itself proof of how deceptive and evil and cunning they really were. Couldn't we see this? He slumped into his seat, apparently exhausted by his diatribe.

After a moment his strength seemed to revive. He jumped to

his feet and continued his harangue. "Won't I ever get it through your numb skulls that they are our worst enemies? They are the most dangerous criminals among us. They're like snakes. They keep themselves hidden from view until they're ready to strike and then it's too late! I'd rather have a hundred murderers running around loose than half a dozen of these poisoners of the people! The murderers we know we can catch any time. But these—you never know what they'll be up to next. They spread their deadly propaganda everywhere and work constantly behind our backs. And you," he shouted, "you let them off!" He went on and on.

"These are the leeches that are sucking the lifeblood of the Russian people," he yelled. "We must crush and destroy these elements. Now, do you still have sympathy for them?"

We were all beginning to see things differently by then. The sheepishness that my men had shown earlier was turning to anger because we had been tricked by the Believers. No one likes to be tricked. We apologized to Nikiforov and mumbled that we hadn't understood properly.

Nikiforov shouted, "Well, next time you'd better understand! What kind of workers for the party are you?"

That really stung. I'd given everything I had to the Communist Party. I was upset and angry—with myself and those people who had deceived me. The next time, I promised myself, I wouldn't be so stupid. *The next time*, I thought, *the next time!*

Nikiforov thought we needed a little more of the regular police operations. So when he called us again, it was for brawls or other regular police work.

Nikiforov knew human nature. He was a master of psychology, a student of the human mind and behaviour who both gained and used his knowledge in his dealings with criminals. And he used his skill on us. He knew just how to spur us on. During the next few weeks especially, he never passed up an opportunity to reward us with high praise after especially violent actions. Once when we arrested two thieves and brought them back, we shoved them through the door at the police station. Nikiforov took one look at them and shouted, "What kind of an arrest is this? Look at these men. Why, they look as fresh as the day they were born! What's the matter with you babies? Won't you ever learn how to change faces? Now take them back out and bring them in looking different!"

Vladimir and Anatoly, our two boxing champions, took the poor fellows outside. Soon we heard the blows and the shouts. They used the thieves like punching bags. When they dragged the two thieves back in, their faces were unrecognizable. "All right, boys," Niki said. "That's better! Now you're acting like the men I thought you were!" We drank vodka, laughed and joked.

That was one step in Nikiforov's brutalization programme. But I can't put the blame on him alone. We responded enthusiastically. We were beginning to enjoy this kind of violent life as much as he.

We had started in May. It was now early August. Most actions had been against the gangsters and brawls. But gradually he began to sandwich a little raid on Believers in between the gang fights and violent arrests. A bar-room raid, a Believer arrest. We soon learned to "change the faces" of Believers as easily as we worked over the drunken, brawling sailors. But still, our raids against the Believers were minor, small groups which met mostly in homes.

13 Sudden death at Elizovo

One Friday in August 1969, Nikiforov called me at the academy. When I got on the telephone, he said, "Kourdakov, I want you to be here at five o'clock this afternoon." From the way he spoke I knew we were at last going to get our big chance to prove ourselves, to once and for all make up for that humiliating first encounter with the detested Believers.

After classes, I got a bus and made my way across the city to the central police headquarters. Nikiforov was waiting for me in his office. I found him looking at his large map on the wall. "Oh, Kourdakov," he said, "come on in." Then, as he always did, he got right down to business.

"Kourdakov, I've just received information from my sources that the Believers are planning a secret baptismal service up here next Sunday," he said, pointing to a spot on the map. I moved closer and saw that he was pointing out the small village of Elizovo, in the foothills, about thirty-five miles north of Petropavlovsk, near the Avacha River.

"They picked quite an area!" I exclaimed.

"Yes," he said, "it's densely forested and from their point of view, it makes an ideal place."

I agreed. The river Avacha started as a small stream high up in the mountainous backbone of the peninsula and as it flowed downward, it became larger. At the town of Elizovo, it was about 200 feet wide but still shallow. From there it flowed to the Pacific, emptying into the bay on which the city of Petropavlovsk was situated.

Nikiforov volunteered more information about the Believers. "This isn't the first time they've used that spot," he said. "They're getting careless. They used it once before for a secret baptismal service, but our informants didn't learn about it until the service was in progress. By the time we got there, they were gone. Usually, these people are pretty smart. They never go to the same place twice. But according to our informant, they're going back. Since it's an ideal spot, they plan to use it once more."

And then he said with ominous delight: "We missed them the first time. We'll not miss them *this* time!"

I understood that he expected me to keep his promise. "When are they meeting?" I asked.

"At four o'clock on Sunday afternoon."

I wondered how he had such specific information. I assumed it could only be from spies among the Believers.

"Kourdakov," he said, "I want you and your group to be here at nine o'clock on Sunday morning. The Believers must not see you coming, so you'll have to get up there and get in place before they show up."

"Yes, comrade!" I exclaimed excitedly, thinking what a great Sunday outing that would be. I went back, contacted my men and told them to meet me at the police station on time and to bring along their guitars. "We're going to have a picnic," I told them, "and make a day of it." *If we've got to be there,* I thought, *why not go early and have some fun?* On Sunday, twelve of us met at 8 a.m., and Nikiforov gave orders to arrest and bring in everyone we caught.

We packed three boxes of vodka and some food in the back of the police truck. Alexander Gulyaev brought his guitar and mine too. We boarded the truck and took off on the road leading out of Petropavlovsk heading north.

As we bounded along, I asked Victor where the vodka came from. "Oh, it's a present from Nikiforov. He had it waiting for us when we got to the station."

I looked in the sack on the floor of the cab, and found some caviare. "Well, old Iceberg Niki may not be so bad after all," I said.

It was almost an hour's drive over winding roads that rose into the foothills until we reached the village of Elizovo. We turned off into the deep, dark forest on to a small side road. What a beautiful, sunny and warm day it was! We drove on deeper into the cool green forest. Checking our map carefully, I concluded we were near the Avacha River which flowed through the dense forest. We stopped and unloaded the truck and I told Victor to park the truck in a ravine so it couldn't be seen. We pulled the vodka bottles out of the back and the sack of sandwiches and caviare out of the cab. Then, walking deeper into the bush, we selected the spot for our picnic. We settled down and relaxed. Alexander began strumming on his guitar, and somebody opened a couple of bottles of vodka, and soon we had a roaring picnic going!

Victor came tramping back over the hill and reported, "Well, nobody will ever see the truck there. I've got it in a little gully completely out of sight."

"Great," I responded. "Here, have a sandwich and a drink."

We spent practically all day there drinking, eating, singing, telling stories and having a good time. As time went by, everyone was getting a little drunker. We thought of the cadets back at the academy. They were rarely let off the base. But we were free to come and go.

I guess I had a little too much vodka and dozed off. When I finally woke up, it was 3.15. The Believers would be heading this way any time. We had to move fast. It had been a restful holiday, but now it was time to go to work. I looked around at my group and, to my chagrin, saw that most of them were half drunk. No one was falling-down drunk, but they were all feeling light-headed and were rousting about, wrestling and rough-housing.

"Hey, you guys," I yelled. "Get ready. We've got work to do. Get your clubs ready."

"Where are they?" somebody asked.

Somebody exclaimed, "We forgot them. They're still in the truck!"

We had to have our clubs. They were made in Czechoslovakia, designed especially for Soviet police work. Made of steel on the inside and solid rubber on the outside, they were heavy and extremely hard. Even a light tap with only one of them could be devastating. They were telescopic, with a lever on the handle that released a spring inside, popping another length of rubber-covered steel out. For close work, we kept it telescoped down to the smallest size. For outside work, like today, we extended it to its full length by flicking the lever. My men and I had become adept with our police clubs, both in tight quarters and outdoors in open spaces.

The clubs were now brought from the truck and distributed around. We then climbed over a high hill and, in minutes, arrived at one of the two spots we thought the Believers might choose for their baptismal service. We began to inspect it.

"This has to be it!" exclaimed Victor. "Look how perfect it is." It was one of the prettiest natural scenes I had ever seen. There was a grassy, gently sloping area leading to the sandy shore. At this point the river was shallow for about fifty feet out. The spot was perfectly secluded, hidden from all approaches by trees and tall rocks. It was difficult to reach, and no one could sneak up on them without warning. *Those Believers,* I thought. *They're stupid to believe in God, but they certainly know how to pick their meeting places.*

As I further examined the spot, however, I noted one point of danger. Because the river was quite shallow, it would be easy for the Believers to try to escape across the river and into the dense forest on the other side once the attack started. My military training told me I'd better assign guards on the other side of the river, in order to cut off any possible escape. Sergei Kanonenko and Yuri Berestennikov got the assignment.

"If any try to escape over there," I said, "you guys cut them off."

"But, Sergei," they protested, "nobody's going to make it that far and we'll miss all the action. We won't have any fun."

That didn't matter one bit to me. Anyway, Kanonenko loved to use his knife too much and I didn't want anyone cut to death. The important thing was to keep anyone from getting away. So Kanonenko and Yuri waded and swam to the other side of the river, grumbling all the way.

I positioned my other men in a semi-circle behind bushes and trees high up on the hillside, so that no matter which direction the Believers might try to run, we'd get them. Every one of my men was perfectly concealed from view. *Those Believers are in for a surprise today!* I thought with satisfaction.

When everything was ready, we lay there waiting. The ambush was all set. Two across the river and ten of us here. We didn't have to wait long. At about 4.15 we heard voices and the sound of feet crunching over dry branches in the forest behind us.

Soon the walking noises and soft voices were very near, and then I spotted a line of people, eighteen or twenty at least, coming towards us in single file along the small path. Their leader was a man about thirty-eight years old. As they walked, they talked quietly. Several of the Believers were wearing white robes, and I assumed they were the ones to be baptized. I was surprised to see how many young people were in the group.

Silently we waited while they assembled at the water's edge. Once the stragglers had arrived and they were all congregated at the river's edge, one of the men began to speak. I strained to hear what he was saying but caught only occasional phrases. Nikiforov had told me their leader was Vasily Litovchenko, a wanted man, from Petropavlovsk. How ironic, I had thought, the same last name as Anatoly Litovchenko, one of my best men. A few of the other Believers were from Petropavlovsk also. Some were from the nearby town of Elizovo, and four were from a nearby collective farm called Pogranishny. Apparently the parasite Vasily had won followers not only in town, but in the country too. It showed me how these people, if left alone, would quickly multiply and spread their poisonous teachings everywhere.

As I looked over the group of Believers, now congregated near the water's edge, I counted seven in white robes. The party kept telling us that religion had no appeal for youth. But this contradicted what I was seeing now with my own eyes and had seen before on other occasions. It worried and somehow angered me.

After speaking for a few minutes and reading to them from a little book, Vasily Litovchenko began to lead the group in singing. Again I strained to hear the words, but mostly without success. It had something to do with God, I knew, for that was the one word I heard most. After the singing, Litovchenko began to walk out into the water, followed by the seven white-robed Believers, one at a time, until they were all about twenty-five feet out in the river, waist deep. The others stood on the river bank softly singing. The sun beat down warmly and the forest was quiet except for the chirping of the crickets. In the background I could hear the sound of running water. I couldn't help but notice the beauty and serenity of the scene.

But now the time for action had come. My men were crouched and ready. Suddenly I jumped to my feet and yelled loudly, "All right, let's go! Now!"

Immediately my men exploded from behind the bushes, racing down from the hill, clubs raised, hitting the sandy shore of the river at full speed. We smashed into the startled group of Believers, knocking them sprawling out into the river. No one remained standing after the first running charge. Knocked into the water and stunned with surprise, they floated about as we went after them one by one.

I came in behind my men. By then the screams of Believers began to rise. A woman's voice cried, "Oh dear Lord, no. No!" Whoever it was soon stopped crying, letting out just one more piercing scream as one of my men got to her. That beautiful mountain scene had erupted into a wild swirling mass of hands, feet and clubs, splashing water and the agonized cries of the Believers.

"Get those in the river," I shouted, and several of my men charged at the white-robed ones standing in the water, ready for baptism, smashing them with our clubs, extended to full length. One young fellow trying to break away jerked his arm from me, but my club was just long enough to enable me to land a blow on the back of his head.

I looked over and saw Alex Gulyaev smash one of the girls on the side of the head with his fist and split her ear wide open. She clutched at it as the blood began to flow. I grabbed one of the Believers around the neck in a judo hold and crushed him until he stopped screaming, then dropped him into the water. The whole scene was a bedlam of curses, shouting, screaming and the Believers frantically praying, "God help us! God help us!"

Their prayers angered me. "Shut them up!" I ordered, then reached down into the water and scooped up a big handful of sand. Jerking open the mouth of one of the Believers, I rammed the sand into his mouth, packing it full until he couldn't pray. The other guys started doing the same. We packed their mouths with sand and mud and the praying stopped.

Hearing an outburst of commotion behind me, I whirled around just as Anatoly Litovchenko reached the pastor, Vasily Litovchenko. The girl who had been waiting to be baptized next had tried to run when she saw Anatoly coming at them. Vladimir Zelenov saw her trying to escape and took off after her, smashing her across the back of the neck with his extended club. Without a sound, she collapsed in a heap in the water. Vladimir dragged her over to the shore and dropped her.

I saw that Anatoly was taking care of the pastor, so I whirled back. All around me my men were following my lead, ramming sand down the Believers' throats—stones, sand, dirt, anything. One man had his mouth open, praying, when I hit him full in the face with my fist and knocked most of his teeth out, cutting my knuckles. I cursed him violently as the blood streamed down his chin.

"All right, all right," I shouted, surveying the scene. "Drag them out of there. Get them on shore!" So we started pulling them out of the water and dragging them up on the river bank and throwing them to the ground. One of the older women with sand in her mouth was bobbing up and down in the water about to drown, gagging and clutching her throat. I grabbed her, pulled her up out of the river and threw her roughly on the beach. Then I looked around to take stock of the scene. There they lay, the choking, gasping Believers, many with blood pouring down their faces. The girl whose ear Vladimir had split open was bleeding profusely. We herded them together and my men stood guard over them. It seemed as if an eternity had passed since we started our attack, but as I looked at my watch I found we had been at it only five minutes. We had taught those people a lesson they wouldn't soon forget. And that was what mattered most.

"Separate those men from the women," I ordered. We grabbed the men roughly and tied their hands behind their backs. Then I looked around and counted. Something was wrong. Somebody was missing.

"Where's Litovchenko?" I demanded.

"Here I am," Anatoly replied.

"I don't mean you, stupid," I growled. "The pastor. That's who I mean."

"I don't know, Sergei. The last I saw of him was when I hit him."

Well, I had more pressing things to attend to and promptly dismissed thoughts of the missing pastor for the time being. We herded the men down the path to the truck. We then turned to the women and girls. Some of my men began ripping the wet, bloody clothes off the young girls. Stripped naked, the girls crouched down on the beach, trying to hide themselves in shame. We prodded them and laughed at them and said, "Hey, guys, so this is what Believers look like!" And we all laughed. The older women bowed their heads and sobbed as we taunted the frightened, beaten young girls.

All this time Yuri and Sergei had been on the other side of the river. Now they made their way back, complaining loudly, angry because they had missed the action.

"Let's get going!" I shouted. Jerking the girls to their feet, my men started running their hands over them. Then we marched off, pushing the Believers ahead of us to the police truck. Many of them were sobbing as they walked.

"Shut up!" Vladimir shouted. But they continued to cry as we pushed and prodded them over the trail to the waiting police truck. Once we arrived, I began counting the men. Yes, one was definitely missing—the leader of the group, Vasily Litovchenko.

"Where is he? Who's seen him?" I demanded of my men. All shrugged except Anatoly.

"The last time I saw him, Sergei, he was floating in the water, unconscious."

Oh, well, I thought, *Nikiforov will understand.* We loaded the men in the front part of the truck, their hands tied behind them, and pushed the women and girls into the back. My fellows sat on the benches around the back of the truck, with the women and girls on the floor in the middle. The four younger girls were still nude. They buried their faces in their hands and sobbed. Up front, the men kept their eyes averted. The older women were praying, I guess, as their lips moved in silent words.

It was about five o'clock in the afternoon when we came back into civilization, passing through several villages and then into the outskirts of the city of Petropavlovsk. It was still quite light, and the people could see the police truck coming down with the nude girls crouching down and being prodded by the big men in the back. By then we had finished what was left of the vodka. Our afternoon's work was done and we were quite drunk. We thought it great fun as some of the men lit up cigarettes and smoked and pressed the lighted ends to the girls' naked flesh and watched them jump and squirm about.

One of the girls, Nina Rudenko, sixteen years old, was singled out for particular abuse because she was so young and innocent looking. Another woman was about twenty-six and Vladimir Zelenov took a liking to her, teasing her and running his hand over her body, laughing boisterously until she turned around and slapped him very hard in the face.

The journey back to police headquarters had been a nightmare horror to these young Christian girls. They had gone out to be baptized as Believers in God, and their baptism turned into one of terror. In the station, I looked again at the sixteen-year-old Nina Rudenko. She had beautiful blue eyes and long brown hair, and was of slight build. Her lips were quivering, and she sobbed and trembled uncontrollably.

Nikiforov, standing at the door, quickly took in the scene and thundered, "Kourdakov! Did you drive these girls through the streets this way?"

"Of course! Why not?" I answered.

"You fool! Don't you know this will turn the people against the police? This makes us look bad," he shouted in rage. "Out of sight, where people can't see you, do what you want with these people; but in the open and in public, *never!*" Nikiforov called for his lieutenants. Several came rushing out, and he ordered, "Put them away, inside. Lock them up."

The men were taken to cells. The girls, including Nina, were left all night in the sobering cell, full of drunken men who tormented and abused them, doing what they wanted with them the whole night. It was a horrifying experience for them and one from which Nina Rudenko never recovered.

At the police station we sat around, and Victor laughed and said, "Did you see poor old Vladimir? Great boxing champion of Kamchatka, but his reflexes are so slow he gets beaten up by a Christian girl!" He laughed uproariously, and for a long time we teased Vladimir about his slow reflexes and how he met his match in a small Christian girl who succeeded in slapping him across the face.

It was part of my job to follow up and make a report of all those we arrested. Days after the arrest, I learned that Nina Rudenko had been expelled from school. The director told me, "Nina was all right until recently, when for no reason that we could determine, she became emotionally and mentally disturbed. She was unable to concentrate on her work; she frequently interrupted the class by babbling incoherently. She often began to shake and weep uncontrollably. We repeatedly had to interrupt the class and take her out. Finally we had to expel her, she was so disruptive. I think the girl's had some sort of nervous breakdown, but I don't know why."

I could have told the school director why, but I didn't.

"We called her mother in for a conference," the director said, "and she told how Nina would awaken at night with a start, sit up in bed and scream in a high-pitched voice that could be heard all through their house and out into the street." The school director concluded the interview with a final remark. "You can well imagine, Comrade Kourdakov, how impossible it would be to keep a child like that in school. We just couldn't let her go on interrupting all the other children." As I listened to the director's report, I was glad he didn't know what had happened to this young girl.

As for the men we brought in from the Elizovo raid, well, first they were loaded into their cells, and Nikiforov said to us, "You boys go in and have a drink and rest up. I'll take care of this bunch and then I'll get your reports." The reports, oral or written, were required as part of our assignment. They were forwarded on to *Gorkom* and from there to Moscow. The party kept close track of everything we did, frequently sending us a complimentary letter on our work.

While we sat in the police station, drinking and waiting to give our reports to Nikiforov, Anatoly said to me, "Sergei, you looked like you were taking a holiday out there. How come you didn't do your share?"

"Listen, you!" I shouted across the room. "Don't you get out of line there, boy, or I'll give you the 'Elizovo treatment'." We all laughed. The "Elizovo treatment" came to be the name for the trick of scooping up handfuls of dirt and sand and packing the mouths of the Believers. From that raid on, any time some of the fellows got into a dispute, we'd say, "Look out, or you'll get the 'Elizovo treatment'!"

Later I whispered to some of the fellows something I didn't want Anatoly Litovchenko to hear. I had been struck by the fact that he and the leader of the Believers, Vasily Litovchenko, had the same surname, and I told the men something out of hearing of Anatoly. Just about then, Nikiforov came into the room, and we quietened down and waited for him to speak.

"Well, my children," he began. *My children?* I thought. *That's the first time he's used that term in a long time.* He was really pleased. "I want to congratulate you. You boys are finally learning how to get things done." He was beaming as we'd never seen him do before. He paused, then asked, "By the way, what happened to Vasily Litovchenko, the pastor?"

I knew he was going to ask that question and had rehearsed my men. When I nodded to them, we all sang out in chorus, "Litovchenko killed Litovchenko."

By that, of course, we meant that *Anatoly* Litovchenko had killed the underground pastor, Vasily Litovchenko. But from what we said, it sounded as if the pastor had committed suicide. Nikiforov caught on to the joke and had a good laugh with the rest of us. We were all in high spirits by now. But then suddenly he sobered and asked sternly, "All right, Kourdakov, now I need to know what happened to Litovchenko."

I smiled and said, "We told you, captain. Litovchenko killed Litovchenko."

With that, everyone joined in laughter again, and finally Nikiforov said, smiling with fatherly approval, "Well, I see I'm not going to get much information out of you boys tonight. Kourdakov, get these men out of here and go out and have a good drink. Come back tomorrow and tell me what happened." We jumped to our feet and started to leave, but Nikiforov stopped us and said, "Before you go I want to tell you how proud I am of you all. You've done a terrific job and taught those Believers a lesson and given them something to remember. You're beginning to really shape up, my children."

That was the second time he had used that phrase that night. I wondered about the significance of it. Maybe we were getting into Nikiforov's good graces at last. Maybe tough old Iceberg Niki was beginning to warm up.

Next day, when I reported back to Nikiforov, he asked, "Kourdakov, are you still holding to that story about Litovchenko killing Litovchenko or was that all a joke?"

I had sobered up during the night and said seriously, "To tell you the truth, captain, I'm not really sure. It was such wild confusion out there, with people shouting, screaming and praying and making all kinds of other noises, I really don't know what happened."

"Well," he said, "I've got news for you. Some villagers down the river a few miles from Elizovo found the body of Vasily Litovchenko this morning snagged on a bush in the river. They called the local police, and the body's on its way here for an autopsy." I shrugged. *So, there's nothing bad about that.* I could tell last night that Nikiforov was proud of his accomplishment in getting rid of the underground pastor. In fact, he had joined in to make a big joke of it with us.

Then looking very serious, he went on, "Kourdakov, I want to review this raid with you. I have no objections to anything that happened on it, except one thing—the way you drove those girls, openly exposed, through the streets. Do whatever you want with the women and other Believers out of sight, but don't ever again bring public ridicule to the police that way."

I said, "Yes, sir." Then I was struck by the fact Nikiforov hadn't raised any objection to the killing of a man, nor any criticism for abusing those girls.

I was at the police station the next day, when the autopsy report was given. It said that Pastor Litovchenko had died from a massive blow across the head that had split his skull and caused instant death through internal haemorrhaging.

That was the first time we had ever killed anybody. As I thought about it, I began to feel bad.

"Listen, Kourdakov," Nikiforov said, sensing my feelings, "you men did an outstanding job at Elizovo. Don't feel bad about it. Remember, these are enemies of the state. They're dangerous and determined to overthrow our way of life and they must be destroyed. Besides, I had arrested this man before. We warned him, we taught him a lesson, but he defied us and went right back to his work among the Believers. Kourdakov, he wasn't an innocent man. Never forget that!"

Well, I felt better about it after that. Certainly Nikiforov was correct. But when I looked at the body of Vasily Litovchenko, a very slight man, he didn't seem like such a terrible enemy. I heard later that he was a man of great character and spiritual stature. He had suffered much for his faith. He was very courageous, never allowing anything or anyone to intimidate him.

"Kourdakov," Nikiforov said, "people in the area have heard that a man was killed and that it was your group that led the raid and was responsible."

"Has his wife heard about it?"

"She has. And you've got to go to her and tell her what happened."

"Tell her what happened!"

"Our version, of course," he said and smiled.

That was something I hadn't bargained for. But I obediently responded. "Yes, sir. Where can I find her?"

"In the hospital."

"Hospital? She wasn't in the raid."

"No, but apparently she is an emotional woman and the shock of her husband's death was too much. She had a stroke. They took her to the emergency ward of Kempi Hospital near the waterfront district. I want you to go down and see her."

"But what can I tell her?"

"Just come up with a good story about how he got that gash in his head."

Why do we have to say anything? I wondered. I didn't see that it was anybody's business what happened. It was police business; and if he got his head torn off, it was his own fault. He'd been warned, but he wouldn't listen. But orders were orders, and I had to go. I left the police station and headed for Kempi Hospital.

When I arrived and inquired for Mrs. Litovchenko, I was

taken to a large ward in which she was lying, four beds down on the right, near the window. She was a pitiful sight.

The nurse reported that she was paralysed from the waist down and was in a state of shock and heavily drugged at that time. I looked at her and thought that at one time she had been a rather beautiful woman. She appeared to be about thirty-five years of age, slight of build, with dark hair and handsome, even beautiful, features. But now she was paralysed and not expected to walk again. She had been devastated by her husband's death. My first thought as I looked at her, was, *What a waste! Such a beautiful woman to be in such a helpless state.*

I felt no real sorrow, just that it was tough luck. My only feeling was the sympathy that one has for anybody in that condition. But I had no regret for what had happened to her husband. After all, enemies of the state can't expect to avoid bringing suffering to members of their families.

The nurse awakened Mrs. Litovchenko, and she looked up at me through heavy-lidded eyes. She was confused and her gaze was bewildered. Sudden sorrow raced through my heart, but only for a moment. I pulled myself together, walked up to her and said, briskly, and with an official tone, "Mrs. Litovchenko, I'm from the Petropavlovsk police. I am the leader of the police operations group which arrested your husband and the others at Elizovo."

I looked for some sign of reaction, some flicker of response. I thought she would surely show anger at seeing me and learning that I was one of the men responsible for her husband's death. But she just lay there in a seeming stupor, apparently not understanding my words. Well, Nikiforov didn't tell me to make her understand. He just told me to tell her. If she couldn't understand, it wasn't my fault.

I went on to say, "I am officially here to explain the reason for your husband's death." Again I peered at her for some reaction as I spoke. But there was none. I wondered if she had lost her mind, as well as having become paralysed. The only sign of life she showed was piteous moans coming from deep within her.

I told her that as we arrested her husband, he made a break for it, jumping into a shallow part of the river and split his head open on a rock. She appeared to be looking straight at me but not seeing me at all. Her unfocusing, unfeeling eyes held a deep, deep look of sorrow.

I explained again that if her husband had obeyed the orders of my police group and had not tried to escape, he would be here today. Then the poor woman tried to speak, but with great effort. Nothing she said was distinct enough to be understood. Finally, she gave a moan and collapsed back against the pillow.

Well, no need to waste any more time here, I thought. I had told her what I had come to say.

As I turned to leave, her eyes caught mine and they sent shivers up my back. I will never forget that last look I saw on the the face of Mrs. Litovchenko. It was as though a deep hidden cry within was bursting to be let out, or a great agonizing scream was futilely trying to be released. Her haunted eyes followed me for days.

I came out into the bright sunshine of Petropavlovsk, with the noise of the waterfront behind me, and walked slowly back to the police station. When I got there, Nikiforov said, "Kourdakov, forget it. You're doing a job for the state. Some will suffer, but they are the worst enemies and criminals. Always remember that."

But I had a hard time forgetting that face.

Later I found that Pastor Litovchenko had had two children —a daughter who had died of illness and an eighteen-year-old son, now serving in the army. We had to write him to inform him officially of his father's death.

Three days later we were ordered to Pastor Litovchenko's home to look for illegal literature. Nikiforov barked out his orders again, "Ransack the house. Do whatever you have to do. Just find that literature!"

Four of us drove to the house in the inner city area of Petropavlovsk. It was a poor, ramshackle, rundown shack. It was evident from our first glimpse of his home that Pastor Litovchenko hadn't lived very well. The furniture was very shabby and poor.

We tore the house up from top to bottom, and our efforts were well rewarded. We found hand-written hymn books, one new Bible, which had been smuggled in from outside the country, and another Bible, very old, worn and tattered.

As we turned the literature over to Nikiforov, he grinned wildly. "Splendid! Splendid!" he said. "We can send this back to Moscow and show them we've been busy out here, getting our job done."

Later that night I did some more thinking about the Litov-chenko home. There would be no husband to return and no wife waiting for him. Suddenly I brought myself up short, thinking, *Sergei, you're getting soft! Remember, these are enemies of the worst kind. Just keep telling yourself that, so you won't forget it.*

Five days after the attack at Elizovo, we were summoned to lead another raid on a group of Believers meeting in an underground church. On this raid we again gave the Believers "something to remember". We arrested their leaders. Several were shipped away to imprisonment in Siberian labour camps, especially to Magadan on the Siberian mainland.

Nikiforov said to me one day after that raid, "Sergei, you and your group have surpassed my expectations. I couldn't ask for a better group of men." I felt there was something more coming—more responsibility with the police, perhaps. I began mentally to total up all I was already doing: my duties as leader of the Communist Youth League, organizing, lecturing, lining up assignments for volunteer work brigades, looking after the political purity of 1,200 future Soviet officers. Then there were also my normal activities in the radio division of the Naval Academy, learning to be a radio engineer in the Soviet navy. I was also active on the academy's sports team and athletic groups. It was during those days that I won the championship in judo wrestling for Kamchatka Province. Also during this period, whenever time permitted, several of my friends and I participated in cross-country hiking and racing.

I was in good with both Nikiforov and my operations group. They were a bit afraid of me because of my position as leader of the Communist Youth League. It was my duty to report on all cadets. One day Yuri Berestennikov got a little drunk and told me, "Sergei, you think you're a pretty big guy these days, don't you?"

Oh, oh, I thought. *Yuri's had a bit too much.*

"I hear you think you're a big shot," he went on. "You're the big shot of the Communist Youth League and all you ever do is spy on the other guys."

"Cut that out, Yuri!" I warned.

"Look at him," Yuri retaliated. "He thinks he can even give us orders here."

I began to understand that beneath his partial drunkenness, Yuri was testing me. So I brought it to a showdown. "Yuri," I said, "any time you think you're the better man, just give me a try."

"How about now?"

"All right, now!"

So we went outside. Yuri was a lot taller than I, but my judo training gave me a big advantage. It wasn't long before I had him down and beaten.

"Don't ever say that again, Yuri," I warned. He got the point and so did everyone else. No one there ever challenged my authority again.

After that incident, I concentrated on my military duties again. Among the most important were two "open house" activities. All the citizens of Petropavlovsk were invited to visit the naval base to observe life first-hand. The main feature of each was a huge dance, to which the girls from town were invited. I had to make sure there would be no drinking, so I had several of my men stand guard at the door, checking the girls' bags to make sure they weren't bringing in liquor.

Vodka is the curse of Russia. It's everywhere. We naval cadets were paid seven roubles at the end of each month and after pay day we promptly headed for town and spent our money on two bottles of vodka. With a bottle inside their pockets, the cadets would go into the street looking for girls. Once they opened their jacket to show the girls the vodka, they could have the girl and anything they wanted. We waged a constant fight against alcoholism among the cadets. And the ironic thing about it all was that we who were responsible to control drinking, which was officially frowned upon, were among the worst offenders.

After one particular open house and dance, we made our regular inspection tour to make sure no one was staying on base illegally. On opening the door to the women's rest room, we couldn't see the floor—it was covered with empty vodka bottles. The next day I had to order a military truck to back up to the building, just below the rest room, and have our cadets throw the bottles into the truck below.

The party blames vodka as the greatest cause for low production in industry. On Saturday nights in Petropavlovsk, and other cities, I'm told, drunks staggering about or falling in the gutters are a common sight.

We in the operations group could see, perhaps as well as anyone, what vodka was doing, especially to the young. In most of the brawls, knifings and shootings, drinking was involved. Yet we who were aware of all this drank our share, especially before raids on Believers. The only thing that kept us from going to the extremes that so many others did was our interest in athletics. To be good athletes and keep in good physical trim, we had to control our drinking. It was for none other than practical reasons that we were concerned.

The steady flurries of directives coming from Moscow to warn us of the problem of alcoholism showed me the great menace it was to youth in the Soviet Union. It was the number one problem of Soviet youth.

14 "Get the literature!"

While studying at the academy one afternoon, I got orders for a small group of my men to meet at the police station at nine o'clock that night. I quickly lined up seven of them to go with me and when we arrived at the station, we went straight to the lounge at the back for our usual briefing with Nikiforov. In the lounge was the ever-present vodka, and this time Nikiforov had laid on some caviare, too. I wondered where Nikiforov got all this expensive stuff. I meant to ask him some time.

Nikiforov told the boys to relax and took me into his office to talk. Very seriously, he explained the night's assignment. "This one's a very important one for us," he said. "We've learned that a group of Believers are meeting tonight at ten o'clock. They've got a Bible—a new one—and hand-written literature. We need that literature for evidence against them. Get it. We'll send it in to Moscow."

"Do we send all the stuff there?" I asked.

"No, only the printed stuff. They don't want the hand-written junk."

"What are we doing with that?"

"Come. I'll show you. Getting rid of it is part of your job." He led me down the dimly lit stairs and into the "cold room", an unheated basement that was at freezing temperature even in summer. That's where we threw the drunks till they sobered up. A small, log-burning stove had been installed to keep the guards warm. The rest of the room was cold as ice. Nikiforov pointed to a box full of old newspapers and sticks of firewood and said, "Just dump the junk in here when you get back. We'll put it to good use—to keep the guards warm!" He laughed at his own joke.

When we were called in advance of a raid, we could be pretty sure that a spy had been at work inside the secret churches. The network of spies Nikiforov had organized and operated was efficient. I asked myself, "Why do those spies do it?" I knew it wasn't for ideological reasons. It wasn't because they were Communists. They were doing it for money, just as we were. "A rouble can change a heart," it is said, and there were a lot more roubles floating around for this work than I ever dreamed possible. The spies working among the Believers were highly paid. They earned even more than we did. And for a good reason. Often they would be beaten up with the Believers because we were never told their identity. In order to keep up a good front, the spies had to attend the Believers' meetings, and if a spy was unlucky enough to be caught with them when we made our raid, he would be beaten up as severely as the Believers. We had no way of distinguishing them from the Believers. That's why they got the extra pay. Without the spies we could have done very little.

The spies never went high in the leadership of the underground churches, I was told. The most information we could get from them was who and where individual underground churches met. But for our purposes, that was all we needed to know. We did the rest.

It was about ten minutes after nine when Nikiforov called me back to his office to check out the street map. "Where is it tonight?" I asked.

The spot he showed me in the suburbs would take us fifteen to twenty minutes to reach. "How many do you expect to be there?"

"Well," Nikiforov replied, "according to our information, between ten and fifteen." Our seven men would be enough to take care of them.

I studied the map closely and decided what route to take. By then it was 9.15 and we still had plenty of time. We made it a policy not to break into a meeting until twenty or thirty minutes after it started. That gave the Believers time to get over their caution, and to relax. They usually figured that if they hadn't been discovered in the first twenty or thirty minutes, the danger was over.

I told my men, "We won't leave until nine forty-five."

A couple of the guys put their feet on the table and sipped vodka and talked. The caviare disappeared fast. Cadets don't often get that kind of food. Victor was reading a book on judo. That struck us all as funny. Victor could have *written* the book on judo! He was judo champion of all East Russia.

Suddenly he put the book down, jumped to his feet and began practising judo holds and karate blows. "I'm going to try this new karate blow tonight," he said. "It looks real effective!"

"Hey! Did you ever try this one, Victor?" I demonstrated

with the flat of my hand across the front of my neck above my Adam's apple. "If you ever want to finish somebody off in a hurry, here's the way to do it." The other guys looked on in amusement.

Vladimir Zelenov and Anatoly Litovchenko, our two boxing champions, began to kid around, too. Being champion of Kamchatka, Vladimir always tried to compete with Anatoly, champion of all Siberia. "Hey, little brother," he teased, "watch and I'll show you a thing or two tonight. I'll show you a punch that will send shivers down your spine."

Anatoly just laughed. "After you get through with your child's play, take a look at me and I'll show you the punch that made me champion of Siberia."

They laughed, and we joined in. We were all getting warmed up. The vodka flowed, the banter continued, and we were ready to practise our arts on those unsuspecting Believers who were already gathering in that small house across town to study their precious literature.

I glanced at my watch and said, "All right, you guys. That's enough of the horseplay and big talk. Let's go and see if you're a bunch of doers or just loud talkers."

Soon we were making our way in the police truck through the darkened streets of Petropavlovsk. As we left the city behind, moving into the suburbs, we left the paved streets and hit the dirt roads that were usually muddy from the frequent rains which deluged Kamchatka. We picked our way along, searching for the street sign we wanted.

"Slow down, Victor, it's around here somewhere . . . There it is," I said, spotting the sign. "It's about three blocks down this way. Drive slowly and quietly."

Victor slowed down and picked his way along the muddy street while I peered through the darkness, searching for the target house. Behind the houses, we could see in dark outline the sloping mountains that characterized this part of Siberia.

"There it is," I said softly. It was a small log house, typical in this area. "Stop here," I told Victor. "We walk the rest of the way."

We got out and the men followed me as I walked down the muddy road towards the house. "You two!" I said, pointing to Alex Gulyaev and Yuri. "You watch the front door and window. Make sure nobody gets out."

133

Alex began to protest. "Look, Alex," I said. "I know what you're going to say. But you've got to guard those exits. As soon as the fun starts you can come and join in." Yuri, as always, complained, but went.

We found the front door locked. No lights were on, except at the back. It was a dark, moonless night. Quietly and quickly we made our way around to the back of the house, where a room had been added on. It was about half the size of the house, with a sloping roof and a back door. The light was on inside. *So that's where they are!*

As we slipped around to the back, somebody tipped something over. A bucket went rolling, and suddenly alarmed voices sounded from inside. People were rushing about.

There was no need for us to keep silent any longer. They knew we were there. "Let's go!" I shouted. "Fast!" We rushed to the back door and found it locked also. But it looked weak, so I told the others to stand back. I backed up about twenty feet and rammed my shoulder against it in a flying run, expecting it to pop open. I felt a sharp pain, bounced off the door and ended up sitting in the mud. As I sat there a brief moment, I couldn't control my anger.

"Over here!" someone shouted, pointing to a small log. They picked it up and brought it to the door to use as a battering ram.

"Knock that door down!" I ordered.

They started battering against it with the log. It was a strong door. Finally the lock burst open. By this time we were very angry, especially me. Inside, by the light of the coal oil lanterns, ten or eleven people were scurrying about. We charged in with all our might, cursing and shoving the Believers to the floor.

I spotted a man in the corner of the room. He had a Bible in his hand and was looking about with terror in his face, trying to find some place to hide it. Rushing over to him, I grabbed at it roughly, but he held on. I jerked it again and tore it out of his hands. Doubly angered because my shoulder hurt from the crash against the door, I started ripping the pages out of the Bible, flinging them to the floor. The man, about sixty-five years old, looked up and cried with a pleading tone, "Don't! Please don't! I beg you!"

His mouth was open, begging, and I whirled around, smashing my fist at his face. My fist landed on the edge of his nose and his upper row of teeth. His nose and mouth began to spurt blood. He struggled back to his feet, grabbing the Bible from my hand.

What kind of fool is he? I asked myself. He values this book more than he values his face! I ripped it away from him again and smashed him again in the face. This time he reeled and fell to the ground unconscious. He wouldn't give us any more trouble. Now my hand was covered with that fool's blood.

I whirled around just in time to see a Believer throw some books under a table covered with a long tablecloth, hanging almost to the floor. As I raced past Victor and Vladimir to get those books, I saw Vladimir aim a blow at a young man about twenty-five. It sent him sailing across the room and crashing into the wall. He fell to the floor, unconscious.

My other men were busy too. Victor picked up one middle-aged man and hurled him across the room as if he was a rag doll. He struck his head against a cabinet and began bleeding. The room was a bloody chaos by this time.

I wanted those books under the table. We had been ordered to take them back to Nikiforov. Anatoly grabbed the man who had thrown them there. Jerking him up by the collar, Anatoly positioned his face and let loose with a devastating blow that must have smashed his jaw in a thousand pieces. He didn't let out a whimper as he fell.

Then it was all over, almost as soon as it had started. There was nobody left standing. The men were lying in bloody heaps and the old man I had beaten was lying with his face in a pool of blood. Three older women lay cowering in the corner, sobbing.

"Get all the Bibles and literature," I barked to my men. Then I crawled under the table to find what had been thrown under it.

About that time, Alex and Yuri came running into the room from their guard posts outside. Angry because they had missed the action, Yuri took one look at my backside sticking out from under the table. Thinking I was a Believer trying to hide, he rushed over and raised his club extended to full length. Before anyone could stop him he brought the club down across my lower back with a powerful, crushing blow.

I felt like the house had fallen on me! I shrieked out in pain. I'll never forget that pain! It was unbelievable. I saw stars and felt hot flashes of pain across my back and collapsed flat. The other fellows were shouting at Yuri, but it was too late. Frantically shoving the table away, he saw who it was he had hit.

"Sergei, I'm sorry!" he shouted. "I thought it was one of the Believers trying to hide."

It hurt so badly I couldn't speak. I just lay there groaning, cursing violently under my breath.

Finally Yuri and Gulyaev helped me to my feet. The lower part of my spine hurt so much I could hardly move my legs. I'd never felt such excruciating pain! Yuri was apologizing all over the place, until I yelled, "Shut up! Just get out of my sight!"

Two of the four Believers we had orders to bring in were still unconscious. The men dragged them through the mud and threw them into the truck. They were pretty battered. I was bent over and hobbling like an old man until a couple of guys gave me a hand. "The literature, did you get it?" I asked Victor.

"Don't worry, Sergei, we got it all. It's right back there," Victor said, pointing to a box stuffed with papers at the back of the truck.

We took off for the police station. Every bump over those rugged roads brought me indescribable pain. After we reached the station and the prisoners were taken in, I walked back and forth, exercising my back. It still hurt terribly. How I wished I had never seen those two books thrown under the table! But I really couldn't blame Yuri. I guess I did look like a Believer trying to escape.

Once I felt better, I went into the station. My men were carrying the Bibles and other literature, piling them on Nikiforov's desk. He looked the growing pile over, exclaiming, "Wonderful! Wonderful! These," he said, pointing to the printed Bibles, "will make great presents for the party back in Moscow. These two," he said to me, "were the ones you were going after when you had your 'accident'." He grinned.

The leader of the group, the man I had smashed in the face twice, was sitting with his head in his hands on a bench. His upper front teeth were missing and the front of his shirt was covered with blood.

"I think he needs a nice shower," Nikiforov said. The fellows laughed and promptly took him downstairs. They threw him in the shower and turned on the cold water that was used to sober up drunks.

Upstairs I was rubbing my back while Nikiforov commended us. "All right," he said, "look what we got. It's a real load. They were hand-copying literature in quantities. We got it all." He spread it out on the table. There were a couple of Bibles, one new and pocket-size, the other almost worn out.

"These will go to Moscow," Nikiforov said. Then he looked at the pile of other literature. Among the pieces were a child's school exercise book with Bible verses scribbled in it, a notebook with a few songs written in it and several pages with hand-written Bible verses.

Nikiforov shouted an order to a couple of the men. "Take this junk downstairs and throw it in the box. At least it'll keep the guards warm!" Then he turned to the others. "Why don't you guys go out and get something to eat?" he said.

We went to eat and drink. My back was still hurting, but I soon forgot it in the noise of the bar. As I was eating, I noticed my fist was still covered with the blood of that Believer. *Oh well, I'll wash it later*, I thought.

The raids were stepping up in frequency. Sometimes we were called out two or three times a week. The Believers were becoming more active. After some raids there were vast amounts of paper work. I had to send someone to the places where the Believers were employed, to get information about them from their fellow workers in order to build a detailed personal file which contained everything about the Believer's life. All this information was sent to the anti-religious headquarters in Moscow. There the complete personal file on every Believer was fed into the computer for immediate retrieval.

Computerized copies of the Believers' files were sent from Moscow back to our local headquarters. This gave us a permanent record in the local police headquarters of every Believer in every district. In addition, a three-by-five-inch card with the Believer's picture, birth date and other data was sent to the police station. These cards were kept in a special file. Any time the party chose, the Believers could be rounded up and removed from society quickly.

15 "You're our Number One man"

During my time off, I sometimes went mountain-climbing and hiking across the mountains of Kamchatka with my friends, just to take a break from my studies and heavy duties in the Youth League. Our military status enabled us to visit places which were restricted to civilians in Kamchatka. During such outings, my friends and I came across something which puzzled us. We saw no fewer than thirty concentration camps and prisons hidden away in the mountains and valleys in the interior. We were amazed, especially because they were new—and empty.

We'd often come around a bend or over a hill, and there would be a new prison complex, with barbed wire around it. Each was completely equipped, even with living quarters for the guards. Caretakers kept the buildings up and closely guarded them. These camps had everything—guards, equipment, dogs—except prisoners.

I wondered about them and what they were for. I asked Nikiforov. He replied, "We have enemies in this country, you know, and we have to be ready for them. In the event of the slightest trouble, we'll find some occupants for those places."

We laughed together, as though it were a joke. But it wasn't. Huge files, such as those on Believers, were set up identifying persons who were to be arrested at the first sign of any disturbance. All that would be needed were orders from Moscow. The prison camps are ready and waiting, hidden in the mountain fastness. I took great pride in all this. Our party was vigilant!

Nikiforov pulled out a confidential police bulletin he had been sent from the anti-religious headquarters in Moscow, giving detailed instructions on the treatment of Believers in the Soviet Union. The document told of a major anti-religious action organization that was being vastly increased, so that every town, hamlet and village in the Soviet Union, stretching the 6,000 miles between Leningrad and the most distant areas of Far East

Russia, would be covered. Specially trained workers were to use films, papers, recordings, lectures, tapes, plays, displays and propaganda of every kind to spread atheism and combat religious faith.

As I surveyed these documents and spoke to Nikiforov, I began to sense the immensity of our party's action to stop the growing menace of religion in our country. I was overwhelmed by it. "What fantastic amounts of money this must cost," I exclaimed to Nikiforov.

"Well, you can imagine," he responded. "You know what your group alone is costing. As I told you, Kourdakov, we have two great enemies, the imperialist Americans and these undermining enemies here at home. They must be controlled, whatever the cost! The Believers are especially dangerous because they are growing so rapidly. We have thirty thousand of them in Kamchatka alone. And that's out of a population of only 250 thousand!"

"That means," I said after some brief mental calculations, "there could be millions of them infesting the nation."

"You're right. And Communism will never fully triumph in our land until their minds are changed or they are destroyed. Frankly, I prefer the latter."

"But what about the Believers saying they have the right to religious freedom?" I asked.

"That's in the constitution for the record," he said. "But you and I are both men. We've lived. We know reality."

His remarks reminded me of a time when I overheard him talk to one of the arrested Believers.

"What are we here for?" the Believer asked.

"You're here because of anti-Soviet literature found in your possession."

"What do you mean, anti-Soviet literature? They were only Bibles."

Nikiforov snapped back, "That's what I'm talking about, you fool. That's anti-Soviet literature."

"But," protested the Believer, who had been roughed up pretty badly, "how could the Bible be anti-Soviet literature? Our government states it is printing Bibles in our own country, and if the government is printing Bibles, how can they be anti-Soviet?"

I wanted to hear Nikiforov's answer to that! "You're wrong!" he shouted. "Our government would never print Bibles."

"Oh yes, it would. It already has. At least, it says it has."

"Shut up," Nikiforov responded angrily and went on with his interrogation.

Later I learned that our government did claim it had printed 10,000 Bibles. But that announcement was for public consumption abroad, to show the Soviet Union as believing in religious freedom. What happened to those Bibles? Well, about 5,000, I learned, were sent abroad for sale to Russian-speaking people in foreign countries. Another 3,000 were sent to the Communist countries of East Europe, and approximately 2,000 were sent to the anti-religious organization in Moscow to be used for study and research, for the purpose of refining our anti-religious propaganda. Virtually none of those 10,000 Bibles ever got to the Russian Believers.

That's why they had smuggled or hand-written Bibles.

As head of the Communist Youth League at the Naval Academy, I had often heard of Comrade Orlov, the party leader for the entire province. Comrade Orlov came to power as the party secretary for Kamchatka Province during the reign of Stalin. He consolidated his control over the party and was known throughout Kamchatka as "Little Stalin", not only because he rose to prominence during Stalin's regime but because his practice, personality and methods of leadership were similar to Stalin's.

Comrade Orlov ranked among the top 200 leaders of the entire Soviet Union. I had heard his name again and again and I greatly respected and admired him. I first met him on 22 April 1970, when we had a great party convention, celebrating the 100th anniversary of founder Lenin's birthday. Party leaders from all Kamchatka Province gathered along with party youth leaders. I was invited to this great conference.

The idea behind this convention was to introduce future Communist leaders to the older leaders. It was to honour the future leaders of the party. I was an invited guest, selected to receive a special award for my work in the Youth League and for being one of the "promising new leaders" of the party. My Youth League had been selected as the top Youth League organization in Kamchatka Province. Since I was the head of it, I was singled out as the Number One Communist Youth of Kamchatka Province. I was given a seat of honour on the platform. On the platform with me were Comrade Orlov and all of the big people I had heard about but never seen. Behind the platform was hung a massive outline of Lenin's profile. I was a little nervous and very excited. It was the greatest Communist celebration in many years.

I was introduced as the head of the winning Youth League organization as TV cameras broadcast the event live. I had been told to prepare an acceptance speech and gave a rousing fifteen-minute talk on the victory of Communism. I gave a detailed report of my work as a youth leader and outlined what we proposed to do in the future. I emphasized we would continue to serve the cause of the party and do even more in the future than we had in the past. I ended with this pledge: "In honour of the memory of Comrade Lenin, I commit my organization to even greater achievements for Communism next year. I pledge to you, and to Lenin's sacred memory, this is only the start!" And I meant every word of it. When I finished, there was great applause, and Comrade Orlov jumped up and put his arms around my shoulder. He called for the special red flag that had been flown in from Moscow. It was brought out, and he ceremoniously presented me with the flag. I kissed it and draped it proudly around my body to the standing applause of the delegates. It was a very big moment for me! Here was the top leader of Kamchatka Province, a man recognized to be one of the highest men in all the U.S.S.R., with his arm around my shoulder, on Soviet television!

When the applause subsided Comrade Orlov declared, "Such young men as this are a perfect example of Communist youth and the future hope of the party in the U.S.S.R. We must support and help them develop, because, comrades, look at this man. In him and thousands like him you see the future of the party and our country." My head was spinning. I hoped my nervousness didn't show on television. What a proud moment it was for me—the proudest moment of my life.

After the ceremony, speeches and the presentation of awards, we were all invited to a great banqueting hall where the tables were groaning with food and drink. Many of the men gathered around, congratulating me. But the very highest leaders, including Comrade Orlov, did not join us. They went to a private dining room apart from the ordinary delegates. After I finished eating, I got up and wandered through the corridor. I didn't drink much, for I was in training for a judo championship match coming up. As I walked down the hall, a door suddenly opened and who was standing there but Comrade Orlov! I had stumbled upon the door of the private banqueting hall for the top party leaders. Orlov saw me and, though quite drunk by now, recognized me. Holding his arms out to me, he said, "Hey, Comrade Kourdakov, come on in here."

I hesitated to go in. After all, I would be out of place in there with the top leaders from our area. Orlov took my arm and pulled me in. About twenty senior party officials were inside, food and drink crowding the large table. I think it was good that they had a private dining room, because of the expensive food and drink they had—sausages, caviare and other delicacies, Greek wines, everything. And vodka flowed like water. I was wide-eyed. This was certainly not what we had been eating out in the banqueting hall.

Orlov excused himself for a few minutes and staggered out of the door looking for a toilet. While he was gone, I looked around. Here were the great Communist leaders of Kamchatka Province, drunk. Several had passed out cold, their heads lying flat on the table. Three lay with their faces in their plates of food. Two pairs of legs came out from under the long dining table. Others were fast drinking themselves into unconsciousness. Another man lay stretched out full-length on the top of the table. His arms and feet were in the big serving trays full of food. I looked at them in disgust. I had ordered cadets dismissed from the academy for less than this. I thought, *The lives of the people of this part of Russia are controlled by these men who are so drunk they don't know their first names.* I was looking at the "cream of the crop" Communist leaders, and the "cream of the crop" were stoned out of their heads. One man had become sick and had vomited over his clothes. The whole scene was incredibly and utterly disgusting.

By now Orlov had come back. He sat me down in the chair next to him. As he drank freely and became drunker, his head began to weave. Suddenly his face fell forward, directly into the food on his plate. He raised his head and shouted, "Hand me a napkin!" I did, and he wiped part of the food off his forehead, chin and nose. Some of the mashed potatoes were still on his nose and chin. He cursed until the air was blue. It was an incredible sight! Food was running down his face on to his coat and medals.

He pulled his uniform up and showed me a long scar, where he had been wounded in the war, and said to me, with his head rolling around, "Comrade Kourdakov, you see this? That bastard Stalin did this to me! Stalin sent me out. Stalin used our bodies instead of weapons. Stalin gave me this and now when it hurts, I curse him."

He cursed Stalin drunkenly, then went on to curse others. "And not only Stalin, but who is this Brezhnev? He's a toad-eater, a lickspittle backslapper, licking the boots of Stalin. That's how Brezhnev survived, and that's how *he* got to be the Communist leader! I listened to him at the party congress in Moscow. He *baaas* like a sheep, *baa baa baa*, one word after another, like a sheep."

I couldn't believe my ears! Orlov rambled on drunkenly, using barnyard terms to describe his "colleague" Brezhnev. I looked frantically around the room to see if anyone was hearing all these incredible words. If they heard what Orlov had said, I was finished! But no one seemed to hear; they were lost in their drinking. Comrade Orlov was himself in some other world, babbling and ranting.

But I had not only the others to fear. If Orlov later remembered what he had said to me, my life wouldn't be worth a kopek. He couldn't afford to let me live, and could silence me with one word. He had that kind of power. I looked at him. His head was on the table, and I thought he was asleep. Suddenly he sat up with a jolt, put up his arms and said, "Communism is the worst curse that has ever come to man!" He nodded and mumbled, "Communism is (a description too foul to print)." I was petrified with fear. Orlov rambled and shouted, "Communists are a bunch of bloodsuckers!"

I fled from the room, left the hall and headed back to the Naval Academy as fast as I could. For days I lived in fear.

Until my encounter with Orlov, I had been a genuine and firm believer in Communism. I had a bedrock belief in its goals and objectives. Often I had been asked by younger cadets, "Why is life so hard in Russia?" The answer I always gave was, "It is difficult now, but we are building a better tomorrow." And I genuinely believed it. I had seen many contradictions between the teachings of Communism and reality. But I was sure they were simply aberrations or personal failures, and that we really were on our way to that better tomorrow.

But my encounter with Orlov and the roomful of Communist bigwigs showed me the hypocrisy of it all. For days my mind went back to that night with Orlov. *So this is what the leaders are really like,* I thought. Calloused, hard, cynical, failing to believe even in Communism, looking merely for a way to get ahead personally.

I had observed that the life of the leaders was rich with everything, but the life of the people was poor and hard. I had seen the great gap between the promises of Communism and the reality in the lives of the people. Always I had justified it and comforted myself by saying that, "Today we sacrifice for tomorrow's victories."

But now I had seen this incredible scene. I decided if those men didn't believe but were using the system to get ahead, then *I* would use it, too. If a man like Orlov wasn't a true believer in Communism, why should I be? If Orlov was wily and clever enough to get to the top, I could get there, too. I had been raised under the system since I was six and I could claw my way up, like the rest of them. My idealism, misguided though it had been, died that night of Lenin's 100th birthday, 22 April 1970.

"Go ahead. Go ahead." That motto I had adopted as a child in the days at the children's home, became my motto once again. From now on, there was only one goal: Get to the top! If the game was played by cynicism and ruthlessness, I'd play it that way. And I'd play it a lot better than Orlov or anybody else. I would serve Communism because that's the way to get ahead.

16 The beautiful religioznik

I answered the telephone after two rings and heard Nikiforov's voice. "This is a big one, Kourdakov," he said. "Make sure you get at least ten men and be here at eight-thirty sharp!" Without waiting for a reply, he hung up.

I began calling my men. Usually I found it difficult to line up more than ten, but today I mustered fourteen. When I arrived at the police station, fifteen minutes early, some of the men were already there. Others drifted in minutes later. "What's up?" they were asking. "Where are we going tonight?" I went into Nikiforov's office to find out.

"Sixty-six Okeanskaya Street," he said, leading me to the wall map and pointing. "You'd better stop about here," he said, and indicated a street intersection three blocks from Okeanskaya Street. "You can make it the rest of the way on foot."

I knew the section well. "That's a heavily populated area," I said. "We're been in that general area several times lately. We're almost certain to be spotted."

"You're a military man, aren't you?" Nikiforov said bluntly. That meant: Use military tactics.

"All right," I said as I studied the map more closely. "I'll put two men here and one over there at that corner. That way I'll be able to block off the street and keep pedestrians away."

"Good."

"How many Believers do you expect?" I asked.

"Fifteen."

"Any special instructions?"

"Same as usual," he said. I was to bring in the two men whose names were on the slip of paper he was handing me. "These are the ones we want."

"What about the rest?"

"The rest?" he bellowed. "Do I have to spell it out to you? Give them something to remember! Let them know it doesn't pay to carry on their kind of activity."

"What time's the meeting?" I asked.

"At ten o'clock. Get there at ten-thirty."

I walked into the back lounge where my men were drinking

145

and joking. Most of them had become close friends. A few were just "vodka friends".

At last it was 9.45—time to go. As we started toward the door, I shouted to Yuri, "Watch what you're doing tonight! Open your eyes before you swing that club."

Yuri laughed and said, "All right, Sergei."

On the way out to the truck, we picked up our police clubs and handcuffs at the door. "Keep the clubs short," I said. "We'll be in close quarters tonight."

The handcuffs we took were special. Once they were on a person, they became tighter as the person struggled, the sharp teeth inside clamping down tighter and more painfully on the victim's wrists. I had once put a pair on myself, just for fun, and was soon yelling for someone to get them off. They were extremely painful, and we used them often against the Believers.

We climbed into the police truck and sped off, racing across the city, lights flashing and siren screaming, playing havoc with traffic. As we came within a few blocks of our destination we shut the siren off, lowered our lights and slowed down. We soon reached Okeanskaya Street. "Pull over here," I said to Victor.

As soon as we had parked at the side of the street, I pointed to a couple of the men in the back of the truck, and said, "You two, get out and block off the street ... And you two, over there, you go around the block and cut off the other end of the street. Remember, nobody gets through. Understand?"

We had strict orders from Nikiforov to keep passers-by away. A couple of recent raids had turned out badly because groups of curious spectators had been attracted by the screams of the Believers. We finally managed to disperse them, but the damage had been done. Word got back to Nikiforov. He was furious and in no uncertain terms ordered me never to let it happen again.

I was determined there would be no spectators tonight. Both ends of the street were completely blocked off. Leaving the guards to their duties, the remaining ten of us walked toward house number sixty-six and its unsuspecting praying occupants. In a few moments we spotted it. It was a simple, plain home, like the others in the area. A light was on inside, shining through a heavy curtain which covered the window. There were two windows on each side of the house and a door at the back. I assigned one man to guard each window and the door. After the usual griping about "missing the action", they went along. That took care of half my men. I told them they could leave their posts when things got going and come inside for the "fun".

Now everything was set. Stealthily we moved toward the front door. After one more check to make sure everyone was in his place and alert, I nodded and said, "Let's go!" Then I hit the door in a flying run and snapped it open.

Inside, fifteen startled people on their knees, praying and singing, looked up in utter disbelief. They knew what was happening and their faces were filled with a mixture of surprise and fear. Yet some kept praying, and three or four continued to sing, not missing a note. These people, I thought, are incredible! I had to admire their courage; but at the same time it infuriated me. I shouted, "What are you doing?"

"Praying," someone replied.

"Who to?"

"To God."

"There is no God, you fools," I yelled. "Don't you know that?" I shouted, "You're praying to empty air. Where's your God now? Let Him help you now!" We shoved and pushed, getting warmed up to the attack. Then suddenly one of my men swung his club and the fight was on. We waded in, shoving, hitting and kicking.

Vladimir grabbed an old man, smashed him in the face and sent him screaming across the room to tumble on the floor in a pool of blood. Anatoly, not to be outdone by Vladimir, grabbed someone else and was pounding him in the stomach, chest and face, toying with him. Then he finished him quickly with a frightful blow in the mouth. The Believers who could stay clear of us rushed about the room trying to hide their Bibles and literature. Seeing what they were doing, I shouted, "Get those Bibles!" Sergei Kanonenko had his knife out and was swinging it wildly, sending Believers diving to avoid the blade. Yuri picked up an old woman, grabbed her long grey hair, pulled her head back and struck her across the throat with a karate chop. Without a sound the old woman crumpled to the floor.

I spotted an old man trying to scurry off and I grabbed him and aimed a blow at his head. But he managed to get his guard up enough to deflect the blow. That made me mad and I raised my fist to let loose with another smash, but someone behind me grabbed my hand and yelled, "Don't hit him, please. Don't hit him. He's just an old man."

I whirled around in a rage. There stood two young men, Believers, one about eighteen and the other about twenty-one. "So you're going to tell me what to do! Well, we'll see!" I looked around the room, spotted Boris and Yuri and yelled to them, "Take these two out the back and teach them not to give us orders." The young men were pushed and pulled outside and beaten until their faces were a bloody pulp. Most of the bones of their faces were broken.

Meanwhile, Sergei Kanonenko had used his knife on a couple of women, and they were screaming and holding their sides. One old man was grovelling on the floor, trying to get up, bloody and beaten. Yuri rushed over and gave him a powerful, arching kick in the ribs with his heavy boot. There was a crunching of bone as several of his ribs were broken. The old man rolled over, writhing in pain.

Nothing in the house—people or furniture—escaped our wrath. We smashed everything in sight. Whoever had turned his house into a secret church building would learn he couldn't do it without losing everything he had. In minutes the house was a shambles—broken tables, chairs, dishes, everything, smashed and scattered all over the room. Half-covered by the debris were the Believers, some unconscious and the rest in agonizing pain.

I saw Victor Matvyev reach and grab for a young girl who was trying to escape to another room. She was a beautiful young girl. *What a waste to be a Believer*, I thought. Victor caught her, picked her up, lifted her above his head and held her high in the air for a second. She was pleading, "Don't, please don't. Dear God, help us!" Victor threw her so hard she hit the wall at the same height she was thrown, then dropped to the floor, semiconscious, moaning. Victor turned and laughed and exclaimed, "I'll bet the idea of God went flying out of her head." But I was thinking, *She's a really beautiful girl*. I wished I had met her under better circumstances.

"Get the books," I shouted. We scoured the room, looking for Bibles and any torn up literature they might have. I grabbed a hand-written child's exercise book with scribbled Bible verses from the hands of an old woman. She was partly conscious and kept moaning, "Why? Why?" It wasn't so much a question, but

an outcry of agony, coming from deep within her soul.
"Why?"

"Get those two men!" I ordered, pointing to the two leaders
who matched the description Nikiforov had given me. "Get
them out to the truck." And while a couple of my men moved
to obey, the rest of us went around the room taking identification papers from the Believers and noting them. I got the beautiful girl's identification card. I had a special interest in her. Her
name was Natasha Zhdanova. After getting their names, we
could find them any time we wanted.

The job was done. It was time to go. I ordered my men out.
As we left, I took one last look around at the scene we were
leaving behind. The room was strewn with broken bodies,
broken chairs, tables, dishes, all in a heap. Everything in the
room was turned upside down. Blood spattered the walls. We
had done our work well.

On the way back to the police station, I began questioning the
two men we had arrested. But first they had a question for us.
"How did you know?"

"Well, what do you think, you stupid fools? We have our
people, our spies. You're the easiest people in the world to find."
They didn't seem surprised.

"You invite people to come to your secret churches, don't
you?" I continued. "If you don't want to be found, why do you
do that?"

"You don't understand," the underground pastor said. "We
know there are spies. We're not that foolish. But we have a great
responsibility to invite people to come to God. How could we
invite people to God and spread our faith and keep outsiders
away? We know, of course, when we talk to people about God,
some will be spies. We know the risk." He paused for a moment,
and I thought he was through, but soon he began again. "But
we feel that our responsibility to share with others is more
important than our own safety."

What stupid fools, I thought. How could our country be en-
dangered by people like that?

It didn't take long to get back to the station, and while the
prisoners were being "processed" below, we rested in the waiting room and had a drink. Anatoly and Vladimir were laughing
about the raid. "These people just don't last long enough,"
Vladimir remarked. "One tap and they're gone." I had seen
Vladimir's "taps". I could understand why the Believers didn't

last long. "It's too easy," he continued. "I wish they'd put up a fight just once and really give us some practice."

But they never did. The Believers never fought back. Try to protect themselves, yes; but they never did fight back.

"Great, my children! Great!" Nikiforov exclaimed, beaming as I reported the raid.

Three days later eight members of my operations group and I were sitting around the waiting room, on duty in case there should be any calls. We did this stand-by duty once or twice a week. At about 7 p.m. Nikiforov's phone rang and seconds later he came hurrying out of his office, shouting, "Kourdakov, Kourdakov, get your men ready and take off right now!"

"Where do we go?" I asked, smelling action.

"Nagornaya Street." And he gave the house number. Either somebody had noticed something suspicious at that address or one of the spies had found the meeting in progress and reported it. At any rate, it was going on right now!

I hurried my men out to the truck, then ordered Victor to drive off at high speed. Either Victor was the world's worst driver, taking so many unnecessary risks, or he was the world's best driver, proving it by his uncanny ability to miss all the traffic on the road by the smallest margin.

"Cut the siren," I shouted, as we neared the target area.

We roared up Nagornaya Street, jumped out before the truck stopped rolling and rushed to the front of the house, crashing through the door. To our astonishment, they were all young people. Not a grey head there! We had found a secret young people's meeting in progress, catching them completely by surprise. We went right to work on them, grabbing them and swinging them about, slapping and shoving them.

"That's him. Grab him," I said, pointing to the twenty-three-year-old youth who was their leader. Some of our guys rushed him and began knocking him around. Some of my men were punching the others around, using them playfully as punching bags. I quickly surveyed the room and saw a sight I couldn't believe! There she was, that same girl! It couldn't be. But it was. Only three nights before, she had been at the other meeting and had been viciously thrown across the room. It was the first time I really got a good look at her. She was more beautiful than I had first remembered, with long, flowing blonde hair, large blue eyes and smooth skin—one of the most naturally beautiful girls I ever have seen.

Victor saw her too and shouted, "She's back! Look, guys, she's back again!"

"Well," I shouted, "it doesn't look like you did such a great job the last time, Victor. You failed to teach her a lesson. Now it's my turn!"

I picked her up and flung her on a table face down. Two of us stripped her clothes off. One of my men held her down and I began to beat her with my open hand as hard as I could, hitting her again and again. My hands began to sting under the blows. Her skin started to blister. I continued to beat her, until pieces of bloody flesh came off on my hand. She moaned but fought desperately not to cry. To suppress her cries, she bit her lower lip until it was bitten through and blood ran down her chin.

At last she gave in and began sobbing. When I was so exhausted I couldn't raise my arm for even one more blow, and her backside was a mass of raw flesh, I pushed her off the table, and she collapsed on the floor.

Leaving her, I looked around, almost exhausted, to see how the rest of our group was doing. The young Believers were lying around the wrecked room. There was no point in prolonging the job so, knowing we already had the leader, I shouted, "We've got our man! Get the names of those people now and let's get out of here."

When we arrived back at the police station, there stood Nikiforov standing at the door greeting us with a smile. "Well, my children," he said, "I see that was quick work."

"Here's your man," I said, shoving the leader of the group at Nikiforov, who had him taken downstairs immediately for "interrogation". I began to look over the names of the other young people who were caught in the meeting. I could understand foolish old people who were infected with religion before Communism. But *young people* believing in God! It was just too much for me to grasp. These were people my age, my generation. It baffled me.

But that one girl had certainly been taught a lesson. I chided Victor once more. "You just didn't have it, old boy," I said. "But I took care of her tonight. We'll never see Gorgeous again."

The next day when I reported back to the police station, I walked in on Nikiforov's interrogation of the youth leader whom we had arrested the night before. I listened, amazed at Nikiforov's skill as an interrogator. Alternating between brutal bullying and sudden kindness, he used both hard and soft tactics to soften up and confuse the young Believer. He was doing what he liked—closing in on a man.

"Do you believe in God?"

"Yes."

"Tell me, are you stupid, foolish or just crazy?"

The young Believer replied, "Well, sir, you can never understand why I believe what I believe, because what I believe is not something that I can completely explain. It's because God is alive that I believe in Him, and He lives in my heart."

Nikiforov exploded in anger, "Why do you say I can't understand? Do you think I'm stupid? I also read this book," he said, pointing to the confiscated Bible. "Do you think I can't read?"

The young man had been beaten up the night before and had been roughed up some in the prison cell as well, but he replied firmly, "You can read, perhaps, but you need eyes to see and ears to hear and a heart to understand what the Spirit of God is saying in this book." I listened in fascination. None of it made the slightest bit of sense to me.

"If you read it only to attack it," the young Believer said, "you'll never know what it really says. Only God can open your eyes so you can see and understand what we believe and why we're ready to pay any price for holding to our beliefs."

Then Nikiforov broke in. "I must admit there are some things I don't understand."

The young Believer replied, "Well, sir, you've answered your own question. You don't understand because your eyes are closed to the truth. If you'd open your heart to God, if you'd open your eyes to understand His word, it would become as real to you as it is to me and those other young people. Why don't you open your heart to God's word? He'll change your life and—"

"Shut up!" Nikiforov exploded. "Don't try to preach to me, you fool, or *I'll* change *your life*—for good!" With that, Nikiforov shouted at the guards, and the young prisoner was taken back to his cell. He was later sent to a labour camp for several years. I had witnessed many such interrogations, and they never made any sense to me. *These Believers never give up*, I thought. *They even tried to convert the police!*

Nikiforov came back and said, "Those people are crazy." I nodded in full agreement.

I was interested in finding out more about Natasha Zhdanova. Since the Youth League is responsible for young people, we keep a record of all the young people in our area. We know exactly who they are, where they were raised, where they went to school. We have all the information about them. I looked up Natasha's file and pulled it out.

She was born in the Donets region of the Ukraine in a small village called Bachnaya. Her parents were workers on a collective farm in the Ukraine and were very poor. To get a better opportunity, Natasha had left the Ukraine when she was a little girl, to live with her uncle in Petropavlovsk. She had attended the schools here and graduated from the Maxim Gorky School Number Four, located in the First District of Petropavlovsk.

After graduating, at the age of eighteen, she became a proof reader at the *Petropavlovsk Pravda* newspaper. As I searched her record I was amazed to find that she had been a member of the Komsomol—our Communist Youth League—in school and had done well. The record showed plainly what had happened. When she got out of school, she fell into the clutches of the Believers and soon became one herself—a perfect example of how Believers catch people in their poisonous web.

I then went to the offices of *Petropavlovsk Pravda* and asked about her and her colleagues. "She's a perfect worker," one of her superiors said. "We've never had any problems whatsoever. She's friendly, reliable, trustworthy and an excellent worker." That kind of report always confused me. With other workers, we had problems of drunkenness, theft of goods, laziness and inefficiency. But whenever I went to fill in one of these police reports on a Believer, the job report was always "perfect worker" or "very good record" or "most trustworthy" or "never drunk". One thing about the Believers, they were serious and hard workers. I had wondered about that. But it wasn't my job to wonder. It was my job to act.

"Why do you want to know?" they asked me as I was inquiring about Natasha.

"We found her twice in secret meetings of underground churches. She's a Believer."

A gasp went up. The workers looked at each other. It was as though I'd said she was a leper or a mass murderer. "Well, now that you mention it," one of them said—then came a torrent of complaints. They suddenly switched and had only bad to say about her.

153

I left a message at her office ordering her to report to me at a certain time at the police station. I knew a visit to the police station would frighten her. That was my purpose.

She came in hesitantly and sat in the chair across from the desk I was using. I could see she was frightened. *Such a beauty!* I thought. *And there she sits, with her head down, just staring at the floor.* I asked why she was a Believer.

"What should I be?" she replied. "An alcoholic? A prostitute?" Then she asked, "Did you find anything wrong in my work record?"

"No, I didn't," I admitted.

"Then why do you object to my personal beliefs? Am I causing any harm to others?"

"No," I replied. "But somewhere you went wrong and are mixed up with people who are a great danger to our country." I lectured and warned her of real trouble if she continued in her ways.

Finally, I saw I wasn't going to shake her. I warned her once more that this was going on her record and she must never be found mixing with Believers again.

Despite her apparent fear, she began to tell me why she believed in God. I had thought that the beatings followed by the interview in the police office, would settle everything, and that Natasha Zhdanova would never give us any trouble again. But Natasha was a most remarkable girl.

While we talked, I was conscious of the deep marks on her lower lip, where she had bitten herself as I beat her. *What a pity,* I thought. The scar marred her otherwise perfect face. *If only we'd met in other circumstances,* I thought. I could go for a girl like that!

Once I had all the information I needed from her and had finished my lecture, I dismissed her abruptly and roughly. It was part of the intimidation. I congratulated myself on a job well done.

About a week later we were called to the police headquarters for another action against a secret church. I went through my routine procedures of finding the location on the map. This secret meeting was in a house on Pograshny Street. We roared off in the police truck. This time we were only six: Alexander Gulyaev, Vladimir Zelenov, Anatoly Litovchenko, Victor Matveyev, Nikolas Olysko and I.

When we reached the meeting place, I posted guards again

154

and blocked off the street. When all was ready, we burst in, swinging clubs wildly.

The shocked, bewildered Believers began to scatter, trying to protect themselves from the rain of blows. The meeting room was small, and with eight Believers and six of us it was crowded. There was lots of noise—shouts and screams. *This isn't going to take long*, I thought. And then I caught a glimpse of a familiar face. I couldn't believe it! There *she* was again—Natasha Zhdanova!

Several of my men saw her too. Alex Gulyaev moved toward Natasha, hatred filling his face, his club raised high above his head.

Then something I never expected to see suddenly happened. Without warning, Victor jumped between Natasha and Alex, facing Alex head on.

"Get out of my way," Alex shouted angrily.

Victor's feet didn't move. He raised his club and said menacingly, "Alex, I'm telling you, don't touch her! No one touches her!"

I listened in amazement. Incredibly, Victor, one of my most brutal men, was protecting one of the Believers! "Get back!" he shouted to Alex. "Get back or I'll let you have it." He shielded Natasha, who was cowering on the floor.

Angered, Alex shouted, "You want her for yourself, don't you?"

"No," Victor shouted back. "She has something we don't have! Nobody touches her! Nobody!"

I had to break this up, and fast. Alex's violent temper would mean a fight. "Look, Alex," I shouted, pointing to another Believer trying to get away. "Get him!" Distracted, Alex took off after him. I breathed a sigh of relief.

Victor still stood with his arms out, protecting Natasha, daring Alex or anyone to take a step toward her. Natasha stood behind Victor, not understanding what was happening. This was not the kind of treatment she had come to expect from this group. I nodded to her, then motioned for her to get out. She turned and hurried out. I nodded a sign of approval.

For one of the few times in my life, I was deeply moved. It was like the time when my friend Sasha died back at Barysevo. Natasha *did* have something! She had been beaten horribly. She had been warned and threatened. She had gone through unbelievable suffering, but here she was again. Even tough Victor had been moved and recognized it. She had something we didn't have. I wanted to run after her and ask, "What is it?" I wanted to talk to her, but she was gone. This heroic Christian girl who had suffered so much at our hands somehow both touched and troubled me very much.

Shortly afterwards Natasha left Kamchatka and returned to her home in the Ukraine. The ridicule and mockery from her co-workers at the newspaper made life all but unbearable for her.

I sent her personal file to the Communist Youth League in her home village in the Ukraine, giving them a detailed record of her life as a Believer.

I was strangely sad that she had left. I felt, for the first time, that these people might not be the fools and enemies I thought they were. Natasha had shaken all my notions about Believers.

17 Police action

May Day, the first day of May, is a great time of festivities, picnics and parades throughout the Soviet Union. It is also a day in which people go to the cemeteries to visit the graves of their relatives and friends and place wreaths and flowers upon them.

On May Day 1970, I received a phone call from Nikiforov. He had an odd request. "Kourdakov," he said excitedly, "get the academy band and go down to the cemetery south of town." The academy band to the cemetery? Had Nikiforov gone out of his mind?

"What's up?" I asked, hoping my voice didn't give away my doubts.

"It's the Believers. They've congregated there, several hundred of them, and they have an orchestra and band playing hymns."

"What are we supposed to do? Join them?"

"This is no time for joking, Kourdakov," Nikiforov said coldly. "Just get your band down there as fast as you can. Set up right next to the Believers and play as loud as you can."

Oh, I thought, *that's the idea!* We were to disrupt their singing by outplaying them. It was crazy, but it sounded like fun. I couldn't help admiring the Believers. This latest stunt was really smart. A meeting in the cemetery on a busy day like May Day made a lot of sense. They knew they'd be surrounded by hundreds of people and that we wouldn't dare arrest them at that time. What an audacious bunch!

I quickly called out as many members of our Naval Academy band as possible on short notice, loaded them into the truck Nikiforov had sent and took off for the cemetery. When we arrived, we found a huge crowd of people had gathered around the Believers. Many were passers-by, gathered on the edge of the crowd to observe the more than 200 Believers. In the middle of the group, a few musicians were playing Christian songs on their instruments.

We started pushing our band through. If it was music the people wanted, then music they would have! "Over here! Over here!" I shouted. "Let us through, move back," I said to the people as we pushed our way toward the Believers. We got as close as possible, and I told the band to strike up. They began playing military songs very loud. The instruments as well as the musicianship of the academy band were far superior to those of the Believers. "Louder," I shouted. "Louder! Drown them out!"

We played *The Internationale* and other Communist and Soviet anthems, easily drowning out the Christian hymns.

Once I got the academy band going, some of the police operations squad who had come along with me took pictures of the Believers to record who they were. All the while, I stormed and fumed about, feeling helpless because we couldn't do anything to them with all these witnesses present. "Never mind, Sergei," Victor said, seeing my disappointment and frustration. "We'll settle the account later. We know who they are."

But for now, we had to allow those irrepressible Believers to go on with their meeting in the cemetery. We couldn't go into action with the holiday crowd around. Finally, after all the Believers had been photographed, I ordered the band to pack up, determined we'd make sure they'd get what was coming to them.

The opportunities came fast. One raid on a secret church followed another in rapid order, an average of one every four days.

Several of our raids were conducted not to interrupt meetings of the secret church but to look for and confiscate secret Christian literature that had been sent into the country or had been hand-written illegally by the Believers.

I often wondered, "How does this insignificant scribbling on a child's school exercise book constitute such a great threat to the Soviet state?" I couldn't see the danger, but Nikiforov kept telling me it existed.

Well, I thought, *if he wants the literature, we'll get him the literature.* And we had found plenty of it. One piece we came upon frequently was a magazine-like booklet published on a hectograph machine somewhere in the Ukraine, several thousand miles away. It was sent to our part of Siberia for the Believers. When I first saw it, I thought, *They're finally getting organized.*

The Believers in Kamchatka, through contacts and communications with other Christians in the Soviet Union, often obtained literature from them. Once Nikiforov picked up one of the hectograph magazines I brought back from one of the raids. He shook it violently and raved, "You see! They have links with Believers in Baku, the Ukraine, Kiev, Leningrad, everywhere! It's a nation-wide conspiracy to destroy our way of life!" He raved on and on.

Underground literature is a way of life in Russia. Not only is it secret, hand-written—*samizdat*—Christian literature; it also includes the works of famous writers who are not allowed to be published openly in Russia, such as Alexander Solzhenitsyn. Since all literature publishing is strictly controlled by the government, a great and thriving *samizdat* organization spreads hand copies or typed manuscripts of banned books, novels and stories throughout the Soviet Union. Though strictly forbidden, they are particularly popular among some of the officers and cadets on the naval base. I had been aware of this and had even read some of these works myself. Solzhenitsyn's works passed from hand to hand among the cadets.

Now I learned the Believers had organized in the same way. They distributed Bible verses, typed or copied by hand. We also found some pocket-sized, new Bibles that had been printed by organizations abroad. Somehow they were getting into our country. I knew that one of the special divisions of the organization in Moscow was established to find ways to block the smuggling of such Bibles into the Soviet Union. I don't know what they were doing, but they weren't doing it very well.

To me, all such literature was trash. I tried to read it but it made no sense to me at all. On one of the raids, I tried to grab a piece of literature from the hand of a tall, well-built man who was a Believer. If he had tried, he could have given me a hard time. I was sure I could lick him, though I knew it would be difficult. But there he was, clinging to those pieces of paper as though they were the most precious things in the world. I smashed him repeatedly in the face, but still he clung to them. Finally I hit him in the lower abdomen, and he doubled up, grabbed his stomach and dropped the paper. I picked up the pages and looked at them. Why did the Believer value them so highly? To us, they were nothing.

One day in 1970 I was called to the police station to see Nikiforov. "Look what we've got, Kourdakov," he said when we met. He pointed to an underground magazine which had been crudely printed on a secret mimeograph machine by Believers. "Where did this come from?" I asked.

"It was given to us by one of our spies. And he gave us information about where we can find a lot more," he said, bubbling with excitement.

Nikiforov, the manhunter, was always happiest on the trail of Believers. I didn't share all of his enthusiasm for the job. I was building a record with the party, making good money and, in the process, slowly becoming attracted to the life of a police officer. The police officer's life seemed a little more attractive than a career as an officer in the military.

"Come over here, Kourdakov," Nikiforov said. "Let me show you something."

We walked up to the map, and he told me, "This is where it is." He pointed to Number 64 Partisan Street.

"Whose house is that?" I asked.

"A Believer lives there. A widow named Annenchenko. She has a younger daughter living with her. An older daughter named Maria, around twenty-two years of age, is somewhere else. We think the widow's got it all stored either here," he said, jabbing at the map, "or in her daughter's place."

"When do you want us to go?" I asked.

"Tomorrow afternoon."

"How many men shall I get?"

"Just four. We've got to watch our budget you know," he said, letting out a laugh.

The procedure for the literature raids was a little different from that for breaking up the underground churches. To preserve the appearance of legality, we had a uniformed police officer go to a home he was about to search. Near the target house, he would stop three or four "comrades" in the streets, and these "disinterested" passers-by would join him and observe him during his investigation and search. They were there as "disinterested citizens" watching the work of the investigating officer, so no one could say later that the officer stole anything. To us, this was a big joke. But we had to observe the formalities. We had conducted many raids, searching for literature, and we followed this same procedure in all of them.

I met the police officer who was in uniform and would lead this "search". The policeman was merely a front, for I was the one held responsible by Nikiforov. The officer and three of my men and I got into the police truck and drove not far from the corner of Pogranichnaya and Partisan streets, high up on a hill overlooking the bay. It is an area of many small, white-walled houses. At the corner we all hopped out of the truck. We innocent "passers-by" stood out on the street. The police officer pulled up in front of the house and knocked on the door. A woman about forty-five years old answered his knock.

The officer said, "I'm here to search your house. We understand that you have illegal materials." Then he turned, pointing to us. "These are citizens who are passing by on the street and I have asked them to witness the search according to the law."

We walked into her house and looked around. It was a small house with poor furnishings, typical of the homes of the Believers. It was easy to understand why Believers lived so poorly. Once a man was known as a Believer, he was treated like a leper and could only get the worst jobs, ones that paid almost nothing.

"Look over there, men," he said. Now we had ceased to pretend to be innocent passers-by and joined him in the search.

"Are you a Believer?" I asked the lady of the house.

"Yes, I am," she said. "I believe in God. But I have no literature, if that's what you're looking for."

"We'll determine that!" I said sharply.

"Well," she went on, "I'm a Believer. Arrest me if you want to." She said it almost defiantly.

I looked at the woman. *Some spirit!* I thought. Then we began our search. We tore up the closet, scattering the clothes around. We opened suitcases, ripped the pillows, cut mattresses open and ripped the house apart room by room. After that, we broke the scattered furniture that remained. I called out, "Well, it's not here." Then I thought maybe she had hidden it under the floor, just as I had once hidden a zip gun back at Barysevo.

The officer was prepared with a crowbar and axe, and we began prying up the boards of the floor, one by one. Soon the poor woman's floor was half ripped up. One of the group jumped down into the huge hole and searched thoroughly with his flashlight.

"Nothing's down here," he called out at last.

"Come on," I shouted. "There's nothing here. Let's go!" We stalked out angry and frustrated, leaving the home completely wrecked inside. Let her fix it.

That treatment was normal and was repeated in most of the literature raids we made. We didn't care. These people were nothing to us. What could they do, complain to the police? We *were* the police. Go over our heads to the higher authorities? Of course not, we were there at the orders of the higher authorities! They couldn't do anything, and we knew it—and acted accordingly.

Soon we were back at the police station reporting to Nikiforov. While we talked, he kept looking into the air and tapping his fingers on the table. "I wonder," he said pensively. "I know she has something to do with that supply of literature to the Believers. I just wonder if it could be her daughter, the one who lives away from home."

"But she'll be alerted by her mother by now," I said.

"Of course," Nikiforov agreed, "and she'll be on guard . . . I've got it!" he said after a moment. "You two," and he pointed to Victor Matveyev and me, "you two lay a trap. Drop by her house; pretend you're fishermen or sailors, in from the sea. Strike up a conversation and casually let it fall that you want to know about God. These stupid Believers will tell anybody about God if they think they're going to convert you."

"Maybe it'll work!" I exclaimed, excited by the prospect of a little dramatics in our police work.

Nikiforov referred to his file and seconds later said, "Her name is Maria Annenchenko." He gave us her address and more information. "She works at a grocery store and finishes at six o'clock every day. You take it from there . . ."

Victor and I left the police station about 4 p.m. We had two hours to plan how we would go about trapping Maria Annenchenko. At about 5.30 we went to the bus stop where she would be getting off the bus in about thirty minutes, on her way home from the store.

"Now listen," I told Victor, "we're supposed to be fishermen home from the sea. We almost drowned out there, and this experience caused us to begin thinking about God and we're here to ask her to help us find God by showing us some literature. That'll get her! When she pulls out the literature, we arrest her. It's that easy."

"Terrific," Matveyev said, responding warmly to our acting roles. "But don't go into that line too fast, or she'll get suspicious."

We lounged around near the kiosk where Maria would soon get off. A few minutes later the bus pulled up and a girl, easily recognized from the photograph Nikiforov had shown us, stepped off and started walking in the direction of her home. "Let's go," I said to Victor.

We walked up behind her and in moments were walking with her stride for stride. To make our performance as seamen more convincing, we had taken a few nips of vodka and as we walked beside her, one on either side, I said cheerily, "Hello, beautiful! May we walk along with you?"

"No, thank you," Maria said coldly.

I took a good look at her. She was not unattractive, though rather plain, with a serious air about her. Victor joked, put his arm around her shoulder and said, "Come on, baby, how about going to your place for a drink and then let's go dancing afterwards. We could have some fun."

As we continued walking with her, she became more embarrassed and said, "No, thank you. I don't drink and I don't want to go anywhere." She tried every way to discourage us, but we kept walking with her.

"All we need is some talk, some drinks and some fun. We've been out to sea for seven months on the fishing boats. We just want to talk and relax a little bit."

She was by now ill at ease. "It looks like you have already had a little too much to drink," she said.

I replied, thinking this was an opening, "We know we have a problem with drinking. But we don't know how to stop. Besides, why should we stop? What else is there in life?" We were giving her an opening to talk about God, but she wasn't taking the bait. We went on, "We've been seamen all our adult lives. Our parents and our grandparents, all of them were Believers. We once thought about God ourselves, but vodka is a seaman's best friend."

She turned and looked us over, as if to assure herself that we really were just fishermen. By then we had reached the front door of a ramshackle little house. "This is where I live," she said. "I'll have to go in now." She paused at the door, as though waiting for us to leave.

"Couldn't we just come in for a quick drink and another little talk?" we said, standing close behind her. "What's your name?"

"Maria," she replied. She opened the door to go in and we walked in with her, uninvited. Inside, we sat down in a tiny, clean two-room house.

"Who knows about questions of life?" I said, pretending to be drunker than I was. "Questions about God, about these big questions and all? They're beyond a simple fisherman." She had busied herself with something. I looked at Victor quickly and shook my head as if to say, "She's going to be a hard one!"

We had been carrying a bottle of vodka and now Victor put it on the table in front of us. "Bring us some glasses, Maria," I said. She brought them over, set them down, and we poured our drinks from our bottle. When she left the room for a minute, I leaned over to Victor and whispered, "She's a smart one—a very smart girl. We're going to have to do better than this if we're going to trap her. Do you think she knows we're police?"

Before he could answer, she came back into the room, and I said, "Oh look, Maria, we're out of vodka. Be a good girl, won't you, and go down to the store and get us another bottle? Please, Maria," I begged, smiling. By this time I think she had swallowed our story that we were seamen. She agreed to go, and I gave her some money.

The minute she left, we jumped up and started searching for literature. We looked in the closets, under the beds, in every place where we thought it could have been hidden. If she had any, it was certainly well concealed. We were careful to put everything back in place so she wouldn't be suspicious. I much preferred doing it the way we did at her mother's, but here we wanted to keep our real purpose hidden. Victor kept a watch at the window, while I searched and ransacked everything. But there was no literature anywhere. "Sit down, Sergei," Victor said, "here she comes."

A few minutes later, she entered, walked across the room and set the vodka bottle down on the table. I could see she had relaxed a little, and I felt sure she believed our story. I winked at Victor. Now we began drinking from the bottle straight, and I began telling how we had sailed to Japan, to Vietnam, off the coast of California, Canada and Hawaii. I made a great story with all the details vivid and alive. Victor sat there, hardly able to keep from smiling as he listened to my wild, made-up story. Then he began to tell about his seven months at sea. His story wasn't too bad, but I thought mine was better.

Nikiforov, with his usual foresight, had given us a big wad of money to show, as though we'd just got off the boat with several months' pay in our pockets. Now we pulled out the money to make sure she saw it. "Come on," I said. "We've got money burning a hole in our pockets and all we want is a nice time. Come on, let's go drink and eat."

Then I began another story how at sea one time I fell over the side of the ship and almost drowned. When I faced death, I told her, I realized there had to be more in life and I began to think about God. But how to find Him—that was the big question on my mind. As I got more and more into my story, a total lie, Victor had a hard time keeping a straight face.

"When our ship docked," I said, "I decided I had been given a warning and I had to find God." I turned, looking at her with all the sincerity I could muster, and said, "We looked everywhere. But nobody can tell us about God. Do you know about Him? Maybe you have some books or magazines or something that would help us find our way to God?"

Now the question was out. How would she respond? She was no fool. "If you're so serious about God, why are you drinking now? Why are you living with alcohol?"

She sure had me there! Smart girl! But no woman was going to get the best of me. So I answered, "Vodka's good company when you're lonely. But if I could find God, I know I wouldn't need this any more, would I? But how to find God?" I shrugged. "It seems nobody knows."

On and on I went, giving her every opportunity to break in and say that she was a Believer, or to give me literature. Finally I finished my emotional story, saying, "If only I could find somebody who would show me how to find God or give me literature to show me the way, I'd give my right arm."

I waited. Victor and I looked at her. She stirred and moved. Was she going to take the bait? *This is it,* I thought. *We've got her!* The minute she'd get the literature out, we'd arrest her and take her off to Nikiforov and regale him with the story of how we tricked her.

"Well, I have no literature," she said. "But I think if you both keep searching, somewhere you'll find God."

Victor and I looked at each other. We knew we had lost the battle. And knowing we had lost, we realized we might as well get out of there. Drunkenly saying, "Good night," we thanked Maria for talking to us and walked out.

Once we were out on the street, Victor said, "Sergei, that was a tremendous story. You almost had me convinced you were a Believer. You're lucky I didn't arrest you!"

I laughed, then cursed and said, "What are we going to tell Nikiforov?" He had told us, "I have two prison cells waiting for mother and daughter. Just bring me one piece of literature, and we'll pick them both up and get rid of them!" Nikiforov's cells were going to stay empty. We knew he would be furious.

When we got back to the police station, we hesitantly told him our story. At first Nikiforov fumed quietly, then suddenly exploded. "Outsmarted by a stupid woman!" he yelled. It was incredible to him that such a thing could happen.

Mrs. Annenchenko and her daughter Maria had escaped Nikiforov that night. But they would not remain free. Eventually they were arrested and sent to the women's prison at Magadan.

"Kourdakov," Nikiforov said one day, "your operations squad is one of the finest. I can tell you, from information I've received from headquarters, you're doing a better job here than most of the groups anywhere in the country. You have one of the leading groups."

I was pleased with those words, because this commendation, added to my successful leadership of the largest Youth League division in the province, was great for my career. Anyone wanting to get ahead in the Soviet Union has to build a consistent, strong record. That's what I was attempting to do. Nikiforov's encouragement sparked my determination to excel, and I redoubled my efforts. And the men responded by becoming more brutal.

One night in a home on the southern outskirts of Petropavlovsk we attacked a group of Believers who had somehow had a few moments' advance notice that we were coming. When we got there and burst through the door with our clubs swinging, three had already managed to escape, and the others were trying to. We attacked them viciously, knocked them to the ground and began beating them. One was an older white-haired man who couldn't move very fast. Alexander Gulyaev caught up with him, whirled him around and said, "All right, grandpa." The old man's lips began to move, muttering a few words of prayer, I supposed.

"So you want to talk to God!" Alexander said. "Well, I'll show you how to talk to God. Maybe you want to go to God right away!" He shook him violently, gave him a hard knee in the stomach and hit him with a karate chop on the back of the neck. Three days later, the old man died of his injuries.

Our squad also developed refinements in its brutal procedures. We used what we called our "quick technique" if we wanted to get the raid over with fast and get the prisoners back to the police station in a hurry. Or if we wanted to play around and have fun, we used our "slow technique", toying with the Believers, getting in some boxing or judo practice.

On the way to the raids, Victor would ask me, "What's it going to be, Sergei, quick or slow?" I'd mull it over a minute and give what I thought should be the answer. Sometimes the fellows agreed, but sometimes not. "No, let's get it over with faster," they would often suggest. "Let's get done and have some fun with the girls."

The quick technique consisted mostly of karate chops and judo throws, with Vladimir and Victor, our boxers, using their own fast punches, knowing just where and how to hit, so that one blow per Believer would finish them off. After subduing everyone, we would drag the leaders out into the truck, pull out the identification cards of the others, record them and take off for the police station to dump our load. As soon as possible, we would then rush off to a bar or club.

It was the quick technique that resulted in the most severe injuries to the Believers. Two women died from their injuries after one of the raids. I learned of their deaths when I was summoned to testify in a court case for a woman who refused to allow her daughter to wear a special Youth League badge. The mother was accused of being a "counter-revolutionary", an enemy of the state. The judge asked her to explain her behaviour. In response, she told how her aunt had died from injuries after being beaten in one of the secret church meetings which had been raided by a "kind of police hooligan group", as she described us. She went on, "I have decided that if my aunt died for her faith, the least I can do to honour her is to take a stand for my own faith, and I will not let my daughter wear the emblem of those who killed my aunt." It had be to my group which killed her aunt. We were the only ones operating.

The court hushed this up, and the report did not get out. But it was another indication that several died from the beatings they suffered at our hands. Sometimes we injured them more than we had planned to, resulting in violent death or permanent incapacity. Sometimes Sergei Kanonenko's knife did the job.

But we felt no remorse. The bloodier the raids, the greater the congratulations from Nikiforov. Each raid was followed by a detailed report given to Nikiforov, and he often came along with us when we investigated the people who had been in the meetings we raided. Reports of resulting injuries and deaths were sent to Moscow, and we never received one word of reprimand. It can't be said that we were gangs of hooligans and anarchists who were exceeding our authority. Every step was known to Nikiforov, our superior officer, as well as to the *Gorkom* and to Moscow. We had proof that Moscow took notice of these reports, because often some official in Moscow singled out something from them for comment.

The raids increased in intensity and violence as time went on. It was especially bad for the older people, who were hit hard or thrown about like pieces of furniture. We made no distinction between women and men. Nikiforov often said, "Is a woman murderer any less dangerous than a man murderer?" By that, we understood that all were the same. We were sinking, degree by degree, into amorality.

I began to realize that this brutalization process was not confined to compartments of my life. It was making its mark upon my every thought and activity. I began to sense the difference in the way I ran the Youth League and in my relationships with the officers and cadets under me. Even some of my men became conscious of the change. One of them remarked to me one day, "Sergei, you're getting hard. What's happened to you?"

His question stopped me in my tracks, and I asked myself, "Sergei, what *has* happened to you?" The cruel, uncaring feelings that characterized me on the raids had permeated every area of my life. I found I could not isolate them or turn them off after I had been on duty with the operations group.

The change in my life was perhaps most noticeable in my job as Youth League director. Whereas before I would try to help the young cadets and use my position to cover many of their errors so they could continue their career, now I had little concern whether a man was dismissed or not or if his career was wrecked forever. At the time these changes first began taking place, I was unaware of them. Later, however, I noticed a sense of general uneasiness in my life, but so ill-defined that I couldn't put my finger on it. There was little time for reflection about it. The raids had to go on.

As the summer months of 1970 came on, the Believers tried to protect themselves by splitting into smaller groups of eight or ten, rarely more. This tactic forced us to conduct more raids to reach the same number of Believers. The Believers were becoming wiser in other ways. They began placing guards on the outside, often children, to warn them upon seeing anything suspicious. At their signal, the Believers would quickly hide their Bibles and other literature, and the tape recorders on which they recorded foreign religious radio broadcasts. On some occasions, the Believers had so much advance warning from guards they had stationed somewhere, that by the time we got there, all had disappeared from the meeting place.

Word of our campaign was getting around the city and the province. With only 250,000 people in all of Kamchatka, and with the devastating and brutal effects of the raids we were conducting, even the general public was beginning to talk. This notoriety enraged Nikiforov, who had warned us repeatedly to keep the people from knowing what we were doing and to prevent word from getting around that the Soviet Union didn't have religious freedom. Orders began coming from Moscow that no news of our activities should be allowed to get out.

Another wearying aspect of our work was that the more vigorously we attacked the Believers, the more rapidly their numbers seemed to grow. Nikiforov had estimated there were 30,000 Believers in the province, out of a population of only 250,000 people. And from what we had seen, he had to be right. In the more than 150 raids I led, rarely did we see the same faces twice. In many of the raids we saw new converts, living evidence of the ability of these Believers to infect others with their religious poison.

To crush them required a greater number of raids, and a severe scheduling problem was created for us. Nikiforov had to put up a special schedule board on the wall, on which we would map out the raids to come. I conducted many conferences with him, standing before that board as we discussed each raid to take place. Often I would say, "Well, we can't do both of these tonight. We'll have to hold this one for next week."

Of course, the multiplicity of meetings was great for us. We got our twenty-five roubles per raid whether there were eight people present or twenty.

Another thing we noticed in 1970, was that more and more of the Believers were turning out to be young people. In some of the meetings we found even small children. Moscow was alarmed by the trend. They regarded it as a dangerous "phenomenon" that must be stopped.

This great upsurge of religious interest among youth bewildered me. I was a youth specialist and thought I understood

Soviet youth. But larger and larger numbers of young people were inexplicably and constantly popping up in the secret churches, knowing full well what it would mean to them, their careers and their future if they were discovered. They were creatures of our Communist state, and here they were, turning to religion in great numbers! I really wondered about this religious appeal. Natasha kept coming back to my mind. She was one of "us", a Soviet youth. What did she see in religion? What did she find in God that caused her to be willing to take those vicious beatings?

The young people's great interest in God also touched a nerve in Moscow. Leaders of the anti-religious organization in Moscow flew out to Kamchatka and conducted special seminars, instructing us on how to oppose this "highly dangerous trend". From their talks, we gathered that the same "dangerous trend" was evident in all other parts of the Soviet Union as well.

I couldn't help comparing and contrasting these young Believers with the youths I dealt with in the Communist Youth League. My young people had been raised in the Communist way of life, just as I had, being taught its doctrines from the earliest years on, believing in it and plunging in to serve its cause with all their hearts. But now they were beginning to see life as it really is and to note the contradiction between the promises and the reality, and they were becoming cynical and hard. Often they turned to alcohol as a way of escape.

I compared this empty, sterile life of hard cynicism with the life of the young people who had turned to belief in God. The contrast was glaring, and it began to create gnawing doubts and questions in my mind.

In July 1970, I sat in the police station waiting room along with Anatoly Litovchenko, Vladimir, Victor and two or three others of my men. We were on regular watch duty at the station, waiting for news of Believers' activities to come in so we could take off immediately. Our time was now divided between answering emergency calls and putting in regular hours of duty at the police station. We often had to spend many hours on duty, for which we drew regular pay.

On this day Nikiforov came into the waiting room and said, "Kourdakov, I want you and one of your men to go and burn some of that junk that's been piling up downstairs."

The raids had become so frequent that we had quickly accumulated great piles of the Believers' confiscated literature. It was worthless and rather pathetic when you looked at it. It was written on very cheap paper, but was characterized by the most precise hand lettering I had ever seen. I once exclaimed, looking at a pile of the stuff, "How do they have time to do anything else except copy this junk?"

"I bet they get writer's cramp!" exclaimed Victor, and we laughed.

All kinds of oddities could be found in that box downstairs. There were some stories, lettered by hand, telling about God in simple terms that children could understand. These were for the children's meetings.

I called Vladimir Zelenov to come with me. We walked around to the stairwell and down to the cold "sobering room" below. There were no drunks in the cell that day. Over to the side, close to the big metal stove, were three deep wooden boxes. Two of them were piled to the brim with confiscated literature. "Start the fire," I said to Vladimir, and he threw in some of the literature, lighted a match and got the blaze going.

Leaving the iron fire door open, we began slinging the copies of hand-written literature into the fire. Even with the fire blazing, the room was cold, and I wanted a drink to warm me up. I asked Vladimir to go and get us a drink. I continued throwing literature into the fire, a handful at a time, watching it go up in flames and thinking a fire was all this stuff was good for.

What did young people see in this trash? I wondered. I thought of Natasha again. A sense of deep curiosity suddenly came over me. Often I had taken a quick look at the literature, out of curiosity before, while riding on the truck back to the police station. I had tried to read it but it never did make any sense to me. All I found was histories of somebody or other. To me it was just like any other history book, only far less interesting. But now, alone, while Vladimir was gone after the vodka, and overcome by curiosity as to what Natasha and the other young people saw in it, I picked up one booklet and began to read.

It was a hand-written portion of the Gospel of Luke, around chapter 11. Some verses were missing. I supposed it was written from memory and the writer didn't recall all the verses, and left gaps to be filled in later. As I read, several words caught my eye. They were some kind of prayer or something. Then, as I was looking, I heard Vladimir's footsteps as he returned with the vodka. Quickly I ripped out a couple of pages from the child's notebook it was written in and shoved them into my pocket.

"Here it is," Vladimir announced as he came downstairs with the vodka. We took a few sips, threw the rest of the Christian literature into the fire, then closed the door to the stove and started back upstairs.

That night, at the first opportunity I had, lying in my bunk at the Naval Academy, I opened up those pieces of paper and began to read them again. Jesus was talking and teaching someone how to pray. I became more curious and read on. This certainly was no anti-state material. It was how to be a better person and how to forgive those who do you wrong. Suddenly the words leaped out of those pages and into my heart. I read on, engrossed in the kind words of Jesus. This was exactly the opposite of what I expected. My lack of understanding which had been like blinkers on my eyes left me right then, and the words bit deeply into my being. It was as though somebody were in the room with me, teaching me those words and what they said. They made a profound impact on me. I read them again and again, then sat thinking, my mind lost in the wonder of it all. "So this is what Natasha believed?" I said to myself.

The words grabbed my heart. I was somehow frightened and uneasy, like a man walking on unfamiliar ground. I read the words and re-read them and put them down, and still they came back to my mind again and again. Those words were leading Natasha to be a better person and help others. They haunted me. It was a feeling totally new to me.

Through the days and weeks ahead, those words of Jesus stayed with me. I couldn't shake them off. I tried. I wished I hadn't read them. Everything had been so organized in my life, but those disturbing words had changed something. I had feelings I had never felt before. I couldn't explain or understand them. I kept those pages, reading and re-reading them during the next several weeks. I could only comprehend so far, and then my understanding broke down into confusion. It was like standing on a shore, in the midst of a swirling cloud, and reaching out. You know there's something beyond, something somewhere to be touched, to be reached, to be known. But it escapes you. All you see is the swirling cloud.

Something deep within me, some tiny ember of humanity was still alive. The life I was leading was not the life that I had wanted to lead. Beating old women was not the kind of life I dreamed of long ago in my early childhood. My first religion, Communism, I believed in wholeheartedly and gave myself to it without reserve. It was the first thing I had to believe in when I discovered it in Barysevo. But that belief was gone now, shattered by the realities of life as I had seen them. Nothing satisfactory had replaced that belief I once held.

It was while I was in this confused state of mind that the time for my next military leave came up, in late July. I flew out of Kamchatka, heading eastward, toward Novosibirsk, and on that flight I made up my mind that I could not continue my way of life. I had no idea what I would be changing *to*, only what I had to change *from*. I decided to escape from Russia and get away from this life. Something was driving and compelling me.

I went to Novosibirsk and there reported to the police headquarters, giving them an address where I could be reached within twenty-four hours in the event of a military emergency. Then, without authority, I boarded a plane for Moscow. When I got there, I went to visit that sacred place I had visited before, the tomb of Lenin. As I stood in line before the tomb in the great, sprawling Red Square, I thought of the last time I had been there, when I was seventeen and on my way to Leningrad at the start of a promising new career as a naval officer. I had stopped, full of optimism, and bowed my knee at the bier of

Lenin. I had prayed, asking Lenin for guidance and direction for my life, for wisdom to be a success, and for obstacles to be removed from my way. I had walked out refreshed and confident, looking eagerly to the future.

This time, in July 1970, I stood in line again, still with a sense of respect for Lenin. He was a brilliant man. He had many good teachings. He had many good goals: the equality of all men; the brotherhood of all people; the helping and the lifting up of the little people. Those were the goals that had attracted me and caused me to be such a dedicated Communist. As I mused, the line was moving forward, and before I knew it, I was only a few feet away from the corpse. Where had all those visions of "equality of men" gone, as Lenin taught them? Was it equality of men when I beat an old woman so severely she died within a few days? Was it equality when a beautiful young girl was twice beaten horribly? Where had all those early dreams and visions of a better life gone wrong? I stood there silently for several minutes as the storm raged inside. *Comrade Lenin*, I thought, *where have men strayed from your teachings? What has gone wrong?*

An agony was taking place inside me as I asked, again and again, what had happened to the promises? What had gone wrong with the future we live for? How could men have so twisted Lenin's good teachings? I hoped that, somehow, being close to Lenin would help me understand and calm the storm inside my heart. But I felt no different.

"Move along," someone was whispering, and I turned and walked out of the tomb of Lenin for the final time.

Down through the streets of Moscow I wandered, lonely, disillusioned, distraught. I was in a state of total confusion, but I decided one thing. I would leave Russia and get as far away as I could. I can't say why I wanted to leave Russia. I only know that I was deeply disillusioned and desperately unhappy, that something was terribly wrong.

I went on to Lvov and stayed there with one of my Ukrainian friends whom I had met in Petropavlovsk. I bought an aqualung on the black market and made plans to go to the border of Russia and Hungary, to the river Tiza, and swim underwater into Hungary. Then I would make my way through Hungary to a river which flows from Hungary into Austria, put on my aqualung again, go back into the water and come up on the other side in Austria. I had Hungarian currency and was ready to go. It was a crazy plan, but I had to escape.

Leaving my friend in Lvov, I went to one of the small towns on the Hungarian border. I took a driver in a car and explained to him that I had seen the far east end of Russia in Siberia. Now I would like to see the west end of Russia here. It made sense to him, so he drove me to the border and left me. I told him I'd find my way back. I could see across to the Hungarian side, and even though it was a Communist country, the border was tightly patrolled. I said to myself, *that border isn't there to keep the Hungarians out of Russia.*

After taking one look at the scene, the constant patrolling and the guard stations, I knew that my plan to escape across the river was impossible. It sounded good from far away; but being here, I saw it was impossible. Something said to me, "Don't go!" I gave up that try, got rid of the aqualung and soon was aboard a train on my way back to Lvov.

I devised another plan, flying first to Baku, then to Yerevan, the capital of Armenian Russia. Arriving in Yerevan, I took a bus into the countryside, heading toward the villages near Turkey. Soon I reached a small village at the end of the bus line and began walking toward the Turkish border. I hid during the day and walked at night until I found myself very close to the Turkish frontier. I could see soldiers on the other side of the border, in a small Turkish town. But Russian soldiers were everywhere on the Soviet side. All night I waited and watched, but still the border was heavily patrolled. There was no getting across here either. My two attempts to start a new life had failed.

Since my military leave was about over, I boarded a plane to Novosibirsk and from there took another flight back to Petropavlovsk, to report to the Naval Academy again. My mind was in a turmoil.

19 The last raid

"Welcome back, Kourdakov," Nikiforov exclaimed as I walked into the police station for the first time after my return from my military holiday.

I thought, *If he only knew what I have been up to, I wonder how welcome I would be.*

"Glad to see you back," he said. "We've got lots of work lined up for you. We will soon have you back in business again. I bet you could use the money, huh?"

Quickly I was back at the raids. The small groups of Believers consisted largely of young people. During interrogations, they reported that they had recently become Believers. Nikiforov was very concerned, and the deluge of directives from Moscow continued, with alarm.

There was no easing up or sympathy from me during these raids. In fact, because I was dissatisfied and ill at ease I was testier than ever. I was sharp and curt with my men and with the Believers. The last raids I led were the most vicious of all. Something was compelling, driving me. I did not understand what it was, and I took out my frustrations and hostilities on any who crossed my path.

One Friday afternoon in October 1970, I got a call from Nikiforov. "Kourdakov," he began, "I want you to be here at twelve-thirty on Sunday. Get as many men as possible."

I called my men, telling them to be sure to be in their rooms at noon on Sunday and I would be around with the police truck to pick them up.

On Sunday at 10 a.m., I went to the police station for a briefing with Nikiforov and to get the location of the meeting place. "How many do you think will be there?" I asked.

"Fifteen or sixteen," he replied.

I was surprised. It had been a long time since we had found that many together in any underground meeting. But I had ten men I could count on, in addition to myself, and there would be no problem.

"I want you to handle this one a little differently, Kourdakov. According to our informants, the Believers are going to meet

176

to pray from noon till two o'clock and then start their regular meeting. I want you to get a man there early with a tape recorder, so we can record their prayers and find out what they're praying about." The police were concerned, he said, thinking that possibly the Believers might be using their praying to cover up plans to overthrow the government.

If Nikiforov wants a tape recording of their prayers, I thought, *he'll get one.*

I told Yuri to get out there at half past twelve, thirty minutes after the prayer meeting was scheduled to begin. Equipped with a small, battery-operated recorder, he was to get as close to the meeting place as possible and secretly tape everything going on inside. The Believers would be meeting in a large bath house, built in the yard of a small home, backed up against a hill. There were no houses behind it and no windows in the back wall of the bath house. Inside it would be impossible to spot anyone approaching from over the hill, from the rear.

Having dispatched Yuri, I made the rounds to pick up my other men. I had no inkling that this raid would be my last.

At two o'clock we quietly approached the neighbourhood in which the prayer meeting was taking place, and parked the unmarked police van out of sight some distance away. We got out and began walking over a hill, to approach the house from the rear. I stationed two men in front in the street to keep away anyone attracted by the screams.

As we came over the hill and approached the house from the back, we could see the bath house closed up tightly. Coming closer, we found Yuri at work. His tape recorder was running and he had taped the muffled voices of the Believers in prayer during the past ninety minutes. These prayers would be heard again and again in Moscow. They would help the state study the Believers' attitudes and thoughts, in order to oppose them more effectively.

I looked at poor Yuri kneeling there, making the recording. I'll bet that was the first prayer meeting he had ever attended —and on his knees for almost two hours! Quietly we walked single file toward the building.

At the door we paused briefly, my men beside me, waiting for the starting signal. Suddenly I shouted, "Now!" And the raid was on. The door was unlocked—obviously they weren't expecting us—and we burst in on them. As the informant had predicted, there were fifteen or sixteen Believers present, packed in tightly and sitting close together. We had caught them in the middle of prayer.

Vladimir Zelenov reached and grabbed a Bible from a Believer, ripping it apart. One of the women cried out, "Why? Why do you do that?" It was a hurt, deep cry, but it irritated Vladimir, and he smashed her full in the face. It was a professional, well-aimed blow that would have flattened any man, much less a frail little woman. She flew back against the other Believers and crumpled to the floor, her face bleeding.

Screams split the air as my men went to work. I pushed the lever on my club, reducing it to its shortest length so it was more useful in this cramped room. Clubs and fists were already flying, and the cries of the Believers were enough to break your eardrums, some screaming in fear, others screaming as they were smashed.

I saw an old woman near the wall, fear on her face, lips trembling in prayer. I couldn't hear what she was saying because of the noise. Her praying infuriated me and I dashed over a few steps and raised my club to hit her. She suddenly saw me poised, ready to strike, and she prayed loudly. I listened for a second to her prayer, more out of curiosity than anything. As my arm was raised, ready to lower my club on her defenceless head, I heard her words, "God, forgive this young man. Show him the true way. Open his eyes and help him. Forgive him, dear God."

I was stunned. *Why doesn't she ask help for herself instead of me? She's the one about to be finished off.* I was angered that she, a nobody, should be praying for me, Sergei Kourdakov, a leader of the Communist Youth League. In a flash of rage, I gripped my club tighter and prepared to smash it against her head. I was going to hit her with all my might, enough to kill her. I started to swing. Then the strangest thing happened to me. I can't describe it. Someone grabbed my wrist and jerked it back. I was startled. It was hurting. It was not imaginary. It was a real squeezing on my wrist until it actually pained. I thought it was a Believer, and I turned around to hit him. But there was no one there!

I looked back. *Nobody* could have grabbed my arm. And yet, somebody had grabbed me! I still felt the pain. I stood there in shock. The blood rushed to my head. I felt hot as fright swept over me. This was beyond me. It was confusing, unreal. Then I forgot everything. Dropping my club, I ran out, with the

178

blood rushing to my head and a hot, flushed feeling in my face. Tears began flowing down my cheeks.

Since I was four years of age I had cried only once that I could remember. Even during the most brutal beatings from Uncle Nichy in the children's home, I never cried. I was too tough to cry, I thought. No one will ever make me cry, I had vowed. Crying was a sign of weakness. But now, as I ran from that nightmare scene, I was crying. Real tears were coursing down my cheeks. I was bewildered, lost. Things were happening I did not understand. I ran and walked, then ran some more, not remembering a thing. Hours passed. I can't recall anything beyond running and crying. I don't know how long I walked, nor where I walked. But when I came to myself, it was dark.

Then I slowly made my way back to the police station. It was about 9 p.m. No sooner had I entered than Nikiforov exploded, "Kourdakov, where have you been?" It was more of a challenge than a question.

"I had to think things over," I replied, "and I've come to a decision to quit this kind of work."

A worried look came over Nikiforov's face, replacing the look of anger. He sized me up for a few moments and said, "Sergei," his voice a little less harsh now, "you're just tired out. Go and get some rest."

"But I'm not, I've . . ." He cut me off, saying, "You're tired. Go and rest and we'll talk about it later."

A few days later Nikiforov called me at the Naval Academy to lead another raid on a secret church. I stammered, searching for a way out, and said, truthfully, "I'm very busy in my studies. We've got tests coming up. I can't do it tonight." Nikiforov hesitated. This was the first time I had turned down a raid. He said no more, then hung up.

A few days later Nikiforov was on the phone again, telling me to report that evening with some of my men.

"I can't make it. I have a Communist Youth League meeting to prepare for," I replied. Several days later he called again, and I told him, "I have my navy studies. I'm graduating soon and I have all my duties as leader of the Youth League. I just don't think I have enough time to continue with the police."

"I'll talk to you later," he said and hung up. I felt relieved. Maybe I was out. I hoped so, very much. I had led more than 150 raids on the secret churches in the past two years, an average of one every five to six days.

I realized I was carrying a heavy psychological load, which I cannot explain. It was as if my heart had been replaced by a heavy rock, pressing me down. There was something very wrong with life, with me. But I told no one.

About two weeks later, around 1 November, it was time for the regular meeting of the Communist Party in Petropavlovsk, at which I was to give a report to the senior Communist Party members on my work as head of the Youth League. I had a good report to give. I had plunged into my Youth League work strenuously, and my organization really was the best in the province. I cited facts, figures and plans for the coming months. I had good reason to expect compliments. But instead, I got a surprise. The minute I finished speaking, a comrade got up and asked, "Comrade Sergei, why have you stopped working with the police?"

Someone exclaimed aloud, "He's not working with the police! Where did you hear that?"

The first man replied, "A little bird told me." As they laughed, I realized Nikiforov had staged all this to pressure me back into the police operations.

The chairman, with mock surprise, leaned over and said, "I can't believe this! It's such a great job with short hours, good money. Is this true, Comrade Sergei?"

"Yes, it is," I replied.

"That little bird also told us you refused to beat the *religiozniki*," the first man said.

"Is that also true?" the chairman asked.

"Yes, sir, it is," I replied.

"Well," he answered, "I think anyone refusing a good job like that is a little crazy to quit. Why?" he demanded.

This unexpected sniping at me, following my excellent Youth League report, was getting to me and I let my guard down and blurted out my feelings, something I had been trained never to do.

"Comrades," I said, "I have been an activist and leader since the Octobrianiks at age eight. I have served the party well and will continue to serve it well. But I have studied the Party Guide Book and the Constitution of the U.S.S.R. It says we are brothers with all men. So I can't beat them. No, I did not beat the *religiozniki* last time. According to our teaching, they are my brothers. How could I beat my brothers? How can I continue? Of course, we have a problem with

these Believers, but it does not say we must beat and
them—!"

The chairman cut me off sharply. "Comrade Serg
said, "you have been the finest youth leader to pass
the Naval Academy in years. You are still very you
much to learn. These *religiozniki* are not our brothers! T
like murderers. They kill the spirits of our children.
cripple people with their poisonous beliefs. We must i
country of these people. This seeming pity for these pe
an infection, nothing less! These Believers are the ones w
disturbing our people and causing troubles. They forc
government to spend huge amounts of money fighting
money which should go toward building our country
helping our people. These people working from the insid
hurt us by undermining the faith of our people in Com
ism and replacing it with a faith in some imaginary
Christ."

He went on, his voice increasing in shrillness. Then qui
his voice softened. "You are a Communist youth leader. W
we are rid of these people, this kind of work will not be ne
sary." I thought, *The way the Believers spread their faith to otl
I'll be dead and in my grave first!*

"Our Central Committee and the Politburo have given
this work to do and we must do it," the chairman told me.

"If it must be done," I replied, "get someone else to do it
not me."

In the tense silence that followed, someone shouted, "Let hi
go. He's young and green. His record is perfect. Give him tim
He'll come round." So they agreed to release me from poli
action and let me continue my work as head of the Yout
League at the Naval Academy.

I left, hurriedly. Behind me I heard the comments, "He'
young. He's got a great future ahead of him. Give him time
He'll see it our way . . ."

My actions would normally have drawn suspicion and I
would have been put under surveillance, but to my knowledge
this did not happen. Possibly it was because they realized that
I was, in fact, extremely busy. Also, my record was without
blemish.

I returned to my studies, which were now nearing completion.
Soon I would be commissioned as a cadet second lieutenant of
the Soviet navy. I continued my work as head of the Youth

League, but it was with a growing dissatisfaction and unhappiness inside me.

Around December first, I received an order to go and see Nikiforov at his office. When I arrived, Azarov, the K.G.B. major who had first recruited me, was also there. I said to myself, "I'm in for something now!"

"Have a seat, Sergei." Nikiforov said, trying to create a relaxed atmosphere. "Sergei, you are really crazy!" he said. "Here you are, with a great career in the police before you, and you are rejecting it to go to sea. Don't you know you'll spend half your life at sea with the fish? What future is there in that?"

Then, adopting a warm, friendly tone, he said, "If you'll just listen to reason, you'll have a great career here with the police. You've done excellent work for us. You have all the qualities we are looking for." As he spoke, I looked at Azarov. I was sure that he had ordered this conversation.

"You're just the kind of man we need. The police needs you more than the navy. Here's what we are prepared to do," he said, nodding to Azarov. "We'll jump your rank from second lieutenant to full lieutenant now. We'll send you to the Party Police Academy in Tomsk." This was a famous élite K.G.B. academy. Most of Russia's top police officers came from there. Graduates of Tomsk were marked for the highest positions in the Soviet police system.

Nikiforov went on, citing my "special experience" with Believers and saying that at Tomsk I would be trained as a specialist in "dealing with Believers". I well knew what *that* meant. My head was spinning. The Tomsk Academy! Only a Russian knows what a career advancement that was. Just look at Azarov. Only around thirty and already a major in the K.G.B.! And I could do even better than Azarov. I knew that. After a year at Tomsk I would be graduated and upgraded from lieutenant to captain, then from captain to major. By the time I was twenty-five, in four years, I knew I could easily be a major in the secret police, in charge of "dealing with Believers". From there, there was no limit to how high I could go. Life can be very good for people who blindly serve the system. I had already seen that. I could have a car, a cottage, plenty of money.

All that flashed through my mind as Nikiforov continued talking. The state needed people like me, he was saying again, and it knew how to reward them well.

Azarov then spoke for the first time. "We know your record, Comrade Kourdakov. It is perfect for this work. It is spotless. You've had excellent experience with the Believers. We need specialists for that work. You will be marked to go far."

Well, I thought, *if they look at my record, it is spotless. But if they could look into my heart, they would see great dissatisfaction.*

I heard them out, then thanked them for the wonderful offer and asked for a few days to think it over, since it would decide my career from that time on.

"We understand," Nikiforov said. "I'll talk to you again soon."

"Comrade Kourdakov," Azarov said ominously and slowly, "the state has a big investment in you—a big investment—and we expect much from you. Don't forget it." I knew what Azarov was saying. I was on the hook and would never get off. I thanked them both again and left. I went back to the Naval Academy, lost in thought.

Most career officers would have given their right arm to get the offer I had just had. For nearly all my life, my driving motto had been, "Go ahead! Go ahead!" Now here was the greatest break of my life. But it seemed hollow. I knew in my heart I could never be a servant of the system which had killed my father and turned me into a hardened animal, beating women and harmless Believers.

If I said yes, I would be a tool of the state to persecute the Believers. Nikiforov had already made it clear that I was marked for that kind of work. There was no question. I couldn't do it.

A few days later, I told Nikiforov my decision. He sputtered and said, "Go and get a few months of life at sea with the fish; and when you get back, we'll have another talk."

I then realized the K.G.B. wouldn't leave me alone until I agreed. "When you get back . . ." Those words rang in my ears. I knew in my heart I would not be coming back—not to that.

With my decision firmly made, I plunged back into my studies and duties as chief of the Youth League, eagerly awaiting the time I could go to sea. A month later, in January 1971, I graduated from the Naval Academy as a radio officer and was commissioned as Cadet Second Lieutenant Sergei Kourdakov of the Russian navy. I was assigned immediately to sea duty and shipped out aboard a Soviet destroyer.

After one and a half months at sea on the destroyer, we returned to the naval base for two weeks. I went to see a friend of mine who worked in the office where naval officers received their orders. I asked to be assigned to a ship operating off the coast of the United States. I told my friend. "I am trained as a radio officer but I need a lot more experience. I want duty with the fleet off the United States coast where there is constant activity in radioing information back from America and I could get a lot of experience quickly." That sounded reasonable enough.

He said, "Well, it is not normal, but for you, Sergei, we can do it."

After two weeks in port I was assigned as the radio officer on board a Soviet submarine heading for duty off the coast of the United States. As I boarded the submarine that raw morning of 4 March 1971, I saw the last of my beloved homeland. I would either be dead or free, but I would not return to serve the system or be another Nikiforov. A normal man has other choices. He can live in Russia and ignore the system as much as possible and live as decent a life as he can. But mine was not such a case. I was part of the system; it had its hands on me.

If I returned from sea, I would have to serve the police system fully. Azarov and Nikiforov had made that clear. And seeing what this system has done to my people and my country, I could never serve it. I am Russian. I love my country. I love my people, who are great and warm and generous. Those conflicting thoughts weighed on my mind very much as I left.

Our submarine cruised the coast of Korea and Japan, then started across the vast expanse of the Pacific, toward the United States. I was honoured, in one sense, to be picked as a submarine officer, for they are the élite, the most carefully chosen of all Soviet naval officers. Only those with spotless records are chosen. They have access to military secrets and handle nuclear weapons which could start a war. Even so, submarine duty was not what I wanted. I couldn't accomplish my plan to escape from a submarine.

As the weeks and months passed, I hoped and waited, faithfully performing my duties in the meantime. Then in mid-June 1971, I was told that the Soviet trawler *Ivan Sereda* was nearby and needed a radio officer. My captain informed me I was to be transferred in mid-Pacific to be the *Ivan Sereda's* radio officer. I could hardly contain my joy ... Things were beginning to go well. We surfaced near Hawaii on 25 June and I transferred to the trawler.

I was on the surface now. We cruised past Hawaii, heading directly towards San Diego, where we came close to shore. We then continued northward along the California coast to a point off Los Angeles. Now everything seemed ready for my flight to freedom. We were just outside the twelve-mile territorial limit. Late in the evening, I gathered several pieces of wood and tied them together into a little makeshift raft. My plan was to use this as flotation and when night came to go overboard carrying some food and water. I would then swim into U.S. coastal waters and hail a passing U.S. yacht or other vessel. My raft was ready and hidden.

In the far distance the lights of Los Angeles could be seen on the horizon. Freedom was so close. But I had to stand duty one more shift as radio operator. That night, as my mind was mostly on the freedom which lay only a few miles away, I routinely carried out my duties. Soon I received radioed notice that we were about to receive a message from Moscow, which would be transmitted shortly. With a pencil I began taking the message. It startled me. I could hardly write it down accurately, due to its impact on my plans. One of our Soviet fishermen, the message said, a young Lithuanian named Simas Kudirka, had jumped from a Soviet fishing vessel on to an American ship off the coast of New England on 23 November 1970. The message said that Kudirka had committed treason to the Soviet Union by his attempt for freedom and had been sentenced to ten years in prison.

Of course, I thought. *What a fool I was to forget Kudirka.* When his escape attempt had happened, I had heard about it. But in the rush now, I had forgotten. Now the comment on his sentencing on the very eve of my escape brought it all back to me with shocking fear. I remembered we were told at the time: "The U.S. Government co-operated fully with the Soviet navy and promptly handed Kudirka back to us. He is now in our custody."

All Soviet seamen were told that his turnover to Soviet authorities was part of a new agreement between the United States and Russia, whereby the United States would hand back any Russian seaman trying to escape, as they had handed back Kudirka. At the time I had wondered what kind of free country is this America which makes an agreement to give back anyone who tries to find freedom?

Suddenly I was angry with myself for forgetting Kudirka and

almost repeating his mistake. Remembering the little raft which, if found, would give me away, I ended my duty in a state of anxiety. The moment I was finished, I headed directly for the spot I had hidden the raft. To my relief, I saw it had not been discovered. I disassembled it and scattered the pieces of wood. That night I stood by the railing, looking at the glow of lights from Los Angeles and wondered, why would the Americans turn back a man fleeing to freedom? (Later I learned that an American admiral had handed Kudirka over without government approval and this was not the American government's policy.)

I looked down at the waters, so warm, so inviting. Now it had to be Canada. It couldn't be America.

20 Search for a new life

We sailed north to a point off Vandenberg Air Force Base on the California coast. Shortly afterward, I received word that I was being transferred to be radio officer on board the *Kolivan*, another Russian trawler, in the large Soviet fleet off the U.S. coast.

As the days passed and July slipped into August, I thought several times of Simas Kudirka and what he faced: ten years of imprisonment at best. Once his trial was over, the Soviets knew the world would forget Kudirka and he could be kept in prison for ever—or have an "accident" in prison.

If such was the fate of a genuine fisherman, what would happen to me, a navy officer, a Communist youth leader? I knew what would happen. I would be dead before I reached Russia if I were caught or handed back.

As the coast of Canada came closer each day, I was coming nearer to the point of life or death. There would be no turning back for me. We crossed into waters off the coast of Canada and remained for a short time off the city of Vancouver. Then our ship was ordered to rendezvous with the Soviet trawler *Shturman Elagin*, and I was informed I was again being transferred, now to the *Elagin*, as its next radio officer. The transfer was completed off the coast of Vancouver, and the *Elagin* immediately set off for Amchitka Island off the coast of Alaska, which was to be the site of the American underground nuclear test blasts.

When I say "trawler", I use the term the Soviet navy uses. Actually, if the ships I was on wanted to catch fish, the fish would have to swim very fast and leap on the deck themselves. We moved swiftly and ignored fishing altogether.

During those days at sea the greatest pleasure I had was tuning in quickly to the Voice of America and hearing what was happening in the world. I had listened to it many times back in Russia and knew that most of the Russian people and many of the naval cadets did the same. It was dangerous, and if caught, one could receive severe punishment. But sometimes the thirst for news and truth is greater than the fear of discovery.

These broadcasts of the Voice of America and religious broad-casts in the Russian language from missionary stations helped strengthen me for the ordeal ahead.

Toward the end of August 1971, the *Elagin* was ordered to head back toward the Canadian coast. For the past weeks I had spent several hours daily lifting weights and doing exercises to build myself up. I would need enormous stamina and strength when my time came. Several of my shipmates joked about my physical fitness work saying, "Hey, are you going to try to be Mr. World?" But I kept at it. Only I knew why.

The *Elagin* had 110 men on board and an officer for every ten men. I found the captain to be a fair, honest man of the sea whom I admired very much. We passed many hours talking and playing chess.

One day as I radioed material to Russia, I received word of an incoming message and started copying it down. It was a message concerning me. In five days the Soviet supply ship, the *Maria Ulyanova*, named for Lenin's sister, was due to rendezvous with the *Elagin* and resupply it. I was to be transferred to the *Ulyanova*, which would then head straight back to Russia.

After acknowledging receipt of the message, I mulled it over with alarm. I had been at sea for almost six months. Five more days on the *Elagin*, and then back to Russia, perhaps never to be near free shores again. I had had my one great chance of freedom off Los Angeles, but I couldn't take the risk of being handed back.

Further communications came over the radio saying that my papers promoting me had been processed and awaited me back in Petropavlovsk. But that was the last thing I was interested in now.

I was gripped by a sense of desperation. As thoughts crowded into my mind, our ship was encountering fierce head winds and heavy seas. We were soon caught in a cyclone. We fought our way forward with every man and machine straining to the fullest. Several of our ships were having difficulty in the storm, and I spent extra hours in the radio cabin transmitting and receiving messages. Above me was a wall calendar which I glanced at often. Time was slipping away; those few remaining days were like the sands of my life running out before my eyes.

"Sergei," the captain ordered, "radio Canadian authorities. Ask for permission to ride out this storm inside their territorial waters."

"Yes, sir," I replied routinely. Then, the importance of that message hit me! *Inside Canadian waters!*

That was it! If we went that close to shore, which we could never do otherwise, I *might* be able to make it. I had planned to go into the water as our ship lay just outside territorial waters, twelve miles offshore, and use some wood as flotation to get me in. But I knew the water temperature and well knew I might die of exposure before I made those twelve miles. But now we were going *inside* Canada's waters! The idea filled me with renewed hope and energy. But whatever happened, I had made up my mind: I would not go back to Russia on the *Ulyanova* in five days. I would not go back to that life.

Making the final decision to go *in any circumstances and conditions* cleared my mind to focus on one thing—my moment of escape. And it was to come during the furious height of the storm.

Around 10 p.m. on 3 September 1971, I plunged into the black, heaving waters. After five hours in the freezing sea, I had climbed the 200-foot cliff, and plunged down a ravine, cut and ripped all the way down. I had been exposed to the cold, wind and rain. I was shaking uncontrollably and bleeding about my legs and feet and hands. I swam halfway across the bay separating me from the village. Then my head began to swirl. I was too cold, too exhausted. I had lost too much blood. I looked up moments before a wave of dizziness swept over me, and the last thing I remember seeing or thinking, was the lights of a tiny village on the coast. *I must make it. I must make it.* And the lights of the tiny village flickered out.

I can't remember what happened afterward. Everything is fuzzy. But later I was told the story by the good people of Tasu village, who found me and took me in.

That morning of 4 September 1971, dawned raw and blustery over the village, a small settlement at the edge of the sea, on the Pacific side of Queen Charlotte Island. Most of the villagers work in mines in that area. A woman whose home faced the sea, about sixty feet away, went to make a phone call at 8.30 a.m. and looked out of her window. It was most unusual that she should be there that day. I was told that almost any other day she would have been at her job; but she had stayed home that day. She looked down toward the sea and saw a surprising sight.

She saw me stagger up from the beach, half naked, exhausted

and bleeding from the cuts. She phoned for help and I was taken to the hospital. The doctor said I had a cardiac irregularity from exertion and I was in and out of a very deep sleep for a long time.

After several hours I could hear distant voices speaking in whispered tones in a language I couldn't understand. I wondered where I was. *Back on ship*, I thought with a rising sense of panic. *But no, no, those are foreign voices! Canada! I must have made it!*

My eyes were beginning to focus, and I looked up into the face of a woman nurse bending over me. She was the most beautiful woman I had ever seen. I was alive! I was in Canada! I had made it! I was the happiest guy alive!

After several hours, a man entered and said he was going to translate for me. "Who are you? Why did you come here?" he asked.

I could hardly speak for the pain. I said, "I don't want to go back to the Russian ship."

He replied, "Very well, we will now contact the Canadian authorities in Prince Rupert and they'll tell us what is to happen to you next."

That same afternoon a plane came and flew me to the capital of Queen Charlotte Island and from there to Prince Rupert in British Columbia. Before I left, I thanked the nurse and the doctor who had taken such good care of me in Tasu. I had nothing to give except my thanks and I couldn't understand their language.

In Prince Rupert I was placed in the prison section of the hospital. I was kept there for some days and given the very best —wonderful food, rest and the finest of medical care. Everybody was very good to me. I was the centre of attention and though I couldn't understand their strange language, I understood that not too many Russian seamen come to Prince Rupert. They looked at me as though I were a creature from outer space. No one could speak Russian, so I spoke a little German and they found someone who could translate. These strangers took such wonderful care of me that I rapidly began to regain my strength.

With my strength coming back, I took more interest in my surroundings. One day an immigration official and an interpreter took me out of the prison hospital and drove me around Prince Rupert. My eyes almost popped out as I looked at the cars and nice homes. I guess I was staring at them. He said, "This is where the people live."

"Who, capitalists and businessmen?" I asked.

He laughed and said, "No, just the plain working people."

Well, I wasn't believing that! I thought, *This is a real propaganda tour, Sergei. Don't fall for it.*

Later, they brought me a photographic magazine to look at. Its name was something like *Interior Decoration Made Easy*, I was told. It was really beautiful, full of pictures of mirrors, chairs, beds, carpets and beautiful homes with expensive furniture. *Aha!* I thought. *This is a special magazine printed by the government to trick me.* I had been raised suspecting everything to be propaganda and had come to learn never to believe the government. I was out of Communism; but Communism, with its suspicion and distrust, wasn't out of me.

I felt a little foolish afterward when I found out that normal workers *did* live in homes like that in Canada and that the magazine hadn't been prepared just to trick me.

Russian propaganda says that the very rich have become rich by exploiting the very poor. But the homes of the workers here were almost like palaces in Russia, and I couldn't fail to notice that everyone was dressed almost the same, with good clothes. I saw a drunk or two, but in Russia you can walk through towns in the evenings and see them spread out on street corners. Our propaganda says that millions are unemployed and have to stage demonstrations to get bread, and that the police beat them terribly. Though I had doubted it, my first exposure to a free country during that short drive showed me what a great tragic lie the Communist propaganda is.

Every day I sensed growing strength and I began to look ahead. Then suddenly, with almost no warning, just as my hopes were highest, I received news which left me reeling in confusion, fear and bewilderment: I might be handed back to the Russians.

The next day a special plane flew me to Vancouver where I was placed in the Vancouver Central Jail. My dream of freedom, a new life and finding something to truly believe in was on the verge of being shattered into a million hopeless pieces. How? Why?

I cannot describe my state of mind in the Vancouver jail. I was alone in a strange land, which I had looked to with great hope and trust, but which seemed now to be turning on me. I had trusted this land. I had chosen the stormy, freezing North Pacific rather than the warm waters of California because I believed in this land. I had placed my life in its hands. I had experienced the most wonderful care, concern and help from everyone I had met. But now this country might possibly hand me back! To certain death! I had never expected that. The sheer possibility of it haunted me.

I was alone in my strange cell. I couldn't speak with others. I felt cruelly betrayed and hurt. I tried to forget my troubles. My guard became a good friend. At times he would take me out of my cell and into the exercise yard. We would throw a ball back and forth to relax.

I had a few physical problems still, not being fully recovered, but they were nothing compared with the pains that tormented my spirit. I had to talk to someone. In my despair I wanted to pray to God. I got down on my knees as I had seen the Believers do. I thought that might help. But I knew no prayers. I was embarrassed; I felt awkward and ashamed. But my heart was so full of problems I began talking to God. It was all I knew to do. I don't know if He heard. I only know that for a little time I felt better.

My court-appointed attorney was a friendly man and a capable lawyer who did his best to help me. He took my case with great interest and worked hard on my behalf, which I shall always appreciate. I asked him why I might be sent back. He told me that Canada was involved in a very large trade arrangement with Russia and was selling her millions of dollars worth of wheat, and so had to have friendly relations with her. The Russian officials had made it clear they wanted me back very much. He explained how my staying here could harm Russian-Canadian relations. On top of that, Kosygin was coming to Canada the next month, and the Canadian government didn't want to offend him.

Alone in my cell, I thought, *I'm finished now, if I'm handed back.*

I had tried and had succeeded through great hardships to find a new home, only to face the danger of being returned. Again that night, in despair, I tried to talk to God. Finally I drifted off into an uneasy sleep.

The next few days were ones of fear and uncertainty for me. Every approaching footstep down the corridor of the jail could be the guards coming to hand me over. Russian ships were in the harbour of Vancouver. It would be so simple to hand me over in a matter of minutes. My mind was tormented and fearful. Once I was in Russian hands, the fate of Kudirka, who was beaten and kicked when he was handed back, would seem merciful compared to mine. During those lonely, fearful days and nights I talked often to God on my knees.

One night I couldn't sleep for worry. I switched off the lights at 2 a.m. and lay awake in the darkened cell. Around 2.30 I suddenly heard men's voices coming from down the corridor, followed by approaching footsteps. They stopped outside my cell. *This is it*, I thought.

The keys rattled and the cell door opened. The light flashed on, and several men in plain clothes stood there. "Come with us," one of them said. "Get all your things. We're going to take you on a little sightseeing trip of the city."

A sightseeing trip at 2.30 in the morning? No, I realized something strange was under way. They hurried me out the back entrance of the jail, into a waiting, unmarked police car. Three officers in plain clothes were in the car. The driver took off into the darkness. Even at 2.30 a.m. the street lights were on and I could see how big and beautiful Vancouver really was. It was the first big city in the free world I had seen. We drove through the main streets, and then began to go through back alleys, down tiny side streets at a fast speed. The driver would swing the car around suddenly and reverse his direction, heading down unlit back alleys, along winding roads, cutting off sharply on to side streets, with his tyres screeching from the abrupt turns.

This "tour" of the city continued for almost two hours. Finally about 4.30, the driver stopped and went into an all-night coffee shop, made a call and came out. He said, "Okay, it's all set. Let's go." We started off again. He headed for the airport and drove on to a runway, up to a large aeroplane waiting there. We went aboard. There were only a few people in the entire airliner, including the officers accompanying me.

We flew across Canada into the dawning new day and landed in Montreal. I was quickly whisked into an unmarked police car and placed between two police officers. I was then driven to Quebec City. There I was taken to a jail on an island in the middle of the St. Lawrence River and was kept in custody in a locked cell. I didn't know then that in a few days the Soviet liner, *Alexander Pushkin* was due to sail up the St. Lawrence and dock only a few hundred yards from where I was being held.

In my mind my being secretly taken out of Vancouver and flown here was apparently set up carefully to prepare for my handover to the Russians in a few days. My case had received a lot of publicity in British Columbia, and many people had befriended me and taken an interest. For this reason I thought I was to be handed over far from where I was known, the other side of Canada. To me there were only two reasons for the great secrecy, the midnight Vancouver ride and the special jet flight across Canada: to protect me from unknown enemies or, far more likely, to hand me over to the Russians quietly, without attention. There was little doubt in my mind at the time that the latter was true.

But back in western Canada, some of my new friends were working to help me. Someone who has never been identified called Pat Burns, who has a popular radio interview show in Vancouver, and informed him that I had been secretly taken out of Vancouver the night before. Mr. Burns had told my story over the radio and had taken an interest in my case. Fearing I might be handed back at any moment, he acted immediately. While broadcasting live on the air, he telephoned Ottawa to speak to a member of Parliament representing Vancouver.

Pat Burns told him what had happened. The member of Parliament then went back on to the floor and demanded to know of the Prime Minister, Mr. Pierre Trudeau, if the Canadian government was planning to give me back to the Russians. He demanded a public answer from the Prime Minister. The press were present and reported the incident.

With my plight now public knowledge, the authorities couldn't give me back, and my danger was past. I never did learn how much danger I actually was in or if I would have been handed back or not. But to me, at least, the danger seemed very real. Meanwhile I paced my cell, nervous, praying and waiting. I didn't know that my awkward prayers to a God I wasn't even sure heard me had been answered.

When I finally was told, "You are allowed to stay in Canada," I realized I was the freest man in the world, even though I was still in jail. And I didn't forget to pray and thank God that He had answered my prayers, as bad as I had been in life to Him and His children.

I stayed in jails in Canada for several more weeks while my papers were being processed and my story was being investigated, but now that I knew I would not be handed back it was wonderful. I played the guitar. I sang. I made up songs. I received letters from people across Canada who had read of my story. I had friends who came to see me. And I was very grateful to the Canadian government for the outcome. I will always appreciate their kindness.

Others also came to see me, less welcome. One day the second secretary from the Russian embassy visited me. He spoke with me in the presence of Canadian authorities, telling me, "We know you are young and made a mistake. If you will just come back, we will forgive you and forget all. We will give you your old position back again, and everything will be the same."

I said I could never do so. He then handed me a letter from my former girl friend, Olga, back in Russia, who pleaded with me to return to her, saying that all would be forgiven—almost word for word the same as the embassy official had said.

When I again said no, the Russian official said, "Kourdakov, some day you will come to us begging to be allowed to return."

Shortly afterward my immigration papers were processed and I was told I was a free man, free to leave jail and start a new life in Canada. During my weeks in jail, someone from a government office came to me and said something to the effect, "Kourdakov, we have checked your story very carefully from start to finish. We have put all the factors into a computer, especially programmed to make an analysis. We have put in the water temperature, the direction and strength of the wind, the severity of the storm, the distance from the ship to shore, the height of the waves—even your physical strength. Our scientists have tested all this on the computer, and the computer analysis is that your swim and survival were impossible. This is the conclusion of our computer. Is there anything, anything at all, that you have failed to tell us about that night?"

I thought for a moment and said, "The only thing I left out is that I prayed to God very much."

He left, then came back a few days later. "Sergei," he said, "you'll be interested to know that when all factors were fed into the computer, including your prayer to God, the computer now reports that your swim and survival were possible. We believe your story." I was amazed. *How could a computer know about God?*

Later it was explained to me that my prayer to God was considered a "psychological strength", and strong psychological strength and will power were the extra motivating factors that made my survival possible.

I left the Quebec jail as a free man and went to a small hotel to get a room. While I was there, and even before, many wonderful people contacted me to offer help, a job or a place to live. But I received one job offer I didn't expect. A swimming competition promoter from Ontario wrote to me that he was sponsoring a great summer swim contest the next year, and since I was now famous across Canada for my swim in the ocean he would give me $150 if I would appear at his swim show and swim twenty-five miles. "Everybody knows you as a great swimmer," he said. "They'll come from everywhere to see you swim. We can make a good business together."

Well, I am a good swimmer, but I told him it was God who helped me swim for so long in the ocean and I could not accept his offer.

I now had two great concerns in my life. My first concern was to keep my promise to God to serve Him. The second was to get a job and settle in Canada, to be the man I wanted to be. The second, I knew, would be far easier than the first.

My first order of business was to find God. But how? Where? I knew virtually nothing of God and I knew no ministers to talk to about Him. But I had seen a large church in the centre of Quebec, Saint Ann's Catholic Church, and decided to go there. I thought, *If this is a church I can find God here.*

I went inside, not knowing what to do. Some people came in and I decided to do as they did. They went up to the front and knelt. I did the same. I watched them carefully to learn what to do next. They began to pray, and I did the same, but not knowing what to say, I felt awkward and unworthy to be in this house of God. I had beaten and killed Believers. I had broken up more than 150 secret meetings in Russia. I had burned Bibles. I had injured old women and many Believers. I was unworthy to be in God's house. But I felt a calm sense come over me and I talked to God, as I had done in the ocean and in the jails.

My heart was so painful, like a man who is looking for bread but cannot find it. I knew I was close to God in the beautiful church, but I wanted to be closer. I felt a beauty, a peace, a lifted burden. I wanted more of this. If this is what God gives, I wanted it very much. After three hours of prayer, I felt as if I had been helped, but my heart was searching for something more, something like what the Believers in the secret churches had. I wanted what Natasha had.

I left the church and went back to my small room. There I had a message that someone wanted to talk to me about a job. I was to come to a certain address and be interviewed. Two Bulgarian young men who had escaped to Canada several months earlier, were helping me as interpreters and showing me around. I left a note for them, saying where I was going, then went to the address written on the message for me. Several people were waiting for me there. But they didn't want to talk about a job. They were members of the F.L.Q., the French separatist terror organization in Quebec which had bombed and killed even diplomats in their struggle to break away from Canada. They had strong Communist support and ties. I looked about and immediately saw it wasn't a job interview. It was a trap.

"Kourdakov," they warned, "if you raise your voice one time and say things you shouldn't you will be silenced."

I tried to talk to them to stall for time and find a way to get out. Then my two Bulgarian friends arrived. They had found the note and rushed over. I left immediately with them, with the warnings ringing in my ears. I now realized that, even here, as a free man, I would not be left alone. Moscow was still reaching out to me.

I was followed in Quebec by a man from the Russian embassy who dogged my footsteps everywhere I went. The Mounted Police warned me that a Soviet ship was docked at Montreal and to be careful. "Call us if you are threatened," they said.

With the danger of the F.L.Q. and the Communists so strong in Quebec, I made plans to leave and go to Toronto. There was a Russian consul in Montreal and the Russian embassy in Ottawa, and I wanted to be far from them. I arrived in Toronto and stayed with a Russian family who had read my story and offered me a place to live.

The Canadian government paid my tuition to study English at the university, and I busied myself learning the new language.

But always on my mind was my need for God. I felt a spiritual hunger which was hard to explain. I felt I would not be a complete man until my spritual needs were met. It was not just a sense of remorse for the beating and killing of Believers. I knew God had forgiven me for that; I had done it in ignorance. What I felt now was a genuine, deep spiritual need in my life. I knew I could never be a really free man until my spirit became as free as I was free physically.

I remembered hearing one of the Believers say, while being questioned, that they often fasted when they were praying for something they wanted very badly. I thought, *Maybe that's what I should do.*

I went to a Toronto church which I had attended with a family who had befriended me. The church was always open for prayer.

There was no one present, so I went to the front and began to pray. I stayed there for two days, only drinking water. I didn't know what words to say, but my heart was praying for me. My heart could express what I felt. After two days, during which time I slept only three hours each night, from 3 to 6 a.m., I left the church and went back to school.

I felt spiritually stronger, but still there was something I lacked. I had received a card from Valentine Bubovich, a Russian girl who was a librarian at a university near Toronto. She told me she was a Christian. I had her address and wrote to her. She invited me to go to church, and I gladly did so.

When I walked into the church, I sensed something familiar. I exclaimed, "This is like in Russia!" thinking of the songs, the spirit, the fellowship which was in the Russian secret churches. Valentine's father gave me a book of Psalms which helped me very much.

I started to go to the Ukrainian churches and found a wonderful spirit there—especially among the young people. I met a pastor who had heard about me, and we talked. I told him how my heart was still empty and that though I was now free physically, I did not feel complete. I explained about the feeling inside me to want to believe in and serve God. He said, "I understand." He answered many questions for me, taught me Bible truths and showed me the way to God. For this I shall always be grateful.

One day during a church service, he said, "Sergei, are you now ready to give your life to God fully and completely?"

"Yes," I replied.

"Let's pray," he said.

As we prayed, something happened in my life—something definite, concrete and positive. I felt the change. I felt the peace of God inside me. I felt my long, long search and yearning was over. I surrendered my life to Jesus Christ, and He entered into my life. My life was born anew that wonderful day, and finally the restlessness, the emptiness, the harshness and the void in my life was filled by Jesus Christ. How wonderful I felt! To know that now I, too, was a Believer, right alongside Natasha, Pastor Litovchenko and the other Believers I had persecuted! Now I was one of them!

The pastor counselled me often, so I would grow as a Christian. One day he said to me, "Sergei, you are a Christian and you need your own Bible in your own language." And he handed me a small, black Russian Bible.

It was as if a thunderbolt had struck me! I couldn't believe my eyes. The pastor saw my shock and asked, "What's wrong? What is it?"

"This Bible." I exclaimed. "I have seen one just like it before."

"Where?"

"This is the same kind of Bible I saw in some of the underground churches in Russia!"

I opened it, looked through it. Yes, it was. It was the same Bible.

"That's very possible," the pastor said. "It's one of the Bibles printed and sent into Russia by the organization called Underground Evangelism."

"Where are they?" I asked. "I want to thank them and tell them their Bibles are getting through."

I learned the address of Underground Evangelism and got a friend to telephone them. I spoke to the president, L. Joe Bass, and he said he would like to speak to me and would be in Toronto soon on his way to Europe. When Mr. Bass came, we met and talked for many hours. I learned of the work this organization is doing to help the persecuted Believers of Russia and other Communist lands, and thanked him on behalf of the Russian people.

My English course was ending and I would soon be ready to take a job. I had a good offer to work in an electronics firm as a radio engineer and I saw many good things ahead in my life. I could make a good salary with the company, buy a car, later get married, raise a family and have my own home. It was all very appealing to me.

But as I thought all those happy thoughts, I could not forget my experiences in Russia. I could not forget the thousands of Believers there who were still being beaten for their faith. I could not forget the youth who had taken my place on the attack squad. I could not forget the Bibles still being burned and the churches still meeting in secret. I could not forget the millions of Russian young people, like me, misled, disillusioned, drifting, looking for the truth. I had to do what I could to help them. I began to speak in churches and on television, telling what my conversion to Christ meant to me and asking prayer for my people, making many public appearances and telling of the religious persecution in Russia.

Then one day I came out of the Dundas West subway station in Toronto and walked toward my rooming house. Feeling I was being followed, I stopped and turned around abruptly. There stood three powerfully built men. One of them spoke in perfect Russian, saying, "If you know what is good for you, Kourdakov, you will keep silent and say nothing more. If you open your mouth, you will have a 'final accident'. Remember, you have been warned."

They turned and were soon gone, and I walked on to my room, thinking about what they had said.

I know the Soviet police, for I was one of them and saw how they worked. This was not an idle threat. I knew I must consider my responsibility to my people, especially those persecuted for their faith. If I kept silent, who would speak for them? Who would know of their suffering? I decided that since I took their lives, I owed them a debt. I decided not to inform the authorities of the threat. After all, it was my decision to speak out, and I had to take the responsibility for it.

Of course I wanted a home, a family and a normal, settled home life, something I never had in all my life. But before I could look to my own life and put it first, I must remember those whom I left behind. I must tell their story and help them. I must show people, especially young people, by my own example, that there is a God and He can change even the worst life, as He has mine.

The soul of the great Russian people is not dead. It has not suffocated under an alien, godless, sterile ideology. It will not, so long as there are men like Alexander Solzhenitsyn, women like Natasha Zhdanova, and millions of others like them in whom the spark of faith and decency has not died out. Indeed, in thousands of secret churches and in millions of lives across Russia today that flicker of faith glows brighter, the commitment to religious principles grows stronger, strengthened by the brutal ordeal of suffering. And one day those millions of flickering candles of faith and decency may burst forth and merge into one gigantic flame of faith.

And I have in my heart a message I want to pass to those Believers in Russia who have helped so much to change my life. I put this message in this book, hoping that in some way, at some time, it can reach them and they will understand.

To Mrs. Litovchenko, the paralysed wife of the pastor whom we killed that Sunday afternoon along the Elizovo River: I wish to tell you that I am sorry, more than you can ever know.

To Nina Rudenko, the beautiful little teenage girl whose life was ruined by my attack group, I ask, "Please forgive us."

And, finally, to Natasha, whom I beat terribly and who was willing to be beaten a third time for her faith, I want to say, "Natasha, largely because of you, my life is now changed and I am a fellow Believer in Christ with you. I have a new life before me. God has forgiven me; I hope you can also."

Thank you, Natasha, wherever you are.

I will never, never forget you!

Publisher's note

Shortly after the draft of this book was completed, Sergei died.

He had devoted what he called his "new life" to awakening Christians of North America to the plight of the Russian Christians, and appealing for Bibles and help on their behalf.

Between January and April, 1972, he told his story in many churches in Canada. On 1 May that year, he joined Underground Evangelism, an organization which provides Bibles and help to the persecuted church throughout the Communist world.

He spoke in churches, on television, gave newspaper interviews and spoke before government officials, telling the story of Communist persecution and the inner workings of his former comrades of the Soviet police. He undertook Bible studies, worked on this book and announced he was especially looking forward to speaking to the youth of Russia by radio broadcasts. These were in the process of being arranged at the time of his death.

Though Sergei had warned that if anything happened to him, it would "have all the appearances of an accident", he was optimistic, outgoing and forward-looking. He made many new friends wherever he went. Among them was a Christian family in Los Angeles, California, for whom he became an "adopted son" and with whom he lived when he was there.

Several times he remarked that he felt his life might be in danger, and borrowed a gun from the father of the family for self protection. He took the gun with him when, accompanied by the daughter of the family, he visited a ski resort close to Los Angeles.

On 1 January 1973 he died instantly from a shot from the gun. Though news of his death was first carried internationally as suicide, this possibility was soon ruled out. An inquest was held and on 1 March 1973 ruled his death to be an accident.

On that very day, Sergei would have been twenty-two.

A special fund has been established in Sergei Kourdakov's memory, to continue providing help for Russia's persecuted Christians to whom Sergei had devoted his short "new life".

Those wishing to enquire or provide Bibles and help to the Persecuted Church may write to:

The Sergei Kourdakov Fund
Underground Evangelism

16 Morden Road
London SW19 3BJ, England

P.M.B. 444
Banktown, NSW 2200, Australia

P.O. Box 26055
Epsom, Auckland 3, New Zealand

Box 49
Claremont, Capetown, South Africa